A BUSH WHICH BURNS
BUT IS NOT CONSUMED

FATHER ELIA CITTERIO

A Bush Which Burns But Is Not Consumed

The Prayer of the Heart in the Singular Romanian Experience of the Burning Bush

TRANS. G. JOHN CHAMPOUX

Angelico Press

Originally published in Italian as
Un Fuoco che Brucia
Ma Non Consuma

info@ilcerchio.it
www.ilcerchio.it

For information, address:
Angelico Press, Ltd.
169 Monitor St.
Brooklyn, NY 11222
www.angelicopress.com

ppr 979-8-89280-169-0
cloth 979-8-89280-170-6

Book and cover design
by Michael Schrauzer

CONTENTS

Make me worthy, O Lord, to know Thee so as also to love Thee, not with knowledge arising from study's exercise and joined to the intellect's dispersion; but make me worthy of that knowledge whereby the intellect, in beholding Thee, glorifies Thy nature in divine vision which steals the awareness of the world from the mind.

Account me worthy to be lifted above the will's wandering eye which begets imaginings, and to behold Thee in the constraint of the cross's bond, in the second part of the crucifixion of the intellect, whose liberty ceases from the activity of its thoughts by abiding in Thy continuous vision, which surpasses nature.

Implant in me the astringent of Thy love, that being drawn away by fervent love for Thee I may come forth from this world. Awake in me understanding of Thy humility, wherewith Thou didst sojourn in the world in the tenement composed of our members which by the mediation of the Holy Virgin Thou didst bear, that with this continual and unfailing recollection, I may accept the humility of my nature with delight.

—Isaac the Syrian, *Homily 36*

Sanctify me in Thy mysteries, let my intellect shine in the knowledge of Thee, let the hope of Thee arise in my heart and make me worthy of a prompting concerning it within me. God, my Father and Lord of my life, make your lamp to shine within me, cast into me something of Thine so that I forget mine, place on me the constraint of the wonder of Thyself so that the constraint of nature may be overcome. Imbue me with the vision of Thy mysteries so that I may perceive what was placed in me at holy baptism. Thou hast placed a guide within me: may it always show me Thy glory.... Cast sweet bridles over my heart, so that my senses do not look outside the paths of Thy law.... May my intellect, in its temptations, receive comfort from the memory of Thee. Illuminate the way before me with the brightness of the knowledge of Thyself, because it is dark.

—Isaac the Syrian, *Conversations on hidden prayer*

FATHER DANIIL
(in the world, Sandu Tudor)

PREFACE

TO DELVE INTO READING A TEXT, ASSUMING it is readable and documented, the reader often just needs to be interested in the topic. The author's personal motivations may well go unnoticed. I think this is not the case with this research. Before willing readers begin their own labor, I would like to recall the background facts that justify the composing of this study, which falls on the fiftieth anniversary of the foundation of our tiny community of the Fratelli Contemplativi di Gesù (Contemplative Brothers of Jesus). What is narrated, investigated, shared, and admired in this study has marked the internal journey of this community. Let me briefly review the story.

In 1982 I had the opportunity to make a study trip to Mount Athos to collect documentation for my doctoral thesis at the Angelicum in Rome on the figure of St. Nicodemus the Hagiorite and the *Philokalia*. I could not find the documents I was seeking, but I had some extraordinary encounters. What turned out to be the most fruitful was a meeting with Fr. Petronie Tănase, the hegumen of the Romanian skete of Prodromu, just over an hour's walk from the Monastery of Great Lavra, on which it depends. Having never met him before, I found him at dawn, in the church, praying alone. He had not noticed my presence. He stood in front of the Holy Doors, singing for a good half hour, with a very sweet melody, the litanic prayer: *Doamne milueste, Doamne milueste... miluieste-ne pre noi* (*Kyrie eleison, Lord have mercy, have mercy on us*). Fr. Petronie prayed with the same sweetness with which he spoke. When I explained the purpose of my trip to him, he sensed the desire I carried in my heart beyond what I was describing and he told me: "But in Romania there are still people and places where the practice of prayer of the heart is preserved. I can put you in touch with someone who can accompany you." I knew almost nothing then about Romania and its hesychast tradition. But in 1984, at the suggestion of his friend Fr. Ioanichie Bălan, a well-known Romanian monk from Sihăstria, in Moldavia, to whom he had turned to get me the indispensable official invitation to go to Romania, I dared to undertake the journey together with one of my brothers. We were still in the midst of the communist period. Trips such as these were daring, but they allowed me to get to know the reality of the Romanian monastic experience and above all to meet the great figures of Romanian spirituality, who over time I understood to be the true pillars of the Romanian church. The discovery of many Romanian hermitages and the life that was led there confirmed for me the possibility of drawing inspiration from the same hesychast tradition in the West too. However, no one, neither monks nor scholars who I gradually got to know, spoke to me about the experience of Antim's Burning Bush movement, whose inception and development over time this study presents. I discovered only later that I had come into contact with the most significant personalities of that movement, who survived the harsh prison to which they had been sentenced in 1958, and with the intellectuals, writers, and theologians who had breathed in its climate and interpreted its legacy. In fact, I was able to meet Fr. Benedict Ghiuș, Fr. Sofian Boghiu, Fr. Dumitru Stăniloae, as well as Fr. Ilie Cleopa and his spiritual father, Fr. Paisie Olaru, along with the group of disciples that had formed around them, like Fr. Iachint Unciulac from Putna, the academic Virgil Cândea, and many others. I was sorry that I never managed to go to Techirghiol in Dobrogea, where the other great charismatic figure of the Burning Bush movement, Fr. Arsenie Papacioc, lived. I was able to visit the most significant places of the Romanian hesychast tradition, both male and female, even the skete of Poiana Mărului, the initial center of the modern philokalic renewal on Romanian soil. I was able to participate in the UNESCO international colloquium for the 500th anniversary of the consecration of the Neamț monastery, held in Iasi on 13–14 October 1997, with a speech on the figure of Paisius Velichkovsky. In the meantime, I have edited several publications relating to the Romanian spiritual tradition with the aim of making it known here. Indeed, I recall that the then Metropolitan of Iasi, His Eminence Dan Ilie Ciobotea, now Patriarch Daniel of the Orthodox Church of Romania, commenting on the publication by our community of the *Autobiography of a Staretz* by Paisius Velichkovsky in 1988, thanked us for uncovering for them what constituted the glory of their history. However, all this was made possible by the friendship and spiritual brotherhood of Fr. Ioanichie Bălan, who did his utmost so that we could get to know places, people, and documents which illustrated to us the liveliness, even if it was hidden at the time, of a great ecclesial tradition, of the great hesychast tradition. Now he, and those spiritual figures whom we have been able to meet through him, have passed the baton to a younger generation. If I could go to Romania now I would have many cemeteries to visit to honor those who have been generous toward us with their wisdom and spiritual experience.

I asked myself how to remember, in gratitude, this precious exchange of gifts, which has proven so fruitful for us. In my research on the *Philokalia* and its fruitfulness in modern times I was able to highlight the importance of the Romanian environment, less known or practically unknown compared to the other two already known environments, the Greek and Slavic ones. All that remained was for me to do something similar within the Romanian environment itself, that is, to return to the original fire, which was rekindled on Romanian soil with the Burning Bush movement. That fire has always been alive in the Romanian monasteries, but with the Burning Bush movement the experience once again became visible, shared, in a broader context, not only in the monasteries but also among intellectuals, among the people, in a terrible moment of recent Romanian history, when the communist dictatorship tried to suffocate any aspiration to freedom and culture, as well as religion.

There had already been signs of growing interest in Romania over the events of the 1950s. In 1995, from his hermitage of Lainici, the elderly Fr. Adrian Fageţeanu, inseparable disciple of Sandu Tudor, came to Bucharest to demand a review of the 1958 trial and the rehabilitation of the condemned people of the Burning Bush group. In 1996 André Scrima's book on the Burning Bush was published. In 2012, on the occasion of the centenary of the birth of Fr. Sofian Boghiu and the tenth anniversary of his death, as well as the fiftieth anniversary of the death of Sandu Tudor, a commemorative symposium was organized by the Patriarchate, the Archbishopric of Bucharest, the Library of the Holy Synod, the Antim Monastery and the

National Council for the Study of the Archives of the Securitate.[1] Articles of various types are appearing in the Romanian public and religious press, both paper and digital, on the Burning Bush movement. Symposiums are organized where the singular experience of the Burning Bush movement is discussed, as in Rome in 2002 and in Bose in 2004. I myself took part in the symposium organized by the Giorgio Cini Foundation in Venice in 2002, on the island of San Giorgio Maggiore: "Romania: religion and spirituality from the post-war period to the present day" with a speech entitled "Movements and prominent figures of Romanian Orthodoxy in the last fifty years." In Romania Ioan Ică Jr., a passionate and far-sighted man, founder of the Deisis publishing house, whose friend and collaborator I became, has done his utmost to raise awareness of the authors Nichifor Crainic and Nae Ionescu of the interwar period, both authors in close relationship with Sandu Tudor, the true driving force behind the Burning Bush movement. He only needed to connect everything and try to take a look from within, especially taking into account the guiding thread of the movement, the discovery of the prayer of the heart. This is what I tried to do in this study, the realization of which would not have been possible without the collaboration of many friends, yesterday and today. I dedicate it especially to the memory of Fr. Ioanichie Bălan who represented for me a precious link to the knowledge of the Romanian monastic world. However, I have many people to thank. The list would be very long. I want to remember at least two of them who, with their help, made my project concretely achievable. First of all, my friend Ioan Ică, who supported me in every way, with his prestigious expertise, his total availability and his long-standing friendship. I am particularly grateful to him. And I thank Sr. Ester, a Romanian sister who lives in the Benedictine community of Isola San Giulio (NO), whose help in the translation of Sandu Tudor's poetic texts was decisive. I cannot help but be grateful also to those who, like my friend Massimo Mascolo, patiently corrected the various

[1] The National Council for the Study of the Archives of the Securitate was the secret service of communist Romania, founded in 1948, with the help of the Soviet NKVD ["People's Commissariat for Internal Affairs"], abolished in December 1989, immediately after the fall of President Nicolae Ceausescu's regime. See further on pages 27 ff.

drafts of the text. Completing this work, which in the end can only be a simple outline to gratefully recognize God's gifts to his Church and which others, I hope, will take up again with more competence and sagacity, has turned out to be the best way for me to bless God for these fifty years of life of our community of the Contemplative Brothers of Jesus. This too is a way of proclaiming that authentic religiosity is ecumenical, as the members of the Burning Bush always repeated.

The work has a bipartite structure. In the first, more historical part, I present a provisional biography of Sandu Tudor, followed by two chapters on the history of Romanian hesychasm and on the prayer of the heart in the rediscovery of the Burning Bush movement. All this is a prelude to enjoying, in the second part, the *Akathist Hymn to the Burning Bush of the Mother of God*, Sandu Tudor's remarkable composition on the prayer of the heart, in its richness and depth, with its Italian and now English translation of the hymn in its hitherto little-known definitive version. I wanted to increase interest in this author by adding an appendix with other poetic compositions by him. In the Italian version it was not possible to convey the poetic musicality of the verses in Romanian, also given the distinctive nature of the language used by our author. In fact, Sandu Tudor wants to imitate the language of the liturgical hymns of the Byzantine tradition and writes in a rather courtly Romanian, using terms that are now out of use or in any case archaic, sometimes difficult to interpret even for a native speaker. The depth of its message and the spiritual experience it describes amply justify the effort of translation, even if impoverished compared to the original. I would be happy if I had managed to pave the way for the prospective reader to follow the author on the arduous paths along which he wants to attract us, so that we too can enjoy the mystery of the prayer of the heart.

By Way of Introduction

ECHOS & COMMENTS BY ANCA VASILIU AND IOAN ICĂ, JR.

ANCA VASILIU[1]

Restitutio

A WORD OF INTRODUCTION

The point is precisely this: to account for the fire. How do we live under the sign of something that purifies and destroys? Burning ourselves, until we are consumed. You will discover that something indestructible always remains. But to discover this ineliminable nucleus, one must pass through fire. Burning your wings, getting lost and starting again, falling and getting back up. Fire does not destroy everything; what does not go up in smoke, is purified and maintained. From the terminal ash comes memory and from fire, faith. Remember and testify. This book speaks only of this: of the memory and of the testimony given to the splendor and misery in which the thirsty human creature burns, near the source.

He whose life we trace, to give us the key to the work, was not afraid of anything. Except, perhaps, for one thing, the one thing that God himself rejects: lukewarmness. The half measure, the fear of fear, the adaptation to circumstances, to "it doesn't depend on us," as the experts say. He, who calls himself Sandu Tudor, dared extremes. Perhaps, all the extremes, or almost all. It is true, moreover, that his own time offered these extremes to him in abundance. He experienced the two wars and the turbulence of

---

[1] Anca Vasiliu, an outstanding Romanian intellectual, editor of the French works of Fr. André Scrima, who was a prominent participant in the Burning Bush movement, has lived in Paris since 1990 and has worked at the CNRS since 1998. She has degrees in philosophy and in art history. Since 2007 she has been Research Director at the CNRS and part of the Centre Léon Robin. Of her numerous studies, the following has appeared in Italian: *L'architettura dipinta. Gli affreschi moldavi nel XV e XVI secolo* [Divine Architecture. Moldavian frescoes in the 15th and 16th centuries (Milano: Jaca Book, 1998)].

a world that, several times, woke up in another world between one evening and the next morning. From archaism to modernity, from the madcap years to the crisis, from one dictatorship to another, in a country that grew or shrank according to international decisions. How was one to live there, without following, helplessly, the flow that drags you along? Without getting into petty controversies and without falling into the prejudices of a chosen party. Simply taking part in it, leaving one's feathers behind, but always continuing one's phoenix flight.

Sandu Tudor's voice resonated everywhere, in newspapers and in literary, intellectual, university, ecclesiastical, military and, at times, political circles. Nowhere was he confined. He was keen to snoop into everything, right from his youth. He got slapped, some did not like his audacity, much less his excesses, he was "baroque" in style, incongruous, too over the top in tone to be admitted into circles where moderation was the norm and there could never be too much caution. However, he saw further than others and attracted those who realized this too. Or, better yet, to put it bluntly, he knew how to recognize the underlying intuition in what others also glimpsed and tried to pursue, as if attracted by something whose precise contours no one knew at the time. He recognized his identity and purpose in what was being prepared. His activity became, then, his strength, but not a brutal activity because it rises little by little like a breath that becomes more certain from one moment to the next, before setting the center on fire.

Sandu Tudor was an essentially unquiet man, in the genuine and extroverted sense of the term. What is he aware of through his vicissitudes, his incessant travels, his spasmodic searches for rare symbols and terms, his timeless writings? He knows that he comes from a world that is always there, but imperceptible due to the noises that cover it as if it says nothing, or at least so little that even a musician's ear can no longer distinguish the delicate timbre of the sound that vibrates below the surface, at the root of the human. He knows it, but even he cannot distinguish what resonates within himself, still unable to define it clearly until the moment he finds himself again. Knowing this, he stayed ready. He had prepared himself to finally listen to that voice that surpasses all noise once the doors of the heart are opened. He knew he would be able to hear it because, from his stay on Mount Athos to the little cell in the bell tower of Antim, in the series of vicissitudes of life in this world, he had kept its echo within himself and it was enough for him to calm his thirst a little so that he could one day reach the source of that dull internal murmur that nourished his faith. At first haughty and proud of his numerous talents, he hurled himself into a frenzy of activity, devoured by the fever of achieving everything. Sandu Tudor ultimately came to want not knowledge, but the only invincible power, that of knowing how to give thanks.

He was sent to a tiny skete on a mountain top. Always endowed with great power of attraction, like a magnet, he organized community life, breathed deeply the pure air of the peaks, spoke to the shepherds about the metaphysical questions of the Elizabethan theater and wrote the Akathist hymn of the Burning Bush in a courtly and archaic language. However, he always remained restless and waited. Not for the state security apparatus that was certainly preparing to come and take him away, but he awaited the true Pascha, that of testimony.

Here he played his role, here was his whole life, collected in an indomitable spirit. He will die, with the shackles still on his feet, for having testified to that fire that does not consume as long as the breath that fuels it does not come from the air, but from the very movement that had brought him there, to keep intact the name that he had given himself and the cross he had embraced. Like the destiny of his people, he entered the splendor that few have recognized, for the sacrifice accepted, becoming the stone upon which one steps to stand in front of the holy doors of the altar.

I had to retrace the pages of this book to reclaim my own story—the history of my country in the twentieth century, as well as the history of my youth in which I was able to meet many of the people whose names are mentioned here and visit the places evoked (with the exception of Mount Athos, of course) without foreseeing all the emotional and spiritual charge. For my generation, it was simply the landscape of the place, with its natural charm, its dignity and its silence imposed by a discretion that was thought to be ancestral and which automatically prohibited any curiosity. The nobility of the people encountered was as evident as the harmony between nature and the environment of earlier times. But all this was called "patrimony"; we learned its history and the duty to conserve it without questioning its transcendent values. Our grandparents didn't speak; our parents worked; at school the benefits of peace were praised and the sciences were learned to ensure future prosperity. Life was elsewhere. You could feel it pulsing silently and you could mention it in a low voice, like something forbidden that passes beneath your thumb and is incomprehensible. Living like this was already a gift. Orthodoxy came to be known only in relation to the Byzantine arts and ancient languages. We were the heirs and we did not even know it, we did not even dare imagine it. As often happens, you discover the treasure hidden in your own garden after traveling around the world.

For almost three decades, works on Romanian intellectuals and spiritual men who lived between the two wars have continued to come to light. The survivors, first of all, have become—fortunately—less discreet. Then came the time for research in the field and in the archives, for the analysis of clues and documents, for interpretations. The field is so vast that no one can boast of having managed to give a faithful summary of that time. We are still at the discovery phase, although the basic lines are now set out before us. In this panorama, that of a surprisingly open, intellectual orthodoxy, responsible for all challenges and all talents, but still torn between rational wisdom and practical, even folkloric wisdom, Sandu Tudor remains the embodiment of the best in the liveliness of the spirit. He must also be thought of as one of those chosen for the consummation of the sacrifice so that it bears fruit and leaves a trace. The "Burning Bush" movement, whose history you will read here, is not only his living creation, but also the intimate expression of his beliefs, of his style, of the ultimate goal that he had set for himself before entering into something much greater than his Pascha. If his experience remains unique, since such is the destiny of every man, the flame of the Burning Bush that he revived in Romanian intellectual circles was transmitted like the trail of light in the night of the Resurrection and continues to set hearts on fire. Has not Fr. Elia Citterio also become one of the members of this ideal "company in spirit" in which one is recognized for the boundless love of beauty and the limitless gift of truth, that is, the gift of oneself in the prayer of intercession for all? "Company in spirit" evidently must be taken as a metaphorical term, completely detached from any ritual practice, from any type of recognition or secret purpose. Instead, we must see the consonance of a brotherhood.

Conducted from a vantage point necessarily external to the terrain upon which this experience developed, this book on the creator of "The Burning Bush" discloses features that are difficult to grasp even from within or in close proximity to that ambience.

More than a practice of Orthodox monasticism, prayer of the heart appears as the very expression of human nature. Compared to the story of the Russian Pilgrim, the prayer of the heart that characterizes the experience of the Burning Bush group is presented from a different perspective, in another, radically different modality, but always with the same intent, that of speaking to all men. The pilgrimage becomes internalized and thus takes on a universal dimension. As for the search for harmony between knowledge, life models and systems of thought, recurring in history under the overused but not untruthful name of "rebirth," it does not necessarily lead to eclecticism; this research depends rather on the vitality of a world that is not content to live solely on the income of its acquisitions. Making a synthesis is a first step to go further, towards meeting what comes to us from afar. The testimony given by the life of Sandu Tudor is not only exemplary for the contemporary history of Christian martyrdom, but makes palpable the eschatological tension that animates the world. Put more simply, Sandu Tudor embodies what is most human, the irrepressible desire to keep one's soul in a state of vigilance until death.

The reader of this book will also discover the poetry of Sandu Tudor, in particular his Akathist Hymn to the Burning Bush of the Mother of God, so rich in that lyrical and hesychastic inspiration which constitutes the guiding thread of his poetics and inner research. The sailor, the pilot, the journalist, the chic intellectual, the university student, the animator of cultural meetings, the theologian and, at the end, the monk Daniil, was first of all a poet; to be more precise, a singer, and this was the case since the beginning. Written in a language that offers clarity of meaning only with some difficulty, his verses are crowns of grace, intertwined with ivy and violets like those placed on the heads of singers of other times, like Orpheus and Dionysus first and foremost. Not that he wanted to forge an obscure style or that he was forced by the eloquence of his time to make his work singular, personal, with no other resonance than that of an imagined past, but because he was looking for what in his eyes could best open things up, for how to give thanks through the intrinsic fragility of words. He sought beauty. For him, it is in fire that beauty appears like a blade that transverberates the heart to open the way to light. For him, the figure of Mary was inspiring. Through the All-Holy the only testimony of a mystery irreducible to words is realized: the incarnation, the birth, the cross, the song of the angelic powers in the cavity of the underworld, the ascension and the glory. But she herself does not speak. She remains as the window through which we look beyond the horizon.

IOAN I. ICĂ, JR.[2]

The Story of a Meeting and a Happy Discovery[3]

BY VIRTUE OF THE BLESSED GIFT OF THE OLD friendship that has bound us for a quarter of a century, Father Elia has given me the privilege of offering some reflections on this extraordinary latest book by him.

The book aims, and fully succeeds, to be an exciting introduction, conceived to put readers in contact with a masterpiece of both intellectual and spiritual depth. Through a masterful

[2] Ioan I. Ică, Jr. (b. 1960), is a prestigious Romanian Orthodox theologian, director of Editura Deisis at Sibiu, a publishing house specializing in theological writings, a university professor at the Faculty of Orthodox Theology of the "Lucian Blaga" University of Sibiu, and a member of the International Commission for Theological Dialogue between the Orthodox Church and the Catholic Church (1997–2007). He is the author of numerous studies, translations and introductions to patristic and contemporary authors. In Italian, in addition to the numerous interventions at Bose's ecumenical conferences, one can read the beautiful presentation of the testimony of a frequenter of the Burning Bush: Roman Braga, *Ogni monaco ha un suo segreto con Dio* [Every Monk has his own Secret with God (Roma: Lipa, 1999)].

[3] This essay has subsequently appeared as part of a tandem introduction by Ioan I. Ică, Jr. and myself to his chapter "Căi spre 'Rugul Aprins'" [Paths to the "Burning Bush"] in his translation and study: Sfântul Nicodim Aghioritul, *Maica Domnului și Intrările ei în Templu în tâlcuiri mistagogice. Cuvinte și poeme* [St. Nicodemus the Hagiorite, *The Mother of God and Her Entry into the Temple in Mystagogic Interpretations. Words and Poems* (Sibiu: Deisis, 2022), 275–307].

transposition into Dante's language—in itself an extraordinary result—readers, and especially the Italian [and English] reader, have here and now the priceless opportunity to come into contact with the *Akathist Hymn to the Burning Bush of the Mother of God*, a flower of fire that has blossomed from prayer and persecution in 1958, a magnificent synthesis of Romanian philokalic spirituality and the pure essence of the experience of Romanian Orthodoxy in the twentieth century.

I have read and reread the manuscript sent to me—a fascinating synthesis of erudition, but also of sensitivity, rigor and beauty—with admiration and gratitude. An exhilarating joy, inevitably tempered by a wave of melancholy, which arises from the inexorable passing of time and times, but immediately overwhelmed by a comforting certainty, that of being projected into another, paradoxical time, that of the Spirit, the time of a spiritual itinerary, lived and witnessed by men of the Spirit, who opposed the general decline with a movement raising up indisputable spiritual fruits.

According to the testimony of Father Elia, it is extraordinary to note that the peculiarity of the experience of his monastic community, that of the Contemplative Brothers of Jesus and the singularity of his spiritual itinerary are the reflection of the decisive encounter with the monastic and philokalic tradition of Romanian Orthodoxy. A study trip with the aim of preparing a doctoral thesis on the figure and the ascetic and spiritual teaching of St. Nicodemus the Hagiorite, also in relation to the origins of the famous *Philokalia* printed in Venice in 1782, was transformed by divine providence into an initiatory and fruitful journey. On the occasion of a double trip—to Athos in 1982, on the occasion of the second centenary of the printing of the *Philokalia* and to Romania in 1984—Father Elia had the extraordinary opportunity to meet and converse with legendary personalities of twentieth-century Romanian Orthodoxy. First of all, with Fr. Petronie of the Romanian skete of Prodromou on Athos, and then, thanks to the friendship with father Ioanichie Bălan, with the Frs. Cleopa and Paisius of Sihăstria of Neamț, Fr. Ciprian of Bistrița, with Frs. Benedict of Cernica and Sofian of Antim, and with illustrious specialists of ancient Romanian history, Virgil Cândea and Dan Zamfirescu.

The majority of these figures who were unable to take refuge in the West passed, in one way or another, through the concentration camp hell of ferocious political repression and anti-Christian persecution in Soviet Romania in the years 1950–1965, years in which the prominent representatives of the political, cultural and spiritual elites of interwar Romania perished. Following some sinister political trials between 1958 and 1959,[4] several dozen[5] intellectuals, monks, theologians, priests and students, who had spontaneously practiced forms of spiritual resistance through prayer and culture, refused to be re-educated by communist ideology. Some of these—such as the monk Daniil (Sandu Tudor) or the archpriest Ilarion Felea—were unable to benefit from the grace of release because they were buried in anonymous graves in Aiud; others—like the elderly poet Vasile Voiculescu—were able to leave only to die soon after due to illnesses that worsened in detention. Thus the second flowering of the philokalic spirituality of Romanian Orthodoxy was brutally annihilated, after the Paisian one of the eighteenth century, which had begun in various centers and under different forms in the years 1939–1958.

Precisely at the moment in which arrests and convictions were taking place in Romania, the extraordinary "*avènement philocalique dans l'Orthodoxie roumaine*" was reported in Paris by "*un moine de l'Eglise Orthodoxe de Roumanie.*"[6] The author of the report was the young and erudite monk Andrei Scrima, who had avoided arrest only because in October 1956 he had managed to leave Romania on a scholarship to India, at the invitation of the president of that country. The latter, being on a visit to Romania, had also been received at the headquarters of the Patriarchate, where Scrima was librarian. The long article which appeared in the magazine *Istina* presented, in a first part, the philokalic rebirth in Moldavia which took place in the second half of the eighteenth century, linked to the charismatic personality and activity of the Ukrainian elder

[4] On the basis of the dossiers prepared by the feared People's *Securitate*, the best known are those that go by the names of the "A. Teodorescu-Burning Bush dossier," the "Noica-Pillat dossier," and the "dossier of the priests of Arad."

[5] Over 4000 were arrested and convicted for counter-revolutionary attitudes and actions in the year 1958 alone.

[6] "Un moine de l'Eglise Orthodoxe de Roumanie," *L'avènement philocalique dans l'Orthodoxie roumaine*, in *Istina* 5 (1958), 295–328, 443–75.

Paisius Velichkovsky, who took refuge, like the elder Vasile a generation earlier, in the Romanian territories. Here the Greek *Philokalia* was translated into Slavonic and then spread into the Russian environment, where, through the Optina monastery, it favored the renowned destiny of the Orthodox Church and nineteenth-century Russian culture. The eighteenth century had highlighted the specific genius of Romanian Orthodoxy. Its vocation was to welcome, give refuge and put itself to service in a spirit of openness, dialogue and synthesis. In his memorable formulas Scrima evoked the main traits: "discretion and sense of proportion in spiritual life," "generosity and openness in dialogue," "a will for synthesis and respect for universal values."

Through the staretz Paisius, the spirit of the *Philokalia*—in other words, the contemplative spirit of activation, through prayer in the Spirit and in the heart, of baptismal sonship—was definitively merged with Romanian spirituality. Under his influence, Romanian Paisian monks created with their translations "an extraordinary Romanian patristic library." Unfortunately, their work remained at manuscript level, although it "already enunciated the program of an integral patristic restoration as our own time would rediscover." "The order, the clarity and the creative vigor of the Paisian period" continued and will continue to remain to this day the ideal plan for a permanent philokalic renewal. All the more necessary for the fact that, from 1830 until 1990, monastic life, as well as the institutional life and academic theology of the new modernized Romania suffered the dramatic impact of many waves of imposed secularizations and assumed secularizations, often bordering on persecution. Once Paisianism disappeared from the monasteries, the contemplative and scholarly spirit of the *Philokalia* retreated like a karst river, or a hidden spiritual vein, "silent but inexhaustible," awaiting "the future flourishing" of this Philokalic "last flourishing" in Romanian Orthodoxy in the mid-twentieth century, to which Scrima dedicated the second part of his study. However certified and liturgically affirmed, the contemporaneity of the patristic tradition in the Orthodox Church, most of the time, remains yet to be made its own and not realized by the Orthodox themselves, with the inevitable result of a lapse into the sclerosis of an external traditionalism. Awareness of the risks of this involution forced them, instead of presenting themselves as defenders and advocates of a venerable, rigid structure of the past, to rediscover in themselves the actuality of the contemplative rigor of an authentic Orthodoxy. This central need implies the understanding of an essential fact, that is, the fact that "building the Church in all the directions of its fundamental unity means continually turning towards our brothers and the world the face that contemplates"; this is the way of the *Philokalia*. If we forget this, the spiritual life of the Church suffers and the presence of the Fathers remains veiled.

The rediscovery of the forgotten philokalic tradition took place in Sibiu through the activity of Fr. Dumitru Stăniloae and occurred initially from the point of view of historical research. Professor at the Andreian Theological Academy of the city on the banks of the Cibin River, Father Dumitru published here in 1938 the first modern monograph on the life and teaching of Saint Gregory Palamas, with the addition of four of his treatises, translated into Romanian, according to the photographs of the codex in the Coislin collection of the National Library of France.[7] Addressing the figure and work of St. Gregory Palamas, however, had a deeper meaning than learned academic research. In the words of Andrei Scrima "it resurrected the primacy of the spiritual from within theological research and entailed the obligation to resume the traditional itinerary to which it bore witness." This obligation was assumed by Father Dumitru himself. In the short interval of the years 1946–1948, precisely the years of the establishment of the Soviet regime in Romania, he managed to publish in Sibiu the translation of the first four volumes of the *Philokalia* into Romanian, covering the first half (sixteen authors) of the powerful folio work of the *Philokalia* printed in Venice in 1782. It was a new, erudite, and documented *Philokalia*, annotated and moreover rearranged through a re-centering around the figure of Saint Maximus the Confessor, to whom the second and third volumes are dedicated, including a series

[7] The translations, the first in a modern language, of the treatises on prayer and divine light (*Triad* I, 2 and 3) were published by the young teacher D. Stăniloae, at the age of 29, in *Anuarul Academiei Teologie Andreiane* from 1932 to 1933 onward.

of writings absent from the Greek *Philokalia*. Scrima presents and comments in detail on the *Philokalia* of Sibiu, hailing it as an initial chapter taken up in Romanian Orthodoxy on the ways of the Philokalic fathers, and considering it as a preliminary condition for receiving their blessing. The particularity of the "Romanian philokalic revival" and, in any case, "the sign of its authenticity," is given by the decisive fact of being located at the point of convergence between the proclamation of its written testimony and the renewal of the life of prayer. Concretely, as the anonymous "un moine de l'Eglise Orthodoxe de Roumanie" has related, the appearance of the *Philokalia* in Romanian is linked to another significant fact that attracted his heart: it developed together with the parallel renewal of hesychast life. In the 1940s, the circles in which lay people met with monks revived, in the light of the teachings of the Fathers, the search for prayer of the heart until the day in which the blessing coming from the line of succession of the elder Paisius was accepted. The moment of fullness had once again been reached: "Still a layman at that time, the leader of the pilgrimage to the place of the heart then subsequently took on the monastic habit and became a hieroschemamonk."

In these few allusive lines, Scrima points out the coincidence between the publication of the volumes of the Romanian *Philokalia* of Sibiu by Father Dumitru Stăniloae and the activity in the years 1944–1948 and 1954–1958 of the circle of lay people and monks gathered around Bucharest's Antim monastery by the journalist and poet Sandu Tudor (Alexandru Teodorescu) in the "Burning Bush" association. Since the autumn of 1945, the group's philokalic research into hesychastic life had enjoyed the blessing and guidance of Father Ioann (Ivan) Kulygin, one of the last monks of Optina before its suppression by the Soviets. Having taken refuge in Romania in 1943, he was arrested in January 1947 by the Soviet army, convicted and sent to the gulag. Along with the blessing, Father Ioann the Stranger brought to the group the hesychast anthology of Valaam and the icon of the Mother of God of the "Burning Bush." On 3 September 1948, Sandu Tudor was consecrated as a monk at Antim with the name of Agathon and, in the following months, completed the first version in 9 + 9 stanzas of the *Akathist Hymn to the*

Burning Bush of the Mother of God. Towards the end of the year, the group was dispersed by the authorities.

Having entered in 1949 as a novice, Andrei Scrima remained at Antim as secretary, then transferred as professor to the Higher Monastic Seminary at Neamț for 1950–1952, and subsequently, until his departure for India in November 1956, to the Patriarchate with the position of librarian. In the summer of the same year he obtained a license in theology with Father Stăniloae and was tonsured a monk by Father Benedict Ghiuș. In 1950 Agathon Sandu Tudor settled in the skete of Crasna (Gorj), where he was consecrated hieromonk. Here he was arrested and detained until 1952 at the Danube–Black Sea Canal. Freed, he went to Sihăstria of Neamț, where in 1952 he was consecrated as a monk of the great habit and took the name of hieroschemamonk Daniil, appointed in the autumn of 1953 as staretz of the skete on the Rarău mountains. Taking advantage of his visits to Bucharest, the "Burning Bush" group resumed clandestine meetings in the homes of its members. In 1958, Father Daniil definitively arranged the last version in 12 + 12 stanzas of the *Akathist Hymn to the Burning Bush of the Mother of God*, before being arrested on the night of 13 June together with sixteen other members of the "Burning Bush"—the last arrested, in September, was Fr. Dumitru Stăniloae—all of whom were sentenced on 8 November to oppressive years of detention. On November 17, 1962, Father Daniil died in the terrible political penitentiary of Aiud. Seriously ill, the poet Vasile Voiculescu was released in May 1962, only to die on 25 April 1963 following serious illnesses contracted in prison. The other members were freed in 1965 and gradually reintegrated into the Church and monasticism,[8] dispersed throughout various areas of the country (some emigrated to the United States). With rare exceptions, they will never be legally rehabilitated for the serious crimes for which they were convicted and imprisoned. Until the fall of the communist regime in 1989, the "Burning Bush" continued to be for the regime a dangerous counter-revolutionary conspiracy of certain mystical

[8] ...a monasticism drastically amputated in November 1959 by a decree that halved the number of monasteries, expelling hundreds of monks and nuns without being able to wear their religious habit anymore and throwing them into factories and farms.

intellectuals with the aim of burning the "achievements" of socialism, which had victoriously imposed itself in the cities and villages. The very name "Burning Bush" was banned and unpronounceable in public discourse in Romania, where this unique phenomenon remained practically unknown until after the fall of communism in 1990.[9]

Since 1965, with Nicolae Ceausescu in power, Romania's communist regime entered a new liberal phase, of openness towards the West (an opening that lasted until 1977) and of marked independence from the USSR. To consolidate his personal power which had now become dictatorial, the communist leader promoted an ideological reorientation in the direction of Romanian national-communism. In the new vision, the Romanian Communist Party no longer legitimized itself as a Romanian variant of revolutionary internationalism led by the Soviet Union, but aspired to gain credibility according to a new image: that of realizing the historical and spiritual aspirations of the Romanian nation of all times. In this sense, in the name of a Romanism that had come back into vogue, it allowed the publication of Romanian cultural and spiritual values, which were clearly in open conflict with the Marxist-Leninist ideology, values censored or harshly repressed in the 1945–1965 years, the two decades of Sovietized Romania. Faced with the opening of borders and the open assertion of independence from Moscow in 1968, on the occasion of the Prague Spring, the new policy attracted international sympathy to the new, apparently "liberalized" Ceausescu regime in its first decade. In exchange for patriotic adhesion to the regime in the name of reaffirmed nationalism, the Romanian Orthodox Church was allowed to connect to the ecumenical movement and participate in theological dialogues. Romanian theologians, including Father Dumitru Stăniloae, were able to circulate and hold conferences in the West and, above all, the editions of the

---

[9] Father Scrima spoke in 1957 in Paris about Father Daniil's Akathist Hymn—the first version of which was also translated into French—and about the "Burning Bush." On the basis of those conferences, Olivier Clément published an enthusiastic article on "L'Eglise Orthodoxe ou le miracle du Buisson ardent" (*Réforme*, No. 644, 20 July 1957), which, if certainly not the starting point for the repression of the group by the communist authorities—Father Daniil had been arrested as early as 13 June—certainly contributed to warning them and provoking the harshness of the sentences.

Romanian Patriarchate obtained permission to publish theological research and the documents of the Christian tradition.[10]

The main beneficiary of this policy was the now venerable professor, Father Dumitru Stăniloae, who retired in 1972. In the years 1976–1979 he published volumes V–VIII of the Romanian *Philokalia* in Bucharest, to which he added a new translation in 1980 of the *Ladder* of Saint John Climacus, which appeared in 1981 as volume IX, together with the *Discourses of Saint Isaac the Syrian*, published as volume X. Alongside these volumes, Fr. Stăniloae published the three summary volumes of Orthodox dogmatic theology in 1978 and in 1981, disguised under the title of "Orthodox Spirituality" as the third volume of a manual of Orthodox moral theology, in essence, his former course on Asceticism and Mysticism, held in 1947 in Bucharest from the teaching chair terminated that year by the communist regime. All references to the terms "mystical" or "mysticism," labeled as retrograde and reactionary by the official ideology of the Communist Party, had to be eliminated, replaced by those of "spiritual" and "spirituality."[11]

Alignment with the new nationalism was also felt in the epilogue *On the History of Hesychasm in Romanian Orthodoxy* with which Fr. Stăniloae concluded volume VIII of the Romanian *Philokalia*[12] in 1979. Despite the historical evidence provided by the dozens of Romanian and Slavic manuscripts and in the libraries at the Romanian Academy or at the Neamț monastery or at the Romanian Patriarchate, which indicate the opposite, the whole essence of the contribution of the

---

[10] In 1979 the Patriarchate editions obtained permission to publish the series "Ecclesiastical Fathers and Writers" which began with the writings of the Apostolic Fathers. In this series, Fr. Stăniloae published the translation of the works of Saint Maximus the Confessor in 1983 and 1990, in 1982 a volume with the writings of St. Gregory of Nyssa, and in 1987–1988 two volumes with the writings of Saint Athanasius the Great, ending with the three volumes of the writings of St. Cyril of Alexandria in 1991, 1992, and 1994.

[11] Reference to the first course in ascetics and mysticism inaugurated in 1933 at the Faculty of Theology in Bucharest by Nichifor Crainic, poet and journalist, but also theorist of a Romanian ethnocratic corporatism with evident sympathy for Italian fascism, was eliminated. Initially sentenced to death by the Soviets and a political prisoner in dramatic conditions for fifteen years in communist prisons as an enemy of the people, from which he was freed in 1962, Crainic lived until 1972, but, despite the nationalism revived by the regime, it was never republished, the regime judging it extremely dangerous.

[12] *Filocalia* VIII, 555–87.

startsy Paisius Velichkovsky and Basil of Poiana Mărului, with the activity carried out by them in the Romanian territories for the purpose of renewing the hesychast life, is mentioned hastily, tied to the past and, in the end, minimized.[13] By avoiding the unilateral excesses of any individualism and singular forms of life and by placing the emphasis on obedience in cenobitic life and on care for the poor, the Romanian Cernican hesychasm would have been a form of *integral spirituality* superior to the typically Slavic paisianism, judged too passive in the contemplative dimension of spiritual life and of a too emotional type.

In outlining the history of Romanian hesychasm, Fr. Dumitru cited several works still in manuscript by the monk Ioanichie Bălan, a leading expert on Romanian historical traditions and the monastic phenomenon, which he had also recommended for publication. In the favorable context of the early eighties, Fr. Ioanichie also received official authorization to publish: *Patericul românesc* (1980), *Vetre de sihăstrie românească* (1981) and the two volumes *Convorbiri duhovnicesti* (1984, 1985) with contemporary fathers, thus constituting a true trilogy on Romanian monasticism.

This is then the general picture of the context and environment in which the 1984 visit to Romania by the Contemplative Brothers of Jesus took place, in search of the origins of the philokalic renewal of modern Orthodoxy. Thanks to the friendship that had been created with Father Ioanichie, the

[13] Ibid. In Fr. Dumitru's opinion, although much has been written about the two Ukrainian startsy who settled in Romanian territory, their inclusion in the tradition of Romanian monasticism has not been sufficiently highlighted, nor what and how much they received from this very much more than they gave. Under no circumstances would they have been concerned with the prayer of Jesus, but only with the introduction of prayer into cenobitic life. And this would in fact have been an influence of the Romanian way of practicing hesychast prayer, affirmed in an even more intense way at the monastery of Cernica by the elder Gheorghe, the disciple of Paisius, in a famous spiritual testament of 1787, some pages of which are presented . The fundamental letter-treatise on the prayer of the mind of staretz Paisius is deliberately omitted, considering it known, but the important introduction to Gregory of Sinai by the staretz Basil of Poiana Mărului is included precisely to highlight the difference between this and the texts collected by the Romanian monks. At a time when the former invited everyone to practice the Jesus Prayer, the latter insisted on the ascetic conditions indispensable for the practice of prayer, including community prayer.

Brothers had the opportunity not only to have memorable meetings with Romania's still living, great spiritual fathers of the twentieth century, but also to establish precious study contacts. The meeting with Archimandrite Ciprian Zaharia of the monastery of Bistrița in Moldavia was providential, who then, together with the historian Dan Zamfirescu, had delineated a program of inventorying and validating the Romanian documents on the staretz Paisius and on the Paisian phenomenon, which had lain forgotten in the manuscripts from the Neamț library and the Romanian Academy. Those documents were collected in a volume, which never saw the light of day. The volume included the three relatively unknown Romanian biographies of the staretz Paisius and the oldest Romanian translation of the famous Autobiography of the staretz still unpublished. A valuable preliminary study on the translations of the philokalic texts found in Romanian monastic manuscripts featured surprising results: the first translations of philokalic texts into a modern language were precisely the Romanian ones made by Paisian disciples, and these preceded the Greek *Philokalia*, published in Venice in 1782, by almost two decades.[14] The Contemplative Brothers of Jesus were able to make abundant use of all this documentation in their excellent doctoral dissertations supported in Rome, one on the staretz Basil of Poiana Mărului in 1986 and the other on Nicodemus the Hagiorite in 1987. They also took care, at the same time, to translate and publish in 1985 and 1988 in Benedictine monastic journals in Belgium and Italy the two articles in which Archimandrite Ciprian summarized the results of the research of the Bistrița center, underscoring how much the context of Romanian Paisianism has remained unknown and so little validated.

Since then Father Elia, with his lucid understanding of and loving regard for Romanian monasticism, has not ceased to be, in his enthusiasm, a tireless and effective interpreter of the spiritual reality of Romanian Orthodoxy. He worked on the autobiography of the elder Paisius, translating it into

[14] This is demonstrated by ms. BAR 2597, called "Filocalia di Dragomirna," copied in 1769, while the ms. BAR 1455, copied in Neamț around the year 1800, contains the Romanian translation, with additions, of the entire first part of the Greek *Philokalia* published in 1782.

Italian and publishing it in 1988 and, in 1991 he presented to the Italian reader a selection of the figures and sayings of contemporary Romanian spiritual fathers, taken from the works of Fr. Ioanichie. To these volumes are added a series of studies and conferences that he has contributed to over the years, having as their theme Romanian philokalic spirituality. The series began with an excellent speech at the international symposium on the *Philokalia* in November 1989 at Rome, in which the philokalic school of staretz Paisius and the 1782 edition of the *Philokalia* by Macarius of Corinth and Nicodemus the Hagiorite are eloquently paralleled, together with the Slavonic edition of Paisius's *Dobrotoljubie* in 1793 at Moscow. The three different environments in which philokalic spirituality spread in the second half of the eighteenth century were clearly highlighted: Slavic, Romanian and Greek. The differences in conception for the use of the philokalic texts were also highlighted: while Macarius and Nicodemus integrated the *Philokalia* into a general missionary strategy with the aim of promoting the patristic tradition as an Orthodox alternative to the Enlightenment, the elder Paisius deemed it to be used exclusively for the monastic environment and under the experienced guidance of a spiritual father (this probably explains the fact that the Romanian Paisian disciples did not publish the philokalic translations that they had created).

We would come to know all this much later. In November 1989, just when the work of the International Symposium on the *Philokalia* was taking place in Rome, Ceausescu's national-communist regime, which had become unbearable in recent years, was experiencing its last moments. The paroxysmal finale of his aberrant dictatorship took place with bloody massacres between 16 and 25 December 1989. The following decades would be often marked by convulsive tensions. These accompanied the difficult and overly long process through which Romania managed to overcome the difficult transition from totalitarianism to democracy, from the Soviet Union to the European Union, of which it became a full member in 2007. A significant moment along this path, in which Romania—a Latin country of Orthodox tradition—found itself unmistakably confirmed in its European vocation, was the historic visit of Pope John Paul II to Bucharest in May 1999.

In this period of time, the Romanian nation, traumatized by the long decades of totalitarian dictatorship, has made the difficult effort to overcome the recent past, to recover the memory and spiritual references repressed by communism, as well as to reconnect with the dynamics and circuitry of European values. Rediscovering its public presence, the Romanian Orthodox Church has initiated a vast program of institutional reaffirmation by engaging in the construction of churches and monasteries, in the multiplication of theological schools and by using the opportunities offered by the mass media: newspapers, television, etc. Unfortunately, not supported by a consistent catechetical program, this dynamic has laid itself open, precisely because of its successes, to the inevitable risk of extroversion and self-secularization. To counter these trends, as well as the seductions of the accelerated secularization of Romanian society, which was rapidly moving from communism to consumerism, the prestigious figures of those spiritual fathers still alive were used through conferences, interviews and television broadcasts. This had a real media impact, but lacked depth and consistency in the absence of an adequate mystagogical and philokalic pedagogy that would guarantee its reception.

In his last three years of life after the fall of communism, the venerable Father Dumitru Stăniloae completed the composition of the Romanian *Philokalia* with volumes XI and XII, including the translation of the *Letters of Barsanuphius and John* and the *Discourses of Abba Isaiah*. Indispensable as pedagogy and ascetic propaedeutics, they have, however, somehow diluted the rigor and programmatic contemplative concentration of the initial Paisian-Nicodemian *Philokalia*. In 1992, Father Dumitru concluded his prodigious theological activity with a volume of *Reflections on the Spirituality of the Romanian People*, exalting an ideal rural Orthodoxy, which was as theologically problematic as it was utopian, since the Romanian peasant world was in fact definitively destroyed in the decades of forced communist collectivization. The nostalgia for a popular Orthodoxy, as well as the ghosts of right-wing Orthodox nationalism between the two wars, partially recycled by Ceausescu's communist ideology, continually surfaced in the interviews of the great spiritual men who survived the communist concentration camps. The external activism of the clergy, the abstract and superficial theology of the theological schools, the liturgical formalism, the popular pietism of the masses and the nostalgic piety of monasticism risked appearing inadequate to the questions of intellectuals, and also to those emerging in the Church, due to dissatisfaction with the language and attitudes of the clergy. The most serious thing was the risk of distance and inadequacy with respect to the authentic Orthodox tradition. A very eloquent indication of the situation that had been created is the fact that, having returned to Romania after 1991 and definitively in 1994, Father Andrei Scrima did not choose to live in Antim, nor in Moldavia, but at the New Europe College, the first for advanced studies in Romania created in 1994 by the philosopher Andrei Pleșu. Until his premature death in the year 2000, he moved among a small circle of intellectuals, not in ecclesiastical or theological circles. The gesture sounded like a tacit protest and an explicit rejection of the horizontal and local conception of Orthodoxy, dominant in the Romanian Church, in the name of a vision of Tradition founded on the vertical-contemplative and universally open axis.

In this context, if I may be allowed a personal remark, as a young assistant at the Faculty of Orthodox Theology of the University of Sibiu—this is how the old Andreian Theological Academy of Father Dumitru Stăniloae of the years between the two wars was reorganized in 1991, which had survived during the years of communism as a university-level theological institute—I insisted on the reintroduction into the study program, under the name of *Orthodox Spirituality*, the title of the interwar course on asceticism and mysticism abolished under communism, and became the first to hold the position in 2003. In 1994, together with a group of students and a monk, we established the Deisis Publishing House. According to the eschatological meaning of the similarly named iconographic theme, the purpose of the editorial activity was and still is the recovery of the contemplative and universal dimension of the Church's patristic tradition, always exposed to risks or distortions. At the center of his program is the ongoing project of an expanded *Philokalia*, the series of writings of the authors present in the classical *Philokalia*, only in an anthologized format.[15]

[15] The complete works of Simeon the New Theologian, Theoleptus of Philadelphia, and Philotheus of Sinai have been published. We are in the process of creating the complete Romanian edition of Gregory Palamas's works.

The task that presented itself as a priority was to bring back the phenomenon of Paisianism in its true dimensions, which was instead minimized in a patriotic sense in the post-war national-communist period.[16] Fr. Ioanichie Bălan's friendship and advice proved essential. It was he who provided me with copies of the doctoral theses and the philokalic and Paisian studies of the Contemplative Brothers of Jesus. Reading them was revealing. Contemplative monks from northern Italy brought enlightening clarifications on the Paisian philokalic phenomenon and for us it was vital and necessary that those clarifications were introduced into the debate and into Romanian culture. I was honored and happy to publish in 1996 for Deisis editions the Romanian version of the monograph on the staretz Basil of Poiana Mărului and that of the autobiography and biographies of the staretz Paisius, restoring them, with the contribution of the brilliant clarifications provided by the "monks of the Church of Italy," to the context of the Orthodox philokalic tradition, Romanian included. Thus was born with Father Elia a friendship rich in contemplative tension and commitment to research, which, due to the luminous faithfulness with which it developed over time, I consider a blessing from above. Born from readings and books, it grew on the occasion of personal meetings in Italy during the first extraordinary symposiums on figures and themes of Orthodox spirituality, organized since 1994 by the monastic community of Bose. A sign of the times and of the work of the Spirit is the fact that, after 1990, such kinds of meetings of a spiritual nature, and not only of a historical-commemorative type, on the main personalities of

[16] They were already outlined in the monograph on the staretz Paisius by Fr. Sergii Chetverikov, existing only in the Romanian version, created by the Neamț staretz and second patriarch of Romania, Nicodim Munteanu, published in 1933 and 1940. The original Russian saw the light of day only in 1976, in Paris. Starting with this publication, the poet, journalist and lay theologian Nichifor Crainic had correctly highlighted, in the first course on ascetics and mysticism in Romania held in the mid-1930s at the University of Bucharest, that Paisianism formed as if it were the golden age of Romanian Orthodoxy and was a pan-Orthodox moment. The course was published defectively in 1993. Deisis editions republished this course on Orthodox mysticism in a critical edition in 2010, together with the course on German mysticism based on the text identified in the Metropolitan Library of Sibiu and that of Fr. Arsenie Boca.

Orthodox philokalic spirituality (from Nil Sorski to Paisius and Nicodemus, or on the Jesus Prayer or on the mystery of the transfiguration) took place not in Orthodox countries, but in Western monastic communities.

Slowly and with difficulty, as always in those years, the true dimensions, meanings and rebirth along the explicit Paisian lineage of the philokalic phenomenon in Romanian Orthodoxy began to be revealed in the first years of Sovietized Romania, known under the name of the Burning Bush. The details of this singular event appeared first of all in the memoir literature of survivors of the hell of communist prisons, to whom the gradual opening of the archives allowed the documents to be revealed.

A prime example in this sense is the unknown work by the hesychast poet and doctor Vasilie Voiculescu, written in the years 1945–1958 but which emerged from lost manuscripts and was then mysteriously found.[17]

The other example is the Burning Bush itself. In 1993, an episcopal publishing house in Transylvania printed, without any type of indication either about the author or the translator, two volumes of an anthology on the prayer of Jesus. It was, as it later turned out, the *Sbornik o molitve Iisusovoi* published by the hegumen Chariton of Valaam in 1936 and the *Besedy o molitve Iisusovoi* published in Serdopol in 1938. They were volumes brought to Romania in 1944 by Father Ioann Kulygin the Stranger and which had been translated from Russian into Romanian by the Bessarabian priest Gheorghe Rosca. Together with Father Paulin Lecca's version from Russian of the *Tales of a Russian Pilgrim*, these two hand-typed and copied translations were the main patristic source for the practice of hesychast prayer in the hands of the members of the Burning Bush and primarily of Sandu Tudor. The second volume (*Besedy*) included the Romanian translation from Russian of the Introductions of the elder Basil and of the six-chapter treatise on the prayer of the mind written in 1770 by the elder Paisius, all seminal texts for Sandu Tudor.

[17] After a first anthology which appeared in 1994, in 2000 the first complete edition of Vasile Voiculescu's poetic work appeared and, in 2004, the definitive edition was published with the facsimile reproduction of the photocopy, from the archives of the *Securitate*, of manuscripts confiscated upon the poet's arrest in 1958.

The first volume (*Sbornik*) also included in the Romanian version an extended summary of the teaching on the hesychast prayer of the startsy Basil and Paisius and ended with an enigmatic text entitled *Word of the Father Ioann the Stranger to His Disciples*. Its secret was revealed a few years later by Father Andrei Scrima, who returned to Romania. The first part of his fundamental volume, published in 1996 with the title *The Time of the Burning Bush*, was an extensive hermeneutic commentary on this letter of blessing and spiritual tradition by Father Ioann Kulygin.[18] A year later, in 1997, the first short variant (9 + 9 stanzas) from 1948 of the *Akathist Hymn to the Burning Bush of the Mother of God* was printed. In 1999 the definitive long variant (12 + 12 stanzas) from 1958 was finally published. Also in 1999 the four notebooks with the recovered notes of Sandu Tudor began to appear. In 2009 the edition of the five akathists by this writer who became a monk was published in full. And in 2018, fragments from the ten folders of the sinister dossier of the 1958 political trial taken from the *Securitate* archives were also published.

The philokalic hesychasm of the Burning Bush was thus one of the strands of Paisian pre-eminence, since Paisianism constituted the distinctive characteristic that defined it. Daniil Sandu Tudor also derived his Mariological synthesis from the same Paisian thread. In the second chapter of his 1770 treatise on the prayer of the mind, which Sandu Tudor read in the Romanian version of the second volume on hesychasm assembled by the monks of Valaam, the staretz Paisius attributed an Edenic origin to the hesychast prayer of the heart. Through a mystical, internalized exegesis, the divine command entrusted to Adam to cultivate and guard the Garden of Eden was accompanied by the command to cultivate and guard, through prayer and attention, the inner sanctuary-paradise of the heart to celebrate the nuptial liturgy of union with God. Having lost, following the expulsion from paradise of our ancestors, the hesychast prayer of the heart as a form of actualization of the dialogue and communion of man with God, this reappears in the Child Mary, in her holiness of life which, according to tradition, she led between

[18] André Scrima, *Timpul Rugului Aprins* (Bucharest: Humanitas, 1996), 25–108.

three and thirteen years of age in the Temple of Jerusalem. In the context of this vision, the elder Paisius cited large fragments of the superb mystical interpretation of the Byzantine feast of November 21, set out in the homily-treatise number 53, written by Gregory Palamas in the years 1333–1335 as an Athonite monk. It was Palamas's second writing, after that of his panegyric for the anchorite St. Peter the Athonite. Sandu Tudor conceived and composed the extraordinary *Akathist Hymn to the Burning Bush of the Mother of God* in the years 1948–1958, grafting Palamite Marian mystagogy onto the traditional contemplative reading of the icon of the Burning Bush, as a theophany of the incarnation of God and transforming it into a theophany of the mystical divinization of man.

In a collection of Byzantine studies and texts published in 2008,[19] I was able to investigate and present in detail the fascinating, little known Byzantine Mariological exposition of the hesychast theology of the fourteenth century in its three variants: the hesychast Mariology of Gregory Palamas, the humanist Mariology of Nicholas Cabasilas and the cosmic Mariology of Theophanes of Nicaea. I have shown that, in a concentrated formula, the novelty and originality of the Byzantine Mariology of the fourteenth century can be perfectly captured by placing it in parallel with the classical patristic Mariology of Andrew of Crete or John of Damascus of the seventh to eighth centuries. If these see the Virgin Mary in the perspective of her role in the descending economy of the mystery of the humanization of God, the Byzantine theologians highlight her place and role in the ascending economy of the symmetrical mystery of the divinization of man—the Virgin Mary seen as the first human deified through mystical union with God.

The editorial circumstances of the Byzantine Mariological texts of the fourteenth century have, to this day, unfortunately blocked their reception and contemporary appreciation. The stages of this process, which I described there at length, are as follows: the three Mariological discourses of Nicholas Cabasilas and the singular masterpiece represented by the extensive Mariological discourse of Theophanes of Nicaea were

[19] Ioan I. Ică, Jr., *Maica Domnului in teologia secoluui XX și în spiritualitatea isihasta a secolului XIV: Grigorie Palama, Nicolae Cabasila, Teofan al Niceei. Studii și texte* (Sibiu: Deisis, 2008).

published in 1925 and 1935 by the Assumptionist scholar Martin Jugie. The edition simultaneously entailed an apologetic purpose, since the orations were used polemically against the Orthodox as Byzantine arguments in favor of the dogma of the Immaculate Conception. Very critical from a strictly Thomistic position of the theology of the uncreated energies of Saint Gregory Palamas, branded as "heresies," Fr. Jugie did not hide his enthusiasm when faced with the singularity of the superlatively appreciated Palamite Mariology. Faced with the barbarity of totalitarianism in Europe, the Catholic Church responded, not by critically denouncing the anti-Christianity of communism and Nazism, but by contrasting it with the luminous figure of the Virgin Mary—for example, by consecrating the whole of humanity in disarray to the Immaculate Heart of the Virgin Mary in 1942 or by establishing the feast of the Queenship of Mary in 1954, or even by proclaiming the Assumption of the Virgin Mary as dogma in 1950. This last act of Pope Pius XII reignited theological controversies throughout the Orthodox world. At the end of the same year, the Romanian Orthodox Church made public an official statement of protest drawn up on the basis of a critical study, written by theology professors in Bucharest and published in the same Patriarchate magazine.[20] Among these, the study of Father Dumitru Stăniloae stood out, which was not limited to providing a widespread comparative presentation of the Catholic and Orthodox Mariologies, but presented for the first time in Romanian theology the Byzantine Mariologies of the fourteenth century, in whose positions he saw the possibility of extracting neopatristics from the polemical polarization of Catholic and Orthodox scholastic Mariologies. The proposed openings were, however, not appreciated by Father Stăniloae's Sibiu colleagues, who, without naming him, responded to his study with a series of critical articles, published in two special issues of the only ecclesiastical newspaper that was printed in Romania at the time.[21] In essence, support for the Mariological positions of the Byzantine theologians of the fourteenth century, edited and promoted by the Roman Catholic theologians,

[20] *Orthodoxia* no. 4/1950.

[21] *Telegraful Român* no. 24–27, 28–30/1951.

was branded as "crypto-Catholicism" and declared incompatible with Orthodox dogmatics. Father Stăniloae then responded, without in turn naming his former colleagues from Sibiu, with an extensive study on the Mother of God mediator,[22] in which he demonstrated the inconsistency of the arguments of the school theologians and once again pleaded the idea of a renewal of Mariology in the spirit of the Byzantine theologians of the fourteenth century, supporting with extensive quotations an ontological vision on the place and key role of the Virgin Mary in the mystery of the divine plan of creation, salvation and the fulfillment of creation and humanity in Christ and in the Church. The theologians of Sibiu returned to the charge with an article of Mariological considerations in 1958, but Fr. Dumitru was no longer able to respond because he was arrested and condemned together with Daniil Sandu Tudor and the members of the Burning Bush. In the trial, Father Stăniloae tried to avoid conviction by dissociating himself from the activity and positions of the Burning Bush. The traumatic experience of repression, but also the depressing previous controversy with his colleagues from Sibiu led Father Stăniloae to never return to the innovative themes of the Mariology of the Byzantine hesychast theologians and made him distance himself definitively from the Paisian philokalic phenomenon (a distance which he explains in volume VIII of the Romanian *Philokalia*).[23]

Both hesychast Mariology and philokalic Paisianism, which lie at the heart of the Burning Bush, would have been reaffirmed, not in a polemical but doxological way, as spiritual resistance in the face of the terror of history embodied by communism, by Father Daniil Sandu Tudor. Two months before his arrest, he finished the masterpiece the *Akathist Hymn to the Burning Bush of the Mother of God*, the spiritual testament of an entire movement and the quintessence of Antim's philokalic renewal: the Virgin Mary, "Holy Bride, weaver of ceaseless prayer." In the years of communist persecution, the feared

---

[22] *Orthodoxia* no. 1/1952.

[23] A distance explicitly stated not only in volume VIII of the Romanian *Philokalia*, but also programmatically in the speech given in October 1955 in Cernica on the occasion of the canonization of the staretz Calinic (†1868 as bishop of Rîmnic).

Orthodox polemicist of the 1930s gave way to the transfigured hymnographer who does not hesitate to sing:

> "Rejoice, rapid spiritual progress granted to firmly established hearts,
> Rejoice, oneness of mind of all the reconciled churches."
> (Ikos 7)

Upon closer inspection, the philokalic renaissance in Romanian Orthodoxy in the 1940s and 1950s presents itself as a many-sided phenomenon. In this period of time, at least four movements emerged to reaffirm philokalic spirituality. Alongside Antim in Bucharest, linked to Sandu Tudor (trip to Athos in 1929, then marked by the meeting in 1944 with the Paisian Ioann Kulygin), the movement linked to the charismatic figure of Fr. Arsenie Boca began in Sâmbata and Prislop. Student of theology in Sibiu and at the Academy of Fine Arts in Bucharest, in 1938, before becoming a monk, Zian Boca lived for a few months on Athos where he met, like Sandu Tudor, the venerable spiritual father Antipa Dinescu, and from there he returned to Romania with a copy of a Romanian philokalic manuscript. Hieromonk Arsenie effectively supported Father Stăniloae in the translation and above all in the diffusion of the volumes of the Romanian *Philokalia* among the monks and the population of believers in the villages of Transylvania. His spiritual sermons with philokalic content[24] enjoyed immense popularity, to which the Securitate responded by arresting him several times. In 1959 the Prislop monastery was closed and Father Arsenie was excluded from monasticism and the priestly rank for life, because the communist authorities always refused to reinstate him for fear of the influence he exercised over believers throughout Romania.

A philokalic renewal nourished by the Paisian manuscripts of Neamț was then established in the 1950s at the monastery of Slatina and also Sihăstria in Moldavia, having as its driving force the imposing figure of a self-taught spiritual father, Fr. Cleopa, the one who, in 1952, consecrated Sandu Tudor a monk of the great habit. To avoid arrest and exclusion from monasticism, Fr. Cleopa hid in the forests of the Rarău mountains where he lived as a hermit, without anyone being able to locate

[24] Published in 1995 under the title *Cărarea Împărăției* [Path to the Kingdom].

him, in the years 1953–1954 and 1959–1964. In this period of time he composed a large cycle of spiritual sermons,[25] which in fact constitute an excellent, popular homiletic initiation into philokalic hesychasm. In the same years, the archpriest Ilarion Felea, professor of theology in Arad and an esteemed writer and preacher, wrote and delivered to the faithful a large cycle of sermons[26] which constituted the translation into homiletic language of the ascetic and mystical courses of Nichifor Crainic and Dumitru Stăniloae. Imprisoned in 1945 and 1950, he was arrested again in 1958 and sentenced to twenty years in prison, and died in Aiud on 18 September 1961.

Among all these movements, the philokalic phenomenon of Antim and the Burning Bush stand out with the uniqueness of its experience—a group of intellectuals in the center of a European capital under Soviet occupation, together with some monks in search of a theorized but also practiced hesychasm—and with an emblematic character, due to Daniil Sandu Tudor's poetic ability to elevate and unify this unique experience into a symbol. As such, both the phenomenon of the Burning Bush and the figures of the group, led by the two poets Sandu Tudor and Vasile Voiculescu, but also the figure and thought of André Scrima, exercise a definite allure in the Romanian cultural space and continue to fascinate people. The reception of the phenomenon, however, is in the order of a predilection according to a historical or intellectual register—documents are published, studies and books are written, symposia are periodically organized with talks and discussions of considerable importance, even in Italy.

However, until now no one had actually addressed the phenomenon in its spiritual core, which is exactly what defines it. A monk of the Italian Church does it now, as a sign of the times, in the wake of the spiritual ecumenism in contemplative communities. Formed by members of the Romanian interwar intellectual elite, which also manifested itself as such in this experience, the Burning Bush was not, however, an intellectual phenomenon, a literary circle of some writer, an artistic

[25] They circulated in typed form, published only in 1992 with the title *Urcus spre inviere* [Ascent towards the resurrection].
[26] Published 2007–2010 in four volumes with the title *Spre Tabor* [Towards Tabor].

or philosophical cenacle, but a prayer group animated by the search for a concrete realization of the philokalic hesychast ideal, considered the mystical essence of true Orthodoxy. For this reason, according to Father Elia's presentation, the impossible biography of Daniil Sandu Tudor, a poet and journalist who became hieroschemamonk, hymnographer and martyr, can only be explained against the backdrop of the philokalic tradition of Orthodox hesychasm, at the center of which lies the mysterious and paradoxical reality of the heart lit in contemplative prayer by the flame of the Spirit. It is a prayer that becomes a journey towards the place of the heart which is the door to heaven in man, the vertical and universal divine dimension of existence. It is the journey-conversion which in fact is a return in repentance, whereby everything stands or falls as a confession of the sinner's state of a prodigal son and the hope of regaining divine sonship through the grace of the infinite mercy of God the Father, rich in love. The Virgin Mary is pre-eminently prayer incarnate, both woven from and weaver of incessant prayer. For this reason, the emblematic symbol of the prayer group, which wanted to be the Burning Bush, could only be a hymn arising from contemplative prayer and aimed at giving birth to contemplative prayer in the person praying, reborn as a temple in the secret sanctuary of the heart. A hymn is a holy Word that cannot be intellectually discussed, expertly annotated or accompanied by an infinity of hermeneutic passages, but must be prayed with a pure heart, capable of absorbing the mystery of God and absorbed in the mystery of an endless love-friendship.

With the simple and clear gaze of an erudite monk, but not the erudition of a monk interested in the spiritual essence of phenomena, Father Elia—a traveler, like the prophet whose name he bears, on the fiery chariot of prayer—gives us here, in the fifth decade of his contemplative life chosen for the sake of Jesus and his Gospel and almost four decades after his encounter with Romanian Orthodox monasticism, the much anticipated contemplative reading of the Burning Bush as an initiatory journey of prayer and hymnody in the place of the heart. Vasile Voiculescu, the other hesychast poet of the Burning Bush, admirably summarizes this initiatory journey in the poem entitled *Calatorie spre locul inimii* ("Journey to the Place of the Heart") written on the night of December 24, 1955. I am happy to transcribe it, as an ending that does not have an end, in Father Elia's inspired translation:

The place of our heart? who ever knows it?
How many are looking for it?
Surely not there does the vortex of thoughts lead us...
The place of our heart in Heaven dwells
and it contains the sweet Light of Him who is immortal.
The harsh abysses in every person fall asunder.
On the mountains of the soul snowed with curses
burns the flower of wonders—the Burning Bush—
which reduces space and time to ashes.
Lord, these steps of prayer exhausted by the journey,
towards the place of our? of your? heart they lead
where the mind suddenly awakens, bright
with the noon of Your Eternity.

An Impossible Biography

PREAMBLE

Since the documents on Sandu Tudor's life are limited to the memories and testimonies of those who loved or opposed him, it is simply not possible to reconstruct his biography in an exhaustive way. Not only that, many of the testimonies and documents that have reached us should be read with caution because the presence of the *Securitate* looms over everything. The truth about events emerges only by comparing the different testimonies with each other. So I thought I would proceed in this way. After a brief biographical overview of our subject, I have chosen some particular moments that characterized his life according to the role he played as an animator and driver of the Burning Bush movement: the trip to Mount Athos in 1929, the tumultuous years of the period between the two wars, the birth of the Burning Bush movement, the trial and prison. I will conclude by outlining a possible portrait.

1. BRIEF BIOGRAPHICAL OVERVIEW

Sandu Tudor, the literary name of Alexandru Teodorescu, was born in Bucharest on 24 December 1896,[1] son of Sofia and Alexandru Teodorescu, a magistrate who was first councilor and then president of the High Court of Auditors. He attended primary school in Bucharest, high school in Ploiești and was drafted into the army during the First World War. He returned to Bucharest to continue his university studies and took a

[1] In his short autobiography, to dispel any misunderstandings and suspicions before the secret police, he noted his date of birth as December 24th. Cf. Daniil Sandu Tudor, *Taina Rugului Aprins. Scrieri și documente inedite* (Bucharest: Anastasia, 1999), 23 (*Scurt itinerar autobiografic*, 23–28). In his biographies, as in the documents of the trial against him now published (Ioana Diaconescu, *"Rugul Aprins." Studii și documente despre exterminare și supraviețuire* [Bucharest: Fundația Academia Civică, 2018], 57–62), the date of birth is given as December 22nd. The biographical data is scant and elusive, so much so that André Scrima notes: "However, we will try to show some—nonfigurative—fragments of Sandu Tudor's 'impossible' biography" (*L'accompagnamento spirituale*, ed. A. Mainardi [Bose: Quiqajon, 2018], 149).

painting course at the Faculty of Fine Arts in Bucharest, but the lack of money forced him to take refuge in his parents' house in Constanța. He obtained his naval officer's license and, over the years 1922–1924, traveled on ships of the Romanian national navy. He himself tells of having participated in the 1922 evacuation, from the docks of Istanbul, of the scions of the Ottoman Empire's aristocracy, abolished that year by Kemal Atatürk.[2] As he relates about himself, "hungry for books" and absorbed by literary interests, he returned to Bucharest and became a teacher at the high school in Pogoanele, in the Buzău district, near Bucharest, dividing his time between school and the literary environment of the capital. In 1925 he published his first volume of poems, *Comornic*,[3] making himself known to the public and critics. He participated in the cultural debates of those years in the conflict between traditionalism and modernism with his contributions to *Contimporanul*, an avant-garde publication of the years 1922–1932, which collected the contributions of the most famous writers of the time, stigmatizing the harmful cultural impact of modernity on Romania.

He was published in numerous magazines as one of the many young talents influenced by the Orthodox current, supported by the magazines *Gândirea* (*Thought*), directed by Nichifor Crainic

---

[2] Cf. André Scrima, *L'accompagnamento spirituale*, 150, note 4.

[3] *Comornic* means *Treasury*, although the literary critic G. Călinescu, (*Istoria literaturii române de la origini pînă in prezent* [Bucharest: Editura Minerva, 1986], 885), says that the title is wrong because *comornic* does not mean "a place with treasures," but is the name of ancient high officials. His opinion is not flattering. He judges Tudor's style in these compositions to be religious, baroque, superficial, and preventing him from becoming a true writer. And in the introduction to the magazine *Gândirea*, edited by Nichifor Crainic, of which Tudor was a collaborator, he ridiculed the "miraculous" thinking of these writers who felt under the influence of a higher calling. Tudor's journey to Mount Athos was made possible by an unexpected grant, and many encounters with the monks are presented in the light of miraculous signs, which Călinescu simply calls coincidences. He recounts that when Tudor arrived in Thessaloniki, he met two Romanian monks who needed to accompany him to the Holy Mountain and relates a passage from Tudor's memoirs about this journey: "The premonition that this whole journey was not accidental was transformed into a sure and vivid feeling. The seeds of faith hidden in my soul led me to think that these incredible circumstances of facts and vicissitudes were evidence of a purpose I still do not understand, were not accidental. At every step the man needed for the journey appeared. This seemed like some gimmick, a prank set up by someone acting secretly. The meeting with the graying Macedonian-Romanian, with the little Thessalonian and now with the two monastic figures are, for me, signs."

(1889–1972),[4] even becoming part of the steering committee, and *Cuvântul* (*The Word*), directed by Nae Ionescu (1890–1940),[5] whose philosophical orientation, called *trăirism*, influenced an entire generation of Romanian intellectuals. His first literary effort in the religious field was expressed in 1927 in the akathist in honor of St. Demetrius the New of Basarabov (thirteenth century),[6] published in the *Gândirea* magazine with the support of Tit Simedrea,[7] at that time vicar of the archdiocese of Bucharest, and was approved the following year by the Holy Synod of the Romanian Orthodox Church and published as an official liturgical text in 1942. At the request of Gala Galaction (1879–1961), translator of the Bible into Romanian from Hebrew and Greek, then member of the Romanian Academy, and director of the School of Theology of Chisinău, in Bessarabia, Sandu Tudor was called to occupy the post of vice-rector of the Theological Student Union in Chisinău, but after a few months he returned to Bucharest because he was offered the position of secretary of the University Student Office and in the meantime obtained a degree in theology. In 1929 he had the opportunity to go to Athos with a scholarship obtained from Tit Simedrea himself, and he remained there for eight months.

[4] On Crainic, see the extensive introductory study by Ioan I. Ică, Jr. in *Nichifor Crainic, Cursurile de mistica* (Sibiu: Deisis, 2010), 5–111.

[5] See the volume, ed. Ioan I. Ică Jr., *Predania și un Îndreptar ortodox cu, de și despre Nae Ionescu teolog* (Sibiu: Deisis, 2001).

[6] The Holy Synod of the Romanian Orthodox Church, on 28 February 1950, decided to generalize his veneration throughout the church and the proceedings for the solemn canonization took place on 27 October 1955. See *Enciclopedia dei santi. Le chiese orientali* (Roma: Città Nuova, 1998), vol. I, col. 635–36.

[7] An important figure in the life of Sandu Tudor, Tit Simedrea (1886–1971) graduated in law from Iași, licensed in theology at Bucharest with studies on the beginnings of monasticism in the Romanian lands and on medieval Romanian culture, became a monk at Cernica in 1924, was a member of the Romanian delegation at the ecumenical and pan-Orthodox conferences (Lausanne, 1927; Sofia, 1929; Constantinople, 1929; Athos, Vatopedi, 1930; Oxford, 1937), metropolitan of Bucovina in 1940 with residence in Cernăuți, and defender of the Jews in Bucovina, earning the title of Righteous Among the Nations in the Israeli National Holocaust Memorial, Yad Vashem. With the invasion of Bessarabia and Bukovina by the Russians in 1944, the ecclesial center moved to Suceava, and in the following year, 1945, he resigned and returned to Bucharest, collaborating with Sandu Tudor and Alexandru Mironescu in the Burning Bush movement of hesychast renewal. When Patriarch Iustinian Marina (1948–1977), started an entire program of restoration of the ecclesial heritage by renovating the Holy Synod's palace at Antim with the adjoining archive and synodal library in 1959, he appointed the former metropolitan president of the commission in charge of the project, together with the Byzantine scholar Al. Elian.

When Tudor returned to Bucharest, his life became tumultuous in every way. He only decided to follow the route he had glimpsed on Athos a good ten years later. These were the years of frenetic journalistic activity, of the intellectual battles and personal controversies of an unconventional and committed intellectual, of tireless frequenting of libraries and monasteries in search of manuscripts of the Romanian hesychast tradition. A considerable library was established (around 8,000 volumes), ranging across various fields and languages—French-language publications in particular. As for his private life, he had had three divorces, all without children.

He would later say that the propensity for monastic life had stirred his heart without finding any way to realize it. He launched the weekly *Floarea de foc* (1932–1936) and the daily *Credința* (*Ziar independent de luptă politică și spirituală*, 1933–1938) promoting the Orthodox vision in its spiritual and social dimensions, rooted in a liturgical purview, with the collaboration of the most famous intellectuals of the time, from both the right and left. He distanced himself from the far-right ideology that was spreading in the country and fought both fascism and communism, taking a clear position with a manifesto condemning anti-Semitism. He harshly criticized the positions of a theological thought that he saw as being emptied of its prophetic and mystical function by aligning itself with a national-popular exaltation of Christianity. He also illegally printed an anti-fascist bulletin. His activities as a left-wing journalist provoked the reaction of the authorities who closed his publications. In 1939 he was called up for military service and immediately became commander of a military school. He was arrested by the fascist authorities due to his anti-Nazi activity but was immediately recalled to the military school that he directed. In 1943, together with the metropolitan of Bucovina, Tit Simedrea, in his see at Cernăuți, he organized a spiritual retreat for a group of intellectuals and prelate friends who would constitute, in the following years, the founding nucleus of the group called "Rugul Aprins" (the "'Burning Bush'"), at the monastery of Antim[8] in Bucharest.

Sandu Tudor, who had already frequented the monastery for some time, pledged, by selling his car and his two apartments

[8] Antim Monastery was built in 1713–1715 by Metropolitan Antim Ivireanul, of Georgian origin, a printer, engraver, theologian, bishop, metropolitan and martyr.

in the capital, to contribute to its restoration after the 1940 earthquake had seriously damaged it. At the beginning of 1945 he abandoned worldly life and entered the community of Antim, choosing Saint Simeon the New Theologian as his patron saint. He settled in a small cell in the bell tower, which would also become the first meeting place for the "Burning Bush."

In the autumn of 1945 he started and in 1946 further developed the hesychast association of the Burning Bush. It was a movement of study, conferences and practice of the Jesus Prayer, composed of clerics and intellectuals and attended by students from the various faculties of Bucharest. The event that would be decisive for the whole group that met in Antim was the meeting on Palm Sunday 1945, in Cernica, between Sandu Tudor, Benedict Ghiuș and Alexandru Mironescu with Father Ioann Kulygin, the Stranger,[9] a providential witness to and master of the Paisian hesychast tradition, and an enlightened practitioner of the prayer of the heart, who would support the Burning Bush group and chose Sandu Tudor as his disciple.

Born in 1885, Kulygin was a pilgrim in various monasteries in Russia, first in Kiev, then in Optino, then in the hermitages of the Caucasus, then in Valaam on Lake Ladoga, where, because still a novice, he survived the extermination of the monks by the Red Army. Returning to Rostov after the war, he was ordained a priest and pastorally served some village churches in the surrounding area; imprisoned in the years 1930–1937 for disobedience to the communist authorities, he became the confessor of Metropolitan Nikolai of Rostov, then was deposed by the Soviets in 1939, restored to his rank in 1942 by the Germans, a refugee in Odessa in 1943 due to the advance of the Red Army and welcomed into exile with his entourage by the Romanian patriarch Nicodim Munteanu (1939–1948) in Cernica. In October 1946 he was arrested by the Soviets for treason and deported in January 1947, after which all traces of him were finally lost.

---

[9] On him see Radu Dragan, "Une figure du christianisme oriental du XXe siècle: Jean l'Étranger," in *Politica Hermetica* 20 (2006), 124–142 (no. 20, entitled *L'ésotérisme au féminin* [Lausanne: L'âge d'homme, 2006]); Gheorghe Vasilescu, ed., *Cuviosul Ioan cel Strain (din arhiva Rugului Aprins)*, afterword by Sofian Boghiu (Bucharest: Anastasia, 1999). On the importance of the meeting between Sandu Tudor and Fr. Ioan Kulygin cf. Scrima, *L'accompagnamento spirituale*, 169–91.

Between 1945 and 1948 the Antim monastery had become the cultural-spiritual center of Bucharest, attracting men of culture, prelates, students and ordinary people around the themes of the mystical tradition of the Orthodox Church—a place of freedom of the spirit, of meeting between culture and church. Meanwhile, communist power was imposing itself in the country with the entire state bent to its aims. In 1946 the communists won rigged elections and unleashed systematic terror against political opponents, whether real or imaginary; King Michael abdicated in 1947, Patriarch Nicodim died in 1948. The new patriarch, Iustinian Marina (1948–1977), more willing than his predecessor to seek some form of collaboration with the communist power, presented a program of "renewal" within the framework rigidly imposed by the regime in an attempt to safeguard the presence of the church in the country. On 3 August 1948, a new Education Law was adopted which provided for the elimination of private and denominational schools, and the nullification of religion as an object of study. On 4 August 1948, the Law of Cults was also approved which regulated the general regime of religious cults, with control over the entire ecclesiastical organization. All ecclesiastical appointments were now part of the Stalinist-style communist project of emptying the religious tradition and taking power away from the communities of believers in the monasteries. On 30 August 1948, the General Directorate of People's Security was established, commonly called the *Securitate*, the new rulers' very powerful means of repression, with an extensive network of informants, which operated among the population and within the prisons to obtain total control over Romanian society. With the Greek Catholic Church outlawed in 1948 and the Catholic Church pushed to the margins of tolerance, the Orthodox Church underwent a process of control and subordination, despite the proclaimed state-church collaboration widespread in official rhetoric. During the same year, the political authority, with the obligatory consent of the patriarch, suspended the meetings in Antim and imposed the change of the monastery's staretz, forcing the predecessor, Fr. Vasile Vasilachi and his brother Haralambie, fervent supporters of the Burning Bush movement, to abandon the monastery.

At Antim, before being tonsured a monk with the name of Agathon on 3 September 1948, Sandu Tudor was arrested for the first time on 12 June and taken to the Jilava penitentiary for interrogation, but remained there for only a few days. Meanwhile he composed the akathist to the Burning Bush of the Mother of God on ceaseless prayer (*Imnul acatist al Rugului Aprins al Maicii Domnului*), perhaps the most beautiful Marian doxological hymn written on Romanian soil.[10] Brother Agathon was called to Craiova and ordained a priest by Metropolitan Firmilian in 1950, who entrusted him with the leadership of the skete of Crasna.[11] Here he invited Adrian Făgețeanu to come and entrusted him with preparations at the monastery for the reception of other intellectual monks. Antonie Plămădeală (the future metropolitan), Iuvenalie Ceanvic from the metropolis of Craiova, Titus Moldovan from the Polovragi monastery and Hristofor from the Lainici monastery came there as well, taking part in the evening conferences held by Sandu Tudor. In those years he managed to complete two other akathist hymns in honor of John the Theologian and Calinic of Cernica, compositions which were published for the first time in Madrid, in 1987, by the Romanian Cultural Foundation. But the communists had set out to destroy any group of Christian intellectuals and did not take long to disperse the community which they had infiltrated. Accused of activity hostile to the state, he was arrested on 16 June 1950 and sentenced to two years in prison (Adrian Făgețeanu was also arrested in December). After two years of prison in Jilava and forced labor on the Danube-Black Sea canal, which saw scores of prisoners die due to inhuman and absurd treatments, he was freed on 9 February 1952.

Having been a political prisoner, when released he could not return to his previous location. With the help of monk friends he repaired to Neamț, settled in Sihla di Sihăstria and from there went to Slatina where, in 1953, he received the habit of

---

[10] The akathist, Sandu Tudor's most famous poetic production, is composed of nine stanzas and, in this guise, was circulated as samizdat and also taken abroad, where it was published for the first time in Madrid in 1983. The translated editions in the various European languages bear this nine-stanza text. In Italian it can be read in *Gloria a Dio per tutto. Inni acatisti* [Glory to God for All Things. Akathist Hymns], edited by the Russian Monastery of the Dormition of the Mother of God (Roma: Appunti di viaggio, 2011), 125–135. In 1957, the now Father Daniil de la Rarău released a second revision of the akathist in thirteen stanzas which we translate here for the first time.

[11] Crasna is a seventeenth-century monastery, located at the foot of the Parâng Mountains, in the village of Crasna-Ungureni in the Gorj district.

a schemamonk from the hands of Fr. Cleopa Ilie, becoming hiero-schemamonk Daniil. Fr. Cleopa sent him to the Rarău skete, where in 1954 he was appointed staretz.[12] Starting in 1954, with prolonged visits to Bucharest, he re-established contacts with the former nucleus of the Burning Bush group, secretly staying at his friend Alexandru Mironescu's house or in the Plumbuita monastery led by Fr. Sofian Boghiu, one of the very first attendees and supporters of the meetings in Antim.

In August 1956 a group of young students spent ten days in Rarău to be introduced to the Orthodox tradition according to the program created by Fr. Daniil: the faculty should, leaving politics aside, adhere to purely scientific activity, to intense spiritual preparation with the practice of prayer of the heart, to faithful participation in liturgical prayer, to a search for spiritual guides, and to insights related to topics on spirituality, with readings and discussions in common. Fr. Daniil wanted them to become 'spiritual men' able, after completing their studies, to face the atheist onslaught. But already in September 1956 the *Securitate* opened a file against the group on suspicion of legionary activity under a religious cover, comparing the group's activity to the phenomenon of Vladimirești, the first monastery of nuns to be dissolved for insubordination to the religious and state authority.[13] In June 1957, informants infiltrated the

[12] According to information from Metropolitan Antonie Plămădeală, *Rugul Aprins* (Sibiu: Editată de Arhiepiscopia Sibiului, 2002), 81–90, it was not easy to get to Rarău. The approval of Metropolitan Sebastian was necessary, who knew Sandu Tudor well for the combative spirit with which he wrote in the literary magazines of the 1930s and whose monastic vocation was suspected to be insincere, given the three divorces behind him and his difficult character. Antonie Plămădeală, welcomed as a monk in Slatina without anyone knowing that he had been condemned in absentia, except Fr. Cleopa, presented himself to the metropolitan with a letter from the same Fr. Cleopa asking to include Fr. Daniil in the community of Slatina with the intention of sending him to Rarău where he could gather some monks around him and revive the skete. The metropolitan was wary of the matter but, in the end, left the responsibility of the decision to Fr. Cleopa and his community and so Fr. Daniil was appointed *staretz* of the tiny Rarău skete.

[13] The Vladimirești (Galați) monastery was founded and directed by Mother Veronica (Vasilica *Gurău*, 1922–2005) in the years 1940–1955, when she and the spiritual father of the nuns, Fr. Ioan Iovan, were arrested, the community dispersed and the monastery closed and transformed into a reception facility for handicapped children. The personal revelations to which Mother Veronica referred, the vitality of the monastery and the innovations adopted (frequent communion, public confession, the acceptance into the community

community and reported Fr. Daniil's intention to create a reactionary philosophical circle with legionaries and intellectuals to fight Marxism, but were not able to prove anything. Between June and December the *Securitate* intercepted the correspondence between Sofian Boghiu, Alexandru Mironescu, Dumitru Stăniloae and Andrei Scrima, who had then arrived in Paris as the patriarch's messenger to make known the situation of the Church, on his study trip to India for which he had received a scholarship to the University of Benares. Olivier Clément collected his confidences and presented them, without his knowledge, in an article in a Protestant weekly: "L'église Orthodoxe Roumaine ou le miracle du Buisson ardent," in *Réforme*, num. 644, samedi 20 juillet 1957. It describes Patriarch Iustinian's efforts to lead the Church within the framework imposed by the communist regime and the spiritual resistance of the monasteries, and makes known the existence of the Burning Bush group.[14] Whether or not this is the triggering motivation, the fact is that the *Securitate* decided to silence the group that revolved around Fr. Daniil. On February 25, 1958, the hieromonk Adrian Făgețeanu, one of the closest disciples of Fr. Daniil, was arrested

of only women who had never married) had caused a great stir in the Romanian church, with conflicting opinions on the sanctity of the type of life led there. Criticism of the official church for submitting to the injunctions of the communist regime led the *Securitate* to begin the destruction of the monasteries there, with the approval of the patriarch. The testimony of Fr. Ilie Cleopa is interesting. In a letter from 1953, published in *Studii teologica*, no. 5–6 (1953), 430–440, the famous staretz of Slatina came to the defense of the monastery, warning against the dangers of departing from tradition. The famous anti-communist writer Petre Pandrea, *Memoriile mandarinului valah. Jurnal 1954–1956*, accused Fr. Daniil de la Rarău and Andrei Scrima of having attacked Mother Veronica and the monastery community in the name of an exasperated traditionalism. When she was released from prison in 1960, mother Veronica found hospitality in Bucharest with the Văsîi family, whose son Gheorghe was in prison for belonging to the Burning Bush group, and with his parents who became monks, his father in Slatina and his mother in Văratec. She then returned to Galați, where she found work with some sisters of the community in a cooperative, and, on a pilgrimage to Jerusalem, had a memorable meeting with the patriarch of Jerusalem himself. In 1990 she obtained permission to rebuild the monastery and the community. Today it is the third largest female monastery in Romania, after those of Agapia and Văratec, with around 200 nuns.

[14] The following year, in 1958, the Scrima article also appeared, but incognito, which defined the Antim environment as the philokalic advent of Romanian orthodoxy: Un moine de l'Eglise Orthodoxe de Roumanie, "L'avènement philocalique dans l'Orthodoxie roumaine," in *Istina* 5 (1958), 295–328, 443–75.

while he was at the Caldarusani monastery near Bucharest. They wanted to obtain detailed information from him on Fr. Daniil de la Rarău's activities. On the night between 13 and 14 June, Fr. Daniil was arrested, in Professor Alexandru Mironescu's house, on charges of subversive activity, which was categorically denied by the interested party. On the morning of June 14, in Rarău, a thorough search of the monastery followed, confiscating everything that could appear compromising: theological, apologetic and anti-communist letters and writings.

The entire group was accused of subversive activity against the social order under a mystical-religious guise and sentenced to prison sentences of up to 25 years, confiscation of assets and deprivation of rights. Fr. Daniil was taken to Aiud prison and subjected to backbreaking work, frightful physical and psychological torture, without ever taking the shackles off his feet. He died on the night between 16 and 17 November 1962. Official cause of death: cerebral hemorrhage; in reality, beaten and tortured, struck on the head and left to die. His body was thrown into the Râpa Robilor (Prisoners' Ravine),[15] Aiud prison's mass grave, and covered with rubbish and soil.

With the famous decree 410/1959 of the Grand National Assembly, the communist power intensified the fight against monasticism, perceived as the only possible reservoir of "counterrevolutionary" energy: 92 monasteries were dissolved, closed or used for social purposes (in January 224 Orthodox monasteries were functioning, in October 194 were functioning and in March 1960 only 132). 4,700 monks and nuns were expelled from monastic life (in January the monasteries numbered over 6,000 people, but following the application of the new regulation, their number dropped to less than 1,500). Article 71 of decree 410 of 1959 stated:

> Monasticism can only function in authorized monasteries belonging to legally recognized cults. The operating authorization for monasteries is issued by the Department for Cults. Graduates of clergy preparatory schools can join monasteries at any age, but only after completing military service. Other

[15] On the Aiud prison, transformed into a large extermination center for the religious and intellectual elite from 1946 to 1965, see *Le catacombe della Romania. Testimonianze dalle carceri comuniste, 1945–1964* (Milano: Rediviva edizioni, 2014), 42–44.

people may be eligible to enter monastic life at 55 (for males) and 50 (for females) if they renounce their salary and pension, if they are not married and if they have no other obligations established by the Family Code. Only if the exercise of worship requires it, the Department of Cults can authorize some monks to assume ecclesiastical positions and receive the salary due. The above provisions also apply to current monasteries and monks.

2. THE JOURNEY TO MOUNT ATHOS

Back in 1929,[16] Sandu Tudor had the opportunity to go to Athos with a scholarship obtained by Tit Simedrea and remained there for eight months. Those eight months on the Holy Mountain would be absolutely decisive for the path he would then undertake several years later. He kept a sort of diary of those wanderings from one monastery to another, from one conversation to another, noting impressions and reflections, material that would constitute the topic of several articles that appeared in *Gândirea* and then collected as *Cartea Muntelui Sfânt* (Book of the Holy Mountain).[17] The journey, begun out of journalistic curiosity, was transformed into a true pilgrimage revealing the profound meanings and especially the practice of the Jesus Prayer. He initially described himself as a tourist, with short trousers and a knapsack on his shoulders, who embarked for the Holy Mountain to check on the slanderous information about the Athonite monks that had appeared in a tabloid newspaper in Paris. As a good journalist, wanting to know more about the hidden secrets of Mount Athos, Sandu Tudor was lucky enough to meet a wandering Romanian monk, Averchie, who instructed him on the way in which he could discover the true secrets of the Holy Mountain: dressing appropriately, maintaining a devout attitude, kissing icons and making prostrations in every church visited. This attitude, fake at the beginning, slowly conquered his heart and opened him to the teachings of the monks who let him share in their deepest secrets, those on incessant prayer.

---

[16] A correction to the 1926 date recalled by André Scrima (*L'accompagnamento spirituale*, 150).

[17] Published by Alexandru Dimcea, collecting the articles from the magazine *Gândirea*, together with other unpublished texts, in A. Dicea, ed., *Ieroschimonahul Daniil Tudor (Sandu Tudor), Scrieri*, I, preface by editor (Bucharest: Asociatia philanthropic medicala crestină / Christiana, 1999), 79–132.

At the time, several hundred Romanian monks were on Athos,[18] suffering somewhat from the Greek supremacy in the administrative organization of the monasteries, with difficulties in travel and contact with their own country. One figure struck him in particular: Fr. Antipa Dinescu, staretz of the Romanian Prodromou monastery from 1900 to 1914, then traveling to Căldărusani in Romania and then again to Athos where he died in 1942. André Scrima remembered that Sandu Tudor jotted down everything that struck him, and in his meetings with Fr. Antipa recalls the latter's reflections on the rupture between East and West, between Orthodoxy and Catholicism, symbolized in the anathemas of 1054. Tudor was interested in the question and Fr. Antipa replied to him: "Until the time of the anathema cast upon you by your brother has passed, you will forget yourself, you will crucify yourself for him, you will suffer in what is the best of your own, so that, in the end, the uncreated light of the resurrection will shine again for both."[19] In Tudor's notes, however, regarding Fr. Antipa we find only this observation:

> Are you asking me what is the meaning of the Holy Mountain? How am I to respond? I tell you: the great fragility, the holy and great monastic weakness, which is all gathered together as a single and powerful prayer, is the sturdy pillar that holds the earth on the celestial waters, at the feet of the Mother of God. If this whole world subsists and does not

[18] Athos had just been shaken by the great theological controversy that broke out among the Russian monks regarding the glorification of the name, masterfully analyzed by Antoine Nivière, *Les glorificateurs du Nom. Une querelle théologique parmi les moines russes du Mont Athos (1907–1914)* (Geneva: Syrtes–CERCLE, 2016). The text, published in 1907, which sparked heated debates on Athos and in Russia, is now published in Italian translation by Adalberto Mainardi: Schimonaco Ilarione, *Sulle montagne del Caucaso* [On the mountains of the Caucasus] (Bose: Qiqajon, 2019).

[19] André Scrima, *L'accompagnamento spirituale*, 150–151; idem, *Teme ecumenice*, (Bucharest: Humanitas, 2004), 127. Scrima remembers these words because he had relived them at the time of the meeting of Patriarch Athenagoras with Paul VI, and with the subsequent annulment of the mutual excommunications. The doubt regarding the real circumstance that Scrima reports on the meeting of Tudor and Fr. Antipa on Athos is given credence by the fact that Fr. Antipa returned to Romania in 1914 with a group of disciples, led the monastery of Caldărusani and returned definitively to Athos in 1934. In his diary, Tudor noted the meeting with Fr. Antipa on his journey to Athos. On Fr. Antipa Dinescu, see Ioanichie Bălan, *Pateric românesc (secole IV–XX)* (Galați: Editura arhiepiscopiei Tomisului și Dunării de Jos, 1999), 551–52.

> founder beneath the curse, this is because it is sustained by the prayers of the Holy Mountain. When, late at night, everyone sleeps peacefully in their beds, and thieves and burglars carry out their evil deeds and the perverse give themselves to their pleasures, the Mountain watches and prays and makes prostrations, with sighs.[20]

In the testimony of Fr. Roman Braga (1922–2015),[21] the Athonite experience of Sandu Tudor, who had spoken to him about it several times, is described thus:

> ...the rumor spread throughout the Mountain that Averchie was traveling from one monastery to another with a very devout pilgrim. All the doors and hearts of the monks who practiced the Jesus Prayer were opened to him. He returned from there with a small prayer stool, having learned the breathing method and the whole secret of the interior liturgy of the hesychasts, learned not from books, not from the *Philokalia*, but directly from those anonymous masters of modern-day prayer: the hesychast monks. There Sandu Tudor understood that our ego is infinite and that in that existential center of our being that the monks call 'heart,' God exists in a 'deep' sense and that God is the seal of our personality...[22]

For Sandu Tudor then began a process of reconsidering all human culture and intellectual development which, having points of reference other than the presence of God in man, became not only superficial, but also demonic. He used to say that to enter the order of the Spirit one must first "brutalize" oneself, and he gave us the example of another wanderer, that of the *Tales of a Russian Pilgrim,* who had become a walking prayer. He told us in detail how on Mount Athos he had started bowing just out of interest, to give the impression of being a devout pilgrim; but, after each bow, something transformed in him. One night, around two o'clock, when the Mountain began to pray, he was at the hermitage of Saint Anne. The sound of bells and semantrons could be heard everywhere, and above the monasteries, hermitages and cells, a full moon shone in

---

[20] *Scrieri,* I, 120.

[21] On him, see Violeta Popescu, *La Chiesa Ortodossa Romena dopo la Seconda Guerra Mondiale. Figure dell'Ortodossia romena nell'Occidente* (Milano: Rediviva edizioni, 2018), 202–219. His testimony is quite interesting: Roman Braga, *Ogni monaco ha un suo segreto con Dio* (Roma: Lipa, 1999).

[22] Braga, *Ogni monaco ha un suo segreto con Dio,* 52.

splendor, silvering the Chalcidian Sea with its rays. The poet's sensitivity, struck by the fire of the Spirit, was strongly moved. The warlike Sandu Tudor began to weep. The elder of the hermitage, seeing him so moved, addressed him with a question that fell like a hammer: "Brother Sandu, tell me, what did you do when you were in the world at this time, late at night?" The shadows of his past began to pass before Sandu Tudor's eyes, from which he would have liked to break away as if from some demonic vision: Capșa,[23] the nightclubs, the Parisian café-concerts, the literary meetings, the entertainment...and the staretz concluded: "We, the monks of Mount Athos, have the conviction that God does not destroy the world just because the monks pray at midnight." Returning to the capital, Sandu Tudor devoted himself to philokalic studies, which he not only read, but practiced, and discovered some unpublished documents on the existence of hermits in the Carpathians, noting in the *Diața starețului Gheorghe* (Spiritual Testament of the *staretz Gheorghe*) of Cernica "the peculiarity of Romanian hesychasm."[24]

Sandu Tudor wondered how to enter the spirit of Athos since he soon realized that the secrets of this Holy Mountain are not revealed to a first-comer. He wanted to enter the heart of things, discover the pure and spiritual soul of Athos, realizing that it was indeed not at all easy to find this "place of the heart"; he too wanted to drink the living water with which the monks quench their thirst, which he gradually came to know and respect, feeling conquered by it. He had the feeling that he did not come to Athos by chance. He would then say that he would return to Bucharest with Mount Athos in his soul, a soul that the disbelief and adversity of the times had lost, had caused to vanish. He found himself confronted with the preconceived ideas about monasticism that the educated

[23] Capșa is a location on Calea Victoriei in Bucharest. After the First World War, the cultural elite of the whole country gathered here, transforming its status from a "gathering spot for the elite" to a "bohemian café bar."

[24] Roman Braga, *Ogni monaco ha un suo segreto con Dio*, 52–53. Actually, Sandu Tudor was already a fervent reader and researcher of patristic texts, but after Athos he continued these interests with a much more interior involvement. However, he would still have to wait many years before the impulse of prayer translated into a consequential life choice. Regarding the startsy Gheorghe and Calinic of Cernica, see Ioan I. Ică, Jr., ed., *Sfinți stareți Gheorghe și Calinic de la Cernica, Viețile, povățuirile, testamentele* [Saints George and Callinicos of Cernica, Lives, teachings, testaments] (Sibiu: Deisis, 2018), 2.

class, to which he belonged, had developed due to its supposed moral superiority and he realized, more here than elsewhere, the falsity of the way of understanding the things of the spirit on the part of a certain secular culture. The level of ignorance, of simple-mindedness, sometimes even of slovenliness, that he encountered on Athos, hid something secret, which does not appear to those who think in worldly terms. He sensed that behind the vaunted "decadence" of the monks in terms of culture and openness to modernity lay an authentic world, a lively spiritual world. He felt stung by the laughter of those who, like Fr. Elisha, looked at him in his inability to understand what he saw, too often scandalized by the examples that presented themselves to him in the circumstances of daily life. This was the first thing he learned: here, the meanings and truths of things cannot be explained directly; they can only be guessed at. Don't be foolish, said the monk friend, Athos has many faces. Learn to see the real one. But how? Here was Fr. Elisha's answer: "Be as patient as you can, everything in its time. It takes patience. You too will discover true monasticism, you did not come this far in vain. With patience and spiritual balance, with peace, with confidence and condescension, since we are all of the earth and born from the womb of sin."[25] Tudor was impressed by the fact that his interlocutors, despite evidently coming from an often tumultuous life and retaining the traits of their human characters, had learned with their arrival in monasticism to live in the shadow of the world of the Spirit, with an interior clarity that constitutes their specific desire, aspiration and hope to see the invisible Holy Beauty. It is a world very close to that of children, very different from the usual world of men. This is how he describes it:

> In their world, of interior lights and illuminations, thoughts and images flourish with wonder and unexpected but, at the same time, ever so true contemplations. Contemplation is the reality here. Along these pathways the marvelous is quite natural, you breathe it and drink it at every step and the signs that reveal it have a power of intelligence and life that we cannot even imagine. Like a child, the monk conforms and regulates the world of his mind and soul beyond ways usual for us.

[25] *Scrieri*, I, 123–24.

> Indeed, what is external and appears as a trivial, vulgar and ugly reality, which he too shares, is in total contrast to that which he is in himself as a creature, as a personal aspect and achievement. It is not surprising then if we discover, taking in the full measure of the monk, let us say, a monk one actually encounters, a side of life that we, with all our acuity and skill, cannot see by remaining in our usual way of being and understanding. Such a life, the life of a spiritual disciple immersed in the vitality, grace and waters of the Spirit, has nothing to do with our intellectual clarity, and yet the materiality of the external world, when not denied by him as the embodiment of sin, of sin's deception and repulsiveness, serves him, just as it is, in its poverty and fragmentation, as a wave in which to hide, to humble himself and lose any high opinion of himself.[26]

Along with this renewed sense of being able to look into an interior world more real than the exterior world, with a spiritual understanding that reads events and situations, both exterior and interior, in the light of the Spirit, discovering the prayer that flows from the heart and recognizing it as the expression of the deepest longing we bear and of the spiritual activity that transfigures life and being, Sandu Tudor returned from Athos with devotion to the Mother of God, queen of Athos and mother of incessant prayer. These poetic verses composed in the spirit of Athos attest to this:

For the great night of the Virgin[27]

Rejoice, sunset of infinite longing.
The heart has glimpsed you and humbly sings,
of your face silvery-white as a holy rose[28]
blooming within the halo of a virginal ring.
Dead is the beauty of earthly flowers,
a figure for worldly ornaments that become corrupted.
Only You, Tabernacle, are of incorruption
for having welcomed the Uncontainable within yourself.
To you I sacrifice the light of my eyes,
so that I might pass inwardly under the night sky,
to gaze in my mind upon your immaculate image
waiting for the longed-for dream to come true.

---

[26] Ibid., 125.

[27] Ibid., 130. See the poem with annotations below, p. 270.

[28] Dog rose, the most common species, which has white petals with pink lobes, pear-shaped red fruit and arched red spines.

And, over the evening of my mind, your seal,
clear, unique and overwhelming,
rests high upon my brow, guiding me
to the azure-betrothal of the star-*logostea*.
Ever lead me with your gentle smile,
through the perils and harshness of the times,
to the destiny of my life,
blind yet full of wonder,
to touch the threshold of the biblical Amen.

3. TUMULTUOUS YEARS: THE PERIOD BETWEEN THE TWO WARS

In the interwar period, as regards the destiny of the country, two positions confronted each other: on the one hand, the liberal intellectuals, partisans of modernization, democratization, industrialization and urbanization and, on the other, the supporters of a tradition linked to village life, the conservation of agricultural structures and Byzantine-Orthodox values, of the peasant community and of authoritarianism. The truly democratic experiment of the years 1918–1930, after the establishment of Greater Romania with the reunion of Bessarabia, Bukovina and Transylvania with the Kingdom of Romania, rapidly collapsed under the influence of the rise to power in Italy and Germany of anti-democratic and anti-liberal corporatism and totalitarianism. In Romania the debate was structured according to the expectations of a whole new generation in search of a new identity, of thought and of society, later defined as nationalist orthodoxism. An indigenous theological-political solution was dreamed of in the face of the social dilemma that opposed liberal capitalist individualism and communist collectivism, both considered symmetrical atheistic materialist systems, with a virulent criticism of the Catholic and Protestant West, whose values were systematically discredited as sources of atheism.

The quite rapid growth in the number of university students (in 1914 there were 8,300 enrolled, while in 1930 over 37,000, with a percentage rate, when compared to the general population, higher than in Germany itself), with the accompanying difficulty in finding employment after studies, greatly exacerbated the contrast between ethnic affiliations, in the sense that national minorities, and Jewish communities in particular, seemed to be favored over Romanians. It was in this context that a young student leader from Iași, Corneliu Zelea Codreanu, organized violent protest riots at the university after a regulation guaranteeing Romanian citizenship only to Christians had been canceled from the Constitution on 28 March 1923, thus opening up the right of citizenship to Jews as well. Incarcerated in Văcărești, in the prison chapel Codreanu saw a depiction of the Archangel Michael defeating Lucifer and from that image was born the impulse that would lead him to fight in the name of the Christian God against the diabolical foreigners, especially the Jews. In that year the Christian National Defense League (*Ligă Apărării Național Creștine*) was created, with Professor Cuza as president and Codreanu as secretary. Codreanu soon moved towards more extremist positions and created the *Legion of Michael the Archangel* in 1927, which later became the *Iron Guard* in 1930. Through the Legion, Codreanu offered a formidable instrument of political struggle and economic-social revenge to thousands of young Romanians, often educated graduates, who would soon be put in enormous difficulty by the arrival of a disruptive economic crisis. In short, he was able to tap into what already in 1929 some acute observers of the Romanian political and social reality had called "the youth offensive." Characters emerged of the caliber of Mircea Eliade (1907–1986), Eugene Ionescu (1909–1995), Constantin Noica (1909–1997), and Emil Cioran (1911–1995) who, through culture, intended to bring the challenge to the very heart of the system to radically change the face of Romania, as Cioran himself wrote bluntly in a 1936 text, significantly entitled *Changing the Face of Romania*. All of these found an ideal reference in the thinker Nae Ionescu (1890–1940), capable of binding an entire generation of young intellectuals to himself with his teachings, imparted from the chairs of Logic and Metaphysics at the University of Bucharest. Ionescu's reasoning started from the observation of a perfect congruence between Romanianism and Orthodoxy. Out of this concept Ionescu developed his idea of national community, modeled on the life of the villages of deepest agrarian Romania, which he contrasted with the individualistic model of the cities, a typical Western imported product, without real roots in the Romanian soul. Democracy and individualism represented a certain and insidious enemy of the Romanian national and Orthodox community and the philosopher did not fail to forcefully criticize those who, among Romanians in recent decades, had moved towards both an external and internal Europeanizing attitude, putting the authentic values of the Romanian nation at risk.[29] An extraordinary megaphone for Nae Ionescu's ideas was the newspaper *Cuvântul* (The Word), a newspaper born in 1924, founded by Titus Enacovici, which immediately gathered famous collaborators such as the philosopher Lucian Blaga, the poet-theologian Nichifor Crainic and the novelist Cezar Petrescu, and which Ionescu joined as a member of the editorial team as early as 1926.

According to Eliade's testimony, discussion about Christianity and Christian philosophy at the university in 1921 was a real revolution. Discussion about redemption, sanctity, orthodoxy, or heresy in metaphysics and logic courses meant moving away from ingrained habits of idealism and positivism. Problems of metaphysics and religious philosophy had long been excluded from academic concerns. Professor Nae Ionescu was the first, with competence and originality, to set these problems at the center of his lessons. On the other hand, only Professor Nae Ionescu could allow himself the freedom to talk about religion, Christianity, mysticism and dogmatics from the chair of metaphysics, because he was at the same time a formidable logician, held courses in the philosophy of science and had presented his doctoral thesis on a mathematical question. His solid scientific preparation could not be disputed by anyone. He could not be suspected of patheticism, mysticism, or amateurism.[30] The titles of his first courses (The Problem of Divinity, The Reality of Spiritual Life, Metaphysics and Religion, The Phenomenology of the Religious Act) are sufficient to show what a radical contrast there was between Professor Ionescu's teaching and the rationalist orientation that dominated the Faculty of Letters. Thus, to oppose the humanistic and moralistic Christianity that had spread in the Orthodox circles of the Romanian capital, Nae Ionescu presented an exclusively theocentric Christianity,

[29] Cf. Emanuela Costantini, *Nae Ionescu, Mircea Eliade, Emil Cioran. Antiliberalismo nazionalista alla periferia d'Europa* (Perugia: Morlacchi, 2005), 54–62.
[30] Cf. Nae Ionescu, *Roza vânturilor 1926–1933* [The Rose of the Winds], Bucharest 1937, 439–40 (anastatic reprint, Bucharest 1990). This is the collection of Nae Ionescu's texts published in the magazine *Cuvântul* which Mircea Eliade comments on with an afterword entitled: ... *și un cuvânt al editorului*, 421–44. The opinions reported in my text are taken from there.

whose only norm was love for God. Theologian of a metaphysical Christianity, Nae Ionescu did not even spare the Patriarch Miron believing that the secularistic, secularizing and Protestant mentality of the head of the Romanian Church constituted an intrusion of the conceptions of the modern world, which he detested, into the spiritual life of the Church.[31] This interest in theological studies culminated in 1927–28, with the publication of *Logos—Revue internationale d'études orthodoxes*. Authoritative exponents of Orthodox thought collaborated on the only two issues that saw the light, including Georges Florovsky (1893–1979) and Pavel Florensky (1882–1937). It was precisely to overcome the lack of a thought tool of this kind that Mircea Eliade with Sandu Tudor and others designed a magazine of religious philosophy, whose title, formulated by Sandu Tudor, should have been *Duh și Slovă* (Spirit and Letter), but the project was unable to materialize.[32] Over the years and following political events, with the dissolution of the legionary movement and the arrest of thousands of legionaries, Nae Ionescu took sides in their defense by placing his prestigious newspaper *Cuvântul* at the disposal of the Guardista militants. Moreover, Nae Ionescu was predisposed to converge on the positions of the legionary movement because of his own way of seeing things.

Another tool for developing and disseminating ideas for young intellectuals, which also includes many legionary militants, was the newspaper *Gândirea* (Thought), founded by Nichifor Crainic and Cezar Petrescu in 1921, a newspaper that promoted right-wing ethno-cultural traditionalism, i.e., aimed at the Orthodox tradition, trying to valorize the Eastern Christian roots in order to reaffirm the autochthonous character of Romanian culture and its national identity.

Over time, Codreanu's legionary movement and the positions of all these young intellectuals had a tendency to come together, constituting the reference horizon for a "new revolution" with respect to Western thought. As demonstrated by Eliade, who celebrated the messianic significance of the legionary doctrine

---

[31] So reports the philosopher Mircea Vulcănescu, *Nae Ionescu. Așa cum l'am cunoscut* [Nae Ionescu. As I Knew Him] (Bucharest: Humanitas, 1992), 43–44, 75.

[32] The project would be taken up again in recent years by Constantin Sigov in Kiev, opening, with the same name created by Tudor, a publishing house that pursues Christian militancy of the same orientation.

in various articles written between 1935 and 1938, Codreanu tended to be seen as an upholder of the primacy of spirituality over politics. The peculiarities of the Iron Guard were exalted, which was not based on the idea of race, like Nazism, nor on the State, like fascism, but could be considered as the only Christian mystical current capable of directing human affairs. It seemed to see embodied in Codreanu the ideal of a "new man" which has its roots in Orthodox mystical religiosity, capable of providing Romanians with a new collective ideal.[33] During one of the trials brought against the legionaries, following the government repression of the movement, an emblematic episode occurred: the accused read in his defense an interview with Mircea Eliade which had been published in December 1937, entitled "Why I believe in legionary victory." Unlike other revolutions that are based on socioeconomic primacy (communism), on the primacy of the State (fascism) or on race (Nazism), the Romanian movement "will win by divine grace," since the legionary revolution is, first of all, a "spiritual and Christian" revolution. These were the underlying beliefs that drove the legionary movement.

The aspect that we are particularly interested in focusing on here is the "religious" tension of these positions, so much so that, especially in the scholastic and ecclesiastical environment, there was enthusiasm for the rediscovery of the roots of one's own Orthodox and national tradition, also induced by honesty, fairness of mind and respect among the members of the organization who advocated this. Many intellectual figures, from the right and the left, as well as many spiritual personalities who would become recognized charismatic leaders in the Romanian church and monasticism, sympathized or joined this movement of ideas. Before founding the Legion of the Archangel Michael, Codreanu had had the idea of starting a movement for students which he called "Confraternity of the Cross" (*Frățiile de Cruce*) for an education in a national and Orthodox spirit. It included, for example, Bartolomeu Anania, later metropolitan of Cluj-Napoca, Teoctist Arăpasu, the future patriarch, Gheorghe Calciu-Dumitreasa, Valeriu Gafencu, Ioan Ianolide, and Horia Sima, Codreanu's successor at the helm of the movement. Many young people, before entering the monastery, had served in the

[33] Cf. Alessandro Mariotti, *Mircea Eliade, Castelvecchi* (Rome, 2017), digital ed., pos. 1062 of 3785.

legionary movement, like Fr. Arsenie Boca, Fr. Arsenie Papacioc, and many who later joined Antim's Burning Bush movement. This means that the disastrous outcome of an ultra-nationalist, far-right, anti-Semitic, illiberal and totalitarian policy on the part of the legionary movement does not account for the climate that had attracted and moved spirits. There was also something else and it is on this other element that we need to focus our attention.

The mentor of the new horizon of thought was Mircea Eliade, who in September 1927 published in *Cuvântul* the first of the twelve articles of *Itinerariu spiritual* (Spiritual Itinerary), in which he addressed his peers in an attempt to describe the specificities of the "Young Generation." Religious experience was, for Mircea Eliade, the most important of experiences, arguing that Orthodoxy could have constituted a global conception of the world and existence, and, had this been achieved, it would have been a new phenomenon in the history of modern Romanian culture. Initially the "Young Generation" defined itself as an apolitical cultural movement; in fact, it appears to align with the "Legion of the Archangel Michael," characterized by a strong mysticism and by revaluation of the native tradition. Two years after the publication of the first article, in 1929, the press presented Eliade as the "prophet" of his generation and the most famous young intellectual in all of Bucharest. In those years, the Capșa café in Calea Victoriei, in Bucharest, became the meeting point for young intellectuals, where philosophy and culture were discussed. Meeting together there were friends Emil Cioran, Mircea Vulcănescu, Constantin Noica, Eugène Ionesco, Mihail Polihroniade, Sandu Tudor, Paul Sterian and Mihail Sebastian, a Jewish writer, one of Mircea Eliade's best friends as well as the author of a diary which is still an important document today on the spread of anti-Semitism and fascism in Romania.

In 1932, the Criterion group came to life among young intellectuals in Bucharest, under the influence of Nae Ionescu—an association of philosophy, art and letters that organized conferences on various themes, followed by public debates, which enjoyed great success in terms of participation. A magazine of the same name was born from Criterion in October 1934, which however could not resist the political tension that had been tearing Bucharest apart for more than five months. Taking part in it were the usual characters we have already met and who found themselves developing their ideas in the various cultural magazines of the capital: Mircea Eliade, Emil Cioran, Mihail Polihroniade, Vasile Voiculescu, Eugen Ionescu, Constantin Noica, Sandu Tudor and others. The happy formula of the conference with public debate would be the same that Sandu Tudor would adopt for the Antim meetings.

What was Sandu Tudor's position in this context of the interwar period's ferment of ideas? From a literary point of view, the work and worldview of Tudor, a poet and literary theorist, influenced by futurism and expressionism, soon took on an Orthodox and neo-traditionalist Christian ethos. He joined Orthodox mystical circles, whose informal leader was the poet-theologian Nichifor Crainic. Starting in 1924, Tudor was among the writers affiliated with the literary magazine *Gândirea*, helping Crainic to orient that publication from its modernist, secular agenda to an Orthodox vision. His first collection of poems, *Comornic*, received negative reviews from literary critics, who described his style as baroque, without managing to rise to the rank of that of a true writer. His contributions to *Contimporanul*, the avant-garde magazine of young intellectuals, both of poetic texts and critical contributions, were framed as Orthodox apocalyptic visions, such as the *Logica absurdului* (The Logic of the Absurd) essay of February 1927 and, the following month, a polemical text on the impact of cultural modernity. It was an attack on modernism, postulating an essential conflict in modern art between the "sons of suicide" and "the warrior art of immortality." However, his synthesis of literary nihilism, in a version combining a modern purism with Orthodox devotion, surprised his critics.[34] He immediately found himself in conflict with the poet-journalist Tudor Arghezi (1880–1967), the idol of the modernists, who with the freshness of his vocabulary represented an original synthesis between traditional styles and modernism. Tudor accused his pseudo-avant-garde poetry of being vulgar and hedonistic and received Arghezi's response in exchange, which antagonized the clerical faction of Orthodoxy: There is no deep connection

[34] Cf. Paul Cernat, "Chipuri' ale poeziei tiner interbelice," *Revista 22*, no. 1118 (August 2011), [under the heading: *Bucurestiul Cultural*, no. 108].

between Orthodoxy and the Romanian psyche; this is just a modernized orthodox vision.[35] Meanwhile Tudor consolidated his reputation as a mystic with the composition of his first akathist hymn in honor of St. Demetrius Basarabov, published in the newspaper *Gândirea* in 1927 and for which Tudor solicited the approval of the Holy Synod with a letter dated 28 May 1928, wishing that it might circulate as a devout reading and spiritual consolation of believers, since it was composed in verse according to ancient Byzantine hymnology. He received, signed by the Metropolitan of Moldova, Pimen, president of the Holy Synod, on 13 June 1928, the approval for the publication entitled: *Acatistul Sfântului Dimitrie cel Nou Basarabov.*[36]

However, Tudor extended his criticism towards Orthodox militant circles. In a November 1928 interview for the magazine *Tiparnita Literara*, Tudor argues that the Orthodox literati of Romania might find themselves deceived by "a spirituality of darkness." Sandu Tudor's response to the question raised by Nichifor Crainic about a new spirituality has a very lucid meaning for what was to happen to the Romanian people, with the challenge of the Iron Guard, the royal and military dictatorships, the war and, finally, communism: "Let us not lie to ourselves. There is a spirituality of darkness, very similar to that of Christ. It is getting closer than ever.... It is necessarily, in this case, not a 'new spirituality' but a form of strong and vigorous penance."[37] With Mircea Vulcănescu and Gheorghe Racoveanu, Tudor wrote the polemical piece *Infailibilitatea Bisericii si failibilitatea sinodala* (Infallibility of the Church and Synodal Fallibility), published on the front pages of the newspaper *Cuvântul* by Nae Ionescu, on 22 January 1929. He reasons that Tradition is superior to the Synod and argues in favor of Ionescu's dissident position on the calculation of Easter, challenging Church policy in subsequent articles to the point of claiming that the Synod was schismatic. However, he always remained within the orbit of Crainic's Orthodox theses

[35] See Z. Ornea, *Anii treizeci. Extrema dreaptă românească* (Bucharest: Editura Fundatiei cultural române, 1995), 105–106.

[36] Cf. Daniil Sandu Tudor, *Taina Rugului Aprins. Scrieri și documente inedite*, 83–84. It was published as a book in 1942.

[37] Sandu Tudor, "Noua spiritualate," *Tiparnița literară*, I, no. 2 (30 Nov. 1928), 45, quoted in Gabriel Hasmatuchi, *Nichifor Crainic and the interwar "New Spirituality"*: http://www.apshus.usv.ro/arhiva/2011II.pdf.

and the position of Nae Ionescu, whom he considered as an awakener of consciences:

> Nae Ionescu is an awakener of consciences...he has never been a contemporary; there is something in him that always attracts further, it is always current. He is not contemporary, but neither is he a man of the past nor of the future. He remains a man of the essential moment, the only point from which to look at the eternal. For this reason, Nae Ionescu is one of the greatest journalists today. He knows how, like no one else, to distill luminous drops of dew from the banality of various political events into the logic of heaven's ideas.... Prof. Ionescu has retransmitted to us, resurrecting it, the ancient mentality of the East that every Romanian should adopt; of course he is not a writer, a maker of books, but he is always a good teacher, an awakener of consciences. He bears something prophetic within himself. His way of seeing is, in fact, the vision of a heavenly Middle Ages, the contemplation of our voievods and monks, who even when they were called Neagoe Basarab or Gheorghe de la Cernica remained only faithful servants of the present, through their word. This is why our Romanian past is not cultural and not even the journalist and professor Nae Ionescu is a simple man of culture. They are only humble servants to always go beyond, the eternal present of the here and now.[38]

He argues with Petre Pandrea,[39] lawyer and memoirist, about his *Manifesto of the White Lily of Revolutionary Youth*, which he had launched from the *Gândirea* newspaper in the August-September 1928 issue, as an echo to the series of articles in the *Cuvântul* newspaper published by Mircea Eliade entitled *Itinerariu spiritual*, from 6 September to 16 November 1927. Although Tudor and Pandrea wrote from the columns of the same newspapers, their paths diverged and the disagreements between them became very bitter to the point of finding vitriolic judgments in their respective positions. This unbearable relationship between the two would explode with the closure

[38] Mihai Radulescu, "Sandu Tudor in deriva spre stânga," *Floarea de foc*, no. 5: http://www.hotnews.ro/stiri-arhiva-1217994-sandu-tudor-deriva-spre-stanga-floarea-foc-5.htm.

[39] On the figure of Petre Pandrea, defender of the persecuted and in turn persecuted by the communist power, who left in his memoirs a merciless portrait of the injustices and abuses of an entire society violated by extremism on the right and left, see Ion Simut, "Justițiar cu orice risc," *România Literară*, no. 3 (2004).

of the Vladimirești (Galați) monastery and the related trial of Mother Veronica and Fr. Ioan, in 1955, where Pandrea championed the nuns against misunderstanding and condemnation, a situation supported to the contrary by Tudor, along with André Scrima and the patriarchate, branding them as obscurantists.[40]

However, the tumultuous years for Sandu Tudor were those that followed his return from Athos where he had stayed for about eight months. He started out as a seasoned journalist who wanted to document the validity of the criticisms of the life of the Athonite monks and returned won over to the true secrets of the Holy Mountain, about which the monks told him, particularly the Jesus Prayer. In his heart he had now decided to dedicate himself to prayer, but it would still take another fifteen years to convince him to leave the world and imitate those holy monks.[41] His life became decidedly tumultuous. He decided to found two newspapers, *Floarea de foc*, a political and literary magazine, with sporadic editions in 1932, 1933, 1936, and *Credința*, a political newspaper, in 1933, where he showed himself to be an energetic polemicist, with a volcanic character, traits he would not ever lose, even in the monastic precincts.[42] The former publication often found itself acting as a sounding board for polemical articles against modernism, which Tudor condemned for its inhuman works of art, not so much because of his Orthodox conservatism as his left-wing anti-capitalism. Regarding his social vision, Tudor moved to the left, and *Floarea de foc* would become a platform for young communists to explain their revolutionary ideas. *Credința* was the mouthpiece for his distancing from the far-right trend affecting many intellectuals. It claimed to be a neutral newspaper, but the staff was left-wing. Tudor had co-opted them

[40] Cf. note 13.

[41] This is how he describes himself in Ikos 10 of his *Akathist to the Burning Bush of the Mother of God*: "After receiving the holy counsel and a blessing / I entered upon the path of my salvation. / I had made the decision, with strength and determination / to spend my energies praying incessantly. / But my intellect, that clay idol, / does not allow me to overcome myself, / to establish myself in prayer as in the place of God / in that contrition of heart for which I long."

[42] Reviews reported by George Enache, *Din arhiva 'Rugului Aprins': Daniil Sandu Tudor, un sfânt in Gulagul românese*, cited in Marius Oprea, *Adevărata călătorie a lui Zahei. V. Voiculescu și taina Rugului Aprins* (Bucharest: Humanitas, 2008), 81.

because he realized that *Cuvântul's* people would be unavailable. Nae Ionescu and his newspaper took positions very close to the Iron Guard and espoused their vision. Mircea Eliade also collaborated with Tudor, who however harshly criticized his friend for his aggressively moralistic columns. And yet both opposed the radical solutions of the far right.

In 1932 Tudor joined the more moderate National Agrarian Party, criticizing radical solutions, both fascist and communist, and defending the young Romanian democracy. In an issue of *Credința* from December 1933, Tudor reacted by writing that if democracy was not a good thing for Romania, this could not even be said because it had never really been tried. From a Christian perspective, Tudor accused Romania's revolutionary youth of aping foreign experiments in totalitarianism, describing Adolf Hitler as the antichrist and equating all revolutionary ideologies to a triumph of animality. With Eliade and thirty other Romanian Christian and Jewish intellectuals, Tudor signed a protest against anti-Semitism in general and Nazism in particular.[43] Again in the columns of *Credința* fascism was branded as the enemy of freedom and communism was judged as left-wing fascism. At a time when many intellectuals were fascinated by the strength that fascism and communism inspired in various European countries, Tudor denounced their falsity and their anti-human character with a polemical verve of great impact. Many of his articles ("Modern bestiality," "The century of the murderers of God," "Between the synod and the soviet," "The lesson of the Moscow trials") were used in the collection of evidence by the *Securitate*, at the time of the trial against him and the Antim movement in 1958, as valid pieces of support for the guilty verdict, with a sentence of 25 years of "hard time" in prison. In this period of intense journalistic activity, but also of the rise of far-right parties, he organized (together with Petre Constantinesc-Iași and Alexandru Mihăilescu) an anti-fascist group which published a *Buletin antifascist* that he wrote almost entirely himself.

Events came to a head with the assassination of Prime Minister Ion G. Duca in December 1933 in Sinaia by activists of the Iron Guard. The authorities closed *Cuvântul* and prosecuted its

[43] Cf. Z. Ornea, *Anii treizeci. Extrema dreaptă românească* (Bucharest: Editura Fundației cultural române, 1995), 68–69.

publisher, Nae Ionescu, in an attempt to suppress the movement, but *Credința*, Tudor's newspaper, continued to be published. The young fascists took revenge, attacking the editorial offices of left-wing periodicals and, in December of 1934, a person unknown to him surprised Tudor in his office at *Credința* and beat him. Tudor refrained from waging a war against his old friends and wrote laudatory words about Nae Ionescu, defining his teaching as nourishing bread and his figure as a goad for consciences, even as a guardian of the true faith.

However, he did not remain silent in the matter of the controversy regarding the *Criterion* association, where he lent himself to slander and blackmail in the different, conflicting political and cultural directions. It is the less noble part of Tudor that is accompanied by his polemicist and intransigent character. The association had opened the doors to many ideological enemies of Tudor who, in the columns of his newspaper, took the opportunity to spark an unprecedented scandal, accusing several members of *Criterion* of promoting pederasty. The slanderous campaign degenerated into a brawl in which Tudor also participated, continuing to write in a slanderous and ignoble way. Tudor's participation in this unseemly campaign, which ended up in the courtroom, where Tudor and his collaborators were forced to recant, seems strange. The scandal, however, undermined the association, which dissolved. The negative fame that accompanied Tudor even as a monk, in addition to his triple divorce in his personal life, dates back to these years in which he expressed himself as an intransigent polemicist, without mincing words, who pursued his goals without stopping at anything and without second thoughts, but this will not be dealt with here.

4. THE BURNING BUSH

a) Before the withdrawal from Cernăuți

Sandu Tudor's fame is linked to the Burning Bush movement which he animated in the years 1945–1948. The first to make that reality known to the world in its specificity was André Scrima, one of the young frequenters of the Antim cenacle.[44] Returning

[44] On Scrima, see the precious interventions by Anca Vasiliu in the magazine *Contacts* 203 (2003), 207 (2004) and her study about Scrima, which I have read in typescript format: *Le Passeur. Voies de l'expression*.

to Antim from his last trip to India in 1991, after the experience of teaching and monastic life in Lebanon, participation in the Second Vatican Council as an envoy of Patriarch Athenagoras, and holding courses in France and the United States, he felt the time had come to view the events he was involved in as a long initiatory journey towards a horizon of interiority. He returned to his origins, to the experience of the Burning Bush, perceived as the hesychast rebirth in Romania, a penetrating sketch of which, like the story of a destiny, he conveys. His book was published by Humanitas in Bucharest in 1996 (2nd ed., 2000) and bears the title *The Time of the Burning Bush. The spiritual master in the eastern tradition.*[45] Some memoirs of those who had participated in that movement were already circulating, after the fall of the regime in 1989 had allowed them to return to the events of that extraordinary and tragic time. Everything seemed lost in 1958 with the trial and conviction of all the exponents of the movement, with Fr. Daniil who died in prison and the others who would be freed in 1964, prostrate and quite exhausted, thanks to the political amnesty of that year, only because by then the whole country had become like a boundless concentration camp. However, no one had yet presented the meaning and destiny of the Burning Bush movement.

Scrima had immediately attracted the attention of Fr. Ioann, the Stranger, the Russian monk who was a refugee in Cernica and whom Sandu Tudor had invited to their meetings in Antim, becoming the spiritual authority for the entire group. Scrima, whom no one would have suspected of being likely to choose monastic life, due to his brilliant and worldly personality and his very lively intelligence, had been introduced to Antim starting in 1946 by Marcel Avramescu (1909–1984),[46] the future

---

[45] It is translated into Italian by Adalberto Mainardi, a monk from Bose. The first edition is entitled *Il Padre spirituale*, 1999; the second is entitled *L'accompagnamento spirituale. Il movimento del Roveto ardente e la rinascita esicasta in Romania.*

[46] In Radu Dragan's study, *La contribution des auteurs roumains à la littérature ésotérique Occidental (xix-xx siècles)*, Avramescu is cited as an exponent of Western esoteric thought, together with Lovinescu, Vâlsan and Eliade, all indebted to René Guénon (1886–1951) and his codification of traditional esotericism: *Conférences de M. Radu Dragan, Annuaires de l'École pratique des hautes études*, Année 2005, vol. 114, 379–85. On Avramescu, see Marcel Tolcea, *De la Marcel Avramescu, la Părintele Mihail Avramescu. Repere ale unei biografii spirituale*, in *Trivium—revistă de gândire symbolica*, no. 4 (13) (2012). More generally, for

Father Mihail of the Nuns' Skete (Schitul Maicilor) in Bucharest, a disciple of the logician and mathematician Anton Dumitriu (1905–1992), who also frequented the Antim conferences, together with many other intellectuals of the time. He was welcomed as a brother into Antim's monastic community, like Sandu Tudor the year before. Once the association of the Burning Bush was dissolved in 1948, due to patriarchal intervention under pressure from the communist government, he arrived as a novice at the monastery of Neamț, where the higher monastic seminary had been opened and where he taught alongside fathers Benedict Ghiuș, Petronie Tănase and Sofian Boghiu, with Fr. Arsenie Papacioc as the community's spiritual father. Once the Neamț seminary was disbanded in 1953, he repaired to Bucharest where he worked, with Bartolomeo Anania, on the reorganization of the Patriarchate Library at Antim. The desire for asceticism and the spiritual life led him to the monastery of Slatina (Suceava), where the patriarch had recalled Fr. Ilie Cleopa from Sihăstria with about twenty monks, with the task of making monastic life flourish there once again, at a time when the destructive policy of the communist party had not yet expressed itself in all its violence. There he found Fr. Petronie and Fr. Benedict Ghiuș, who tonsured him as a monk in 1956. Also in 1956, Scrima took his license in theology with Fr. Stăniloae, who had been transferred several years earlier from Sibiu to Bucharest. When, in 1958, the entire Burning Bush group was imprisoned, Scrima escaped condemnation because he had left for India at the invitation of the Indian vice-president Sarvepalli Radhakrishnan who, visiting Romania in May–June 1956, was surprised to hear a very young Orthodox monk reciting a passage from the *Katha Upanisad* in Sanskrit. On his journey to India, he stopped for five months at the Chateaux de Bossey, an ecumenical institute organized by the World Council of Churches. At the invitation of the Dominican Christophe Dumont, publisher of the well-known magazine *Istina*,[47] he came to Paris where he

the comparison between hesychasm and Guénonian esotericism found as a cultural background in intellectuals who were part of the Burning Bush, see Enrico Montanari, *La fatica del cuore. Saggio sull'ascesi esicasta* (Milano: Jaca Books, 2003), 81–179, and *Un'umile regalità. Percorsi dell'esicasmo in Occidente* (Milano–Udine: Mimesis, 2022).

[47] His article on the history of hesychasm in Romania appears anonymously in this magazine: Un moine de l'Eglise Orthodoxe de Roumanie, "L'avènement

met some representatives of the Parisian Russian emigration. On that occasion, as we know from a long letter written from Benares on 6 August 1957 to Fr. Benedict Ghiuș, listening to him speak about the situation of monastic life in Romania and the phenomenon of the Burning Bush was also Professor Olivier Clément, who then reported this in the Protestant weekly *Réforme*, num. 644, Saturday, 20 July 1957: "L'église Orthodoxe Roumaine ou le miracle du Buisson ardent."[48] From there he passed through Mount Athos and continued to New Delhi. Returning from India he settled in Lebanon, invited by the local Orthodox community that he had met while stopping in Beirut on his journey to India. He remained there for about twenty years as a professor at the French University of Kaslik affiliated with the Lyon campus and as a monk in the new Orthodox monastery of Deir el-Harf. He returned to Romania in 1991 and died there in 2000. He rests in the cemetery of Cernica.

I have gone to great lengths to present the events of this exceptional figure of Romanian monasticism precisely because of the interpretation he gave of the Burning Bush movement,[49] having rightly placed it within and following the Romanian hesychast tradition. This is based on his own recollections and those of many others who have gradually brought forward their own testimonies about having participated firsthand in that prodigious movement, several of whom I was able to get to know personally while visiting the Romanian monasteries in the period of the communist dictatorship and afterwards. I would now like to outline the unfolding of events so to perceive their spiritual fruitfulness.

---

philocalique dans l'Orthodoxie roumaine", in *Istina* (1958), no. 3: 295–328 and no. 4: 443–75.

[48] The letter was published in André Scrima, *Ortodoxia și încercarea Comunismului* (Bucharest: Humanitas, 2008), 394–417. Clément published the article in *Réforme* without his knowledge. Scrima construed it as the result of the meetings in Paris, one of which Prof. Clément had also attended. He was enthusiastic about the article's title, inspired by the akathist of Fr. Daniil which he himself had translated on the spot (it was the composition in eight stanzas), in one of those meetings. However, he regretted speaking so openly about Fr. Daniil and other Romanian intellectuals, evidently fearing repercussions from the communist government.

[49] Another interesting presentation is that of Ioan I. Ică, *Il "Roveto ardente": una fioritura dell'ideale esicasta all'alba del comunismo in Romania*, in *Il monachesimo tra eredità e aperture*, ed. Maciej Bielawski and Daniel Hombergen (Roma: Studia anselmiana, 2004), 471–88.

The political context, first of all. In 1938, to eliminate the political threat of the Iron Guard, King Charles II seized power, banned the Iron Guard, and had their Captain, Corneliu Codreanu, imprisoned and murdered. The Second World War then broke out and, after the annihilation of Poland and the collapse of France, Romania, under Marshal Antonescu, could only align itself with Nazi Germany. However, in 1939, the latter had made a pact with the Soviet Union, allowing it to demand from Romania the cession of the territories of Bessarabia and Northern Bukovina by invading them in June 1940. Furthermore, in August, Romania would also be forced to cede part of Transylvania to Hungary and part of Dobruja to Bulgaria. In this series of dramatic events for the country, the king sought a way out by appointing General Antonescu as prime minister. He was pro-Nazi and capable of bringing the Iron Guard under his direct control, but immediately afterwards found himself forced to abdicate in favor of a dictatorial regime, which became known as the "State National Legionary" (*Statul național-legionar*). The agreement between Antonescu and the Iron Guard did not last long due to the latter's claims to have more power, so much so that Antonescu repressed the revolt. When Germany invaded the Soviet Union in June 1941, Romanian troops supported it, liberating the territories of Bukovina and Bessarabia from the Russian presence but also committing the great mistake of penetrating deep into Soviet territory and perpetrating reprisals and massacres, above all against the Jewish population. After the Battle of Stalingrad, which caused the annihilation of the German troops, the Red Army advanced westwards and entered Romania between March and August 1944. The Romanian losses were huge and there was a sense of inevitable defeat. On 23 August 1944, King Michael decided to arrest Marshal Antonescu and sided with the USSR and the Allies. On August 31, the Red Army entered Bucharest and remained its true master, thus mortgaging the future of Romania.

Under arms since 1939, Sandu Tudor returned from the front in 1941 to direct the Motorcycle-Mechanization technical school. Imprisoned by the fascist authorities for his anti-Nazi positions, he was immediately freed thanks to the intervention of the Ministry of War which wanted him in military school. In his autobiography he reports that he was discharged in 1942 and returned to his activity as a publicist, without managing however to republish his newspaper *Floarea de foc*. He recognized that his family life was a failure and decided to change his life: "From now on I want to dedicate all my strength only to the most powerful and profound calling of my life. I have decided to serve only Christ and his eternal truths. I have had enough of transience."[50] And, in 1945, he entered the monastic community of Antim as a brother.

But there was a whole movement that preceded and accompanied this decision, leading him to become a tireless and inspired animator of a true spiritual fraternity. In a celebratory volume in honor of the academic Virgil Cândea, whom I met several times and who encouraged me in my research on the Romanian hesychast tradition, Dr. Cornelia Bodea recalls that around the monastery of Antim, founded in the years 1713–1715 by the Metropolitan of Wallachia, Antim Ivireanul, a general interest had coalesced in the restoration of the monastic complex and in the publication of the works of its founder. A famous speech by the historian Nicolae Iorga in 1937 had rallied the intellectuals and clergy of Bucharest to support the interventions of the Commission for Historical Monuments. The monastic community of Antim was flourishing again with the presence of exceptional personalities such as Fathers Benedict Ghiuș, Sofian Boghiu, Felix Dubneac, and Petronie Tănase, who, with their spiritual gifts, were able to attract many intellectuals and thinkers.[51] The distinguishing feature that emerged was that of

[50] Daniil Sandu Tudor, *Taina Rugului Aprins. Scrieri și documente inedite*, 27 (*Scurt itinerar autobiographic*, 23–28).

[51] Benedict Ghiuș (1904–1990), with a doctorate in theology in Strasbourg, admirer of Benedictine life having stayed at Maria Laach monastery in Germany, elected bishop of Hotin, in Bessarabia (an appointment later canceled due to the intervention of the vice-president of the Council of Ministers Mihai Antonescu), university assistant at the Faculty of Theology of Bucharest for the chair of Ascetics and Mysticism, first with Nichifor Crainic and then with Dumitru Stăniloae who had been moved from Sibiu to Bucharest in 1946, a highly popular lecturer at the Sunday meetings of Antim and in the evenings with the monks of Antim reading and commenting on philokalic texts together with Sandu Tudor (it must not be forgotten that many young monks, coming from the monastic seminary of Cernica, were enrolled in the Faculty of Theology and the other Faculties of Medicine, Letters and Fine Arts). Arrested with the entire Antim group in 1958, in prison he was loved by everyone for his amiability, sweetness and depth of thought. Released in 1964, he resumed his service at the Cathedral of the Patriarchate and then retired to Cernica, where he died in 1990. Sofian Boghiu (1912–2002) and Felix

a form of confraternity between thinkers and those who pray.[52] From the fiery cultural debates of the interwar period of writers, poets and journalists, initially with rather uniform positions, then increasingly antagonistic due to the various choices of field, roughly two divergent orientations emerged: on the one hand, ethno-cultural traditionalism oriented towards a political nationalism of an extremist right; on the other, Orthodox traditionalism, lived in faith and open to a certain cultural universality of left-wing positions. Tudor would become the champion of this second trend. Bucharest in the interwar period was like a large village: intellectuals and spiritual men knew each other, and had personal relationships, even if they argued with each other in various newspapers. Among the various literary circles of the capital, the *Duh și slovă* (Spirit and Letter) group should be remembered, which met precisely at Antim under the leadership of Archimandrite Iuliu Scriban, a well-known theologian.[53] Informally, Mircea Vulcănescu, Sandu Tudor and Paul Sterian were part of the group, the same ones who would be found later in the Burning Bush movement. The circle of friends was thus organized slowly and fundamentally for a spiritual search.

The first concrete step in this direction took place in August 1943 with Tit Simedrea,[54] then metropolitan of Bucovina, inviting significant personalities in the field of culture and a

---

Dubneac (1912–2008), both from Bessarabia, church painters, attending the seminar in Cernica, then together at Antim, imprisoned in 1958 and freed in 1964. The first returned to Antim, while the second was transferred to the United States. Petronie Tănase (1916–2011), a monk at Neamț, then at Antim, with studies in theology, mathematics and philosophy, librarian, secretary of the patriarch Nicodim, transferred to Mount Athos in 1978 and became hegumen of the Romanian skete of the Prodromou [in Italian, cf. Ionichie Balan, *Volti e parole dei padri del deserto romeno*, introduction, translation and notes by the Fratelli Contemplativi di Gesù (Bose: Qiqajon, 1991), 90–108].

[52] Cornelia Bodea, "L'esprit du 'Buisson ardent' du monastère st. Anthime-Bucharest," in *Omagiu Virgil Cândea la 75 de ani*, ed. Paul H. Stahl (Bucharest: Academiei Române-Roza Vânturilor, 2002), vol. I, 87–95.

[53] This information is provided by Antonie Plămădeală, *Rugul Aprins* (Sibiu: Arhiepiscopia Sibiului, 2002), 24 and repeated by Marius Vasileanu, *Rugul Aprins, un simplu cenaclu?* in *Ziarul Financiar*, 19 Feb 2015. Iuliu Scriban († 1949) was transferred from Chisinău (1928–1941) to the Faculty of Theology in Bucharest (1941–1943), a sympathizer of the association *Oastea Domnului* [The Army of the Lord]. This movement began in 1923 within the Orthodox Church of Romania by the Transylvanian priest Iosif Trifa, a movement later declared outlawed in 1948.

[54] Cf. note 7, supra p. 41.

monastic sphere that he knew personally. This was in northern Moldavia, in Bessarabia, the region liberated from Russian occupation by the Romanian army, a region grappling with pastoral renewal in the wake of tradition. A man of refined culture, a defender of the Jews, concerned with revitalizing the country's religious practice, he invited first-rate personalities to his residence in Cernăuți to meditate together on themes of tradition and Christian mysticism. Paul Henri Stahl, then eighteen years old, participated with his father and decided to tell of it after having read André Scrima's book on the Burning Bush, thinking to add an interesting piece of information to Scrima's memoirs.[55] He followed his father, Henri H. Stahl, and disclosed that the various people who participated in that week of retreat had already met previously. The American bombings had persistently hit railway communications, so much so that various lines were interrupted. Having arrived through perils at Cernăuți, he remembered having seen Jews walking about with the yellow star on their chest and having noticed the remains of anti-religious exhibitions, which were organized at the time of the Soviet occupation. The meetings took place on 1–7 August, during the fasting period for the feast of the Dormition of the Mother of God. The days were marked by conferences followed by debate, by a common table presided over by the metropolitan, in silence, with a reader who read excerpts from the saint's life according to the liturgical commemoration of the day, and by a religious service in the evening, in an atmosphere of intense meditation. Of the participants, some he already knew from Bucharest, others he met there and he lists them: Sandu Tudor, Alexandru Mironescu, Constantin Noica, Mac Constantinescu, Paul Sterian, Viorel Solutiu, Fr. Benedict Ghiuș and many others.

Plămădeală also lists Nicolae M. Popescu, Anton Dumitriu, Alexandru Elian, Petre Manoliu. To underscore the importance of the meeting, according to a style that we could call Western, a brochure was published with the presentation of the program: "By the desire of a handful of men of culture, priests and lay people, looking for greater depth in the Orthodox spiritual experience, both personally and as a community, thanks to the

[55] *Dilema*, IV, 1996, no. 193, 20–26 September, 2: *Intâlnirea duhovnicească de la Cernăuți*, August 1943.

extraordinary understanding, hospitality and blessing of His Excellency Tit, Metropolitan of Bucovina, these seven days of spiritual retreat [*priveghere*] were able to be organized in the wonderful spiritual city of the Archbishopric of Cernăuți." A program of prayer and spiritual retreat, as in the pattern of the Ignatian tradition's spiritual exercises, were divided as follows:

> *Sunday*, Nicolae Popescu, professor of church history: "Liturgical calendar and spiritual retreat"; Alexandru Elian, Byzantine scholar: "From the icon to spirituality."
>
> *Monday*, Alexandru Mironescu, doctor of physical sciences in Paris, assistant professor of organic chemistry in Bucharest, who would publish in 1945 *The Limits of Scientific Knowledge: the Contribution of Science to the Epistemological Problem* and, in 1947, *Certainty and Truth*: "The relics of St. Stephen and the eternity of the body."
>
> *Tuesday*, Anton Dumitriu, mathematician and professor of logic in Bucharest: "Knowledge and asceticism."
>
> *Wednesday*, Paul Sterian, writer: "The seven youths of Ephesus and the evidence of the resurrection."
>
> *Thursday*, unexpected guest, Constantin Noica, philosopher: "Pathos and Patmos."
>
> *Friday*, Petre Manoliu, writer: "Transfiguration and redemptive beauty."
>
> *Saturday*, Benedict Ghiuș, hieromonk: "The spiritual father and healing."

Lastly, the one who, at the beginning of the week, introduced the course, Sandu Tudor: "The prayer of the heart and holy hesychia."

Beyond the conferences, it was the spiritual program of the week that was important. The presentation brochure introduced the retreat like this:

> "Brother in Christ, if you also tend towards this good thing, be welcome among us." The meeting was open to the public. There was no special invitation, all that counted was the desire to live according to the Spirit. The motto for the week was taken from the letter to the Ephesians 5:16: "making good use of [redeeming] the time, because the days are evil."

Towards the end of the same year (1943) was another event that would later be recognized as providential. Welcomed by the Romanian patriarch Nicodim, a fellow student at the Kiev Academy, Metropolitan Nikolai of Rostov with his entourage, fleeing from Rostov due to the advance of the Red Army, took refuge in the Cernica monastery. Accompanying him was Fr. Ioann the Stranger, heir to the Paisian hesychast tradition, whom Scrima remembered very well:

> "Father Ioann's teaching combined the rigor of exact knowledge—acquired both from the study of texts and from lived experience—with the sweetness of a heart rooted in mercy. We cannot forget how he commented on *Tales of a Pilgrim*, and he asked questions that we were not at first able to answer. I thought to myself, even then, that Father Ioann must travel with the *Philokalia* but also with the *Tales of a Pilgrim*, just as the latter traveled with the *Philokalia*. With him the hesychast tradition was actually 'at work,' as well as legitimately transmitted to and received by the hearts of those seekers attracted by the foundation at Antim."[56]

In his suitcase he carried numerous texts of the Russian tradition, which were soon translated into Romanian by Fr. Gheorghe Rosca, a refugee from Bessarabia who knew Russian perfectly and circulated material "in samizdat" at a time prior to this coinage of this term.[57] This was St. Seraphim of Sarov's *Conversation with Motovilov*, the *Letters* of Theophan the Recluse, the *Tales of a Russian Pilgrim*, the famous anthology *What is*

---

[56] André Scrima, *L'accompagnamento spirituale*, 172. See my "La dottrina spirituale dello starets Paisij. Radiografia di una comunità" in N. Kauchtschischwili, et al., *Paisij, lo starec* (Bose: Qiqajon, 1997), 55–82. Translated into Romanian in *Românii în reînnoirea isihastă*, ed. Virgil Cândea (Iași: Trinitas, 1997), 121–48, with a valuable intervention on the theme of Romanian hesychasm by the same academic Virgil Cândea: *Locul spiritualtății românești în reînnoirea isihastă*, 17–38. It should not be forgotten that in 1938 a student house was opened in Antim with around twenty students from the Cernica seminary and the various university faculties of Bucharest. The *staretz* at the time, Nicodim Ionita, who was educated and charismatic, re-established the ancient liturgical order with well-attended and participatory celebrations. He also restarted the old Ecclesiastical Music Academy.

[57] Roman Braga, one of the Antim group, recalls in *Ogni monaco ha un suo segreto*, 53–54: "The manuscripts brought to Antim by Father Kulygin were immediately translated into Romanian and multiplied with the typewriter, mimeographed in secret and distributed in hundreds of copies. We, who were the witnesses of those days, cannot forget that during communism books on mysticism and asceticism, on prayer and the lives of the saints were distributed in secret, they were sought by the *Securitate* in order to be destroyed and whoever owned them ran the danger of being thrown into prison."

the prayer of Jesus according to the tradition of the Orthodox Church, published at Serdobol in 1938 by the Valaam monastery, with an appendix, "A dialogue between a monk and a secular priest on the practice of prayer." I recall this publication effort with a certain emotion because I was able to hold some of Fr. Gheorghe Rosca's typewritten Romanian versions in my hands too, before I managed to obtain the original Russian texts. With the coming of this staretz, the whole group felt that they could reconnect to a living tradition, to a true "spiritual fatherhood."

Nicodim had been elected patriarch of Romania in 1939 and before that he had been superior of the Neamț monastery, the largest and most well-known monastery in Romania. He knew Russian from having studied at the Kiev Academy and had translated several Russian texts into Romanian. In particular, he had distributed in Romania the monograph of the Russian archpriest Sergii Chetverikov[58] on the personality and work of Paisius Velichkovsky, a figure that Sandu Tudor knew very well, together with that of his master and spiritual father, Basil of Poiana Mărului, who had preceded him in emigrating to Romanian territory.[59] Tudor referred to them—whose manuscript texts he had found in the libraries of Romania—precisely in relation to teaching on the prayer of Jesus. I think I see in this openness to the Slavic tradition a kind of historical predisposition. Two centuries earlier the Slavic tradition became accessible

[58] Serghie Četverikov, *Paisie starețul Mânăstirii Neamțului din Moldova. Viața, învătătura și influența lui asupra Bisericii Ortodoxe* (Neamț, 1933). The Russian text was only published in 1938 in Petseri, Estonia. Only in the Romanian text, however, can we consult the perspective table on the spread of Paisian influence with its impressive list of disciples and monasteries. See my "Paisij Velickovskij e il contributo delle terre romene alla storia della spiritualità ortodossa," *Storia religiosa dello spazio romeno*, ed. Luciano Vaccaro, under the direction of Cesare Alzati, vol. 2 (Milan: Centro Ambrosiano, 2016), 515–36.

[59] Roman Braga also testifies to the fact that Sandu Tudor always carried with him the Rule of the elder Gheorghe of Cernica, in the line of the spiritual inheritance of Paisij Velickovskij, recognizing in this text the particularity of Romanian hesychasm. He also recalls that when he attended the seminar in Cernica, Sandu Tudor, then a journalist for *Credința*, showed up in short trousers, arousing the ire of Archimandrite Scriban, but spoke to the students about the Prayer of Jesus: "Sandu Tudor had an innate zeal for spiritual things; this zeal led to his future transformation." Cf. Roman Braga, *Ogni monaco ha un suo segreto*, 51 and 53. On Basil of Poiana Mărului see Dario Raccanello, *La preghiera di Gesù negli scritti di Basilio di Poiana Mărului* (Alessandria: n. p., 1986), Romanian translation: *Rugaciunea lui Iisus in scrierile staretului Vasile de la Poiana Mărului* (Sibiu: Deisis, 1996).

to the Romanian tradition, since, first Basil of Poiana Mărului and then Paisius, emigrating from Ukraine, had sought refuge in Moldavia and there revived the great Orthodox hesychast tradition, making use of a large group of Romanian monks, good Greek scholars, in their activity of correcting and translating patristic, especially philokalic, literature. Paisius, coming from Athos, had stayed from 1763 to 1794 in the monasteries of Dragomirna, Secu and Neamț, making the latter the center of monastic renewal, capable of extending his influence on the Romanian and Russian churches.[60]

Furthermore, this openness to the Slavic tradition was also favored by the monks of Bessarabia, who knew Russian due to having lived in territories under the influence of the Russian Orthodox Church. After the Soviet occupation of Bessarabia in 1940, they swarmed into the monasteries of Romania, and were welcomed in particular in the monasteries of Cernica and Căldărușani near Bucharest. The professor Virgil Cândea remembers this in the preface to the writings of one of the leading exponents of the Burning Bush group, a very close friend of Sandu Tudor, Professor Alexandru Mironescu, someone we will always find as Tudor's companion in all the spiritual adventures of those prodigious years in Antim and following.[61]

Of his visits to Cernica and Antim as a young student, as was the custom then for many who went there on pilgrimage, he remembers how first-rate spiritual men lived there, practicing uninterrupted prayer of the heart, with the gift of tears. From those places the texts on the prayer of the heart were distributed, in typewritten form, translated from Russian. Roman Braga summarizes the climate of the time in Cernica thus:

> Father Dionisie was there, who is still alive, and Father Teodosie. When they heard what we were doing in Antim, the old monks began to smile and said: "Look, these people are giving lectures on the Jesus Prayer!" It was a surprising thing

[60] Cf. E. Citterio, "La scuola filocalica di Paisij Velichkovskij e la Filocalia di Nicodimo Aghiorita. Un confronto" [The philokalic school of Paisij Velichkovskij and the Philokalia of Nicodimus the Hagiorite. A comparison], in Tomas Spidlik, et al., *Amore del bello. Studi sulla Filocalia* [Love of beauty. Studies on the Philokalia] (Bose: Qiqajon, 1991), 179–207.

[61] Alexandru Mironescu, *Calea inimii. Eseuri în duhul Rugului Aprins*, foreword by Virgil Cândea (Bucharest: Anastasia, 1998), V-XVII. Contains a series of essays written in the 1940s but never published.

> for them. How can we talk about the Jesus Prayer, something that must be practiced instead. No! These things shouldn't have been talked about. These are secret things. And from them I learned that their spiritual fathers did not give the blessing to practice this prayer to everyone, but only to a few and with much supervision and parsimony.[62]

Another fact not to be forgotten is the movement of rediscovery of the philokalic tradition in the Romanian monastic environment in Transylvania with the research of Fr. Dumitru Stăniloae (1903–1993),[63] and, in particular, with the figure of Fr. Arsenie Boca who had caused the monastery of Sâmbăta de Sus (judetul Brasov) to flourish again. The first four volumes of the Romanian edition of the *Philokalia* saw the light between 1946 and 1948, but it was not simply a publishing event, but rather a true spiritual event, which was of great benefit to Antim's visitors, with the presence of Fr. Stăniloae himself at their meetings, who was also later condemned together with the whole group. In the preface to the edition of the first volumes of the *Philokalia*, Fr. Stăniloae expresses his gratitude for the support given him by Fr. Arsenie Boca, both with help in the

---

[62] *Ogni monaco ha un suo segreto*, 58.

[63] On the figure and work of this great theologian, see Ioan I. Ică, Jr., ed., *Persoană și communiune* (Sibiu: 1993). Fr. Stăniloae tried to build a "neopatristic synthesis," creating an existential approach to the genuine tradition of the Church Fathers. He dedicated his entire life to this purpose. What is important in his work are not individual ideas or approaches, but an overall vision, a positive underlying tension in seeing God linked to the world created by Him rather than a world that has lost God. Theology is precisely the effort to see the Invisible and to look at the world and man through His eyes. The vision of the world and of life is closely linked to the spiritual purification and asceticism of man, and it is the vision of God that changes the human intelligence of the world. In his virtues and his defects Fr. Staniloae remains tied to the context of the traditional Romanian rural village where he was born, experiencing in a particular way the fusion between Orthodoxy and Romanian rural culture. The key themes of his theological reflection are "person" and "communion," crucial points of ecclesial and social life and of the understanding of man, although he combined them in a "nationalistic" type of communitarian personalism, as if there belonged to the Romanian Orthodox vocation a measure, a harmony that would be lacking in the Greeks as well as the Slavs, in the East as well as the West, an evidently very weak position. This is a weakness that is often seen in today's Romania both in the religious (the conflict and coexistence between the different Christian confessions) and cultural fields (the debate on modernity and the relationship with the West) and which one hopes can be overcome despite the pride of those who know they can count on a rich and precious tradition and despite the humility of those who struggle with others, as Jacob fought with the angel, in order to ask for a blessing.

translations and above all in procuring subscriptions for the purchase of the work. It had never happened that farmers and shepherds could have the philokalic texts in their own hands, even subsidizing their publication to the point of making Fr. Staniloae say:

> Fr. Arsenie can rightly be called *ctitor de frunte* (main founder) of the Romanian *Philokalia*... [the publication of the *Philokalia*] will remain linked to a large extent to his name and to the religious movement that he was able to inspire around the monastery of Sâmbăta de Sus, on the most authentic foundations of the Orthodox tradition and through his work as a spiritual father both for the solidity of his doctrine and for the love of his soul.[64]

I have reported on this expanded context to better understand the particularity of the experience of the Burning Bush which would soon be established at Antim, after the experience of the Cernăuți retreat. The people who participated in that retreat and who were soon meeting in Antim were not monks, but intellectuals, seekers of meaning and truth, each starting from their own skills and their living and working environments. They were moved by a profound yearning that sought a way to be realized, aware of participating in an experience that preceded and accompanied them, the experience of the Church. A lecture by Tudor at Cernăuți, found among his papers, is particularly illuminating.[65] He shows how the program for the

[64] From the Preface to vol. II of the *Philokalia* (Sibiu: 1947), IV. Arsenie Boca (1910–1989), graduated from the Theological Academy of Sibiu in 1933, having as a teacher Fr. Dumitru Stăniloae. He enrolled at the Institute of Fine Arts in Bucharest and simultaneously audited Nichifor Crainic's course on mysticism, and spent three months on Athos in 1939, where he collected manuscripts of philokalic authors in Romanian and Greek. In 1942, he was formally received into the monastic community of Sâmbăta de Sus, was ordained a priest and appointed staretz of the monastery. An avid supporter of the spiritual rebirth movement of national-legionary inspiration, and a translator of Greek patristic texts under the supervision of Nichifor Crainic, he collaborated on the edition of the first four volumes of the *Philokalia* in Romanian. Arrested several times, also for the support given to the anti-communist fighters, former legionaries, in the Făgăras mountains, in 1948 he was sent to the monastery of Prislop and after the transformation of the monastery into a female community, he remained as a father confessor, prevented from carrying out pastoral activity until his death, suffering imprisonment and forced labor on several occasions, and constantly monitored by the *Securitate*.

[65] See the text in Antonie Plămădeală, *Rugul Aprins*, 123–55, recounted together with two other lectures.

retreat days was conceived in conversations between himself and the metropolitan. The problem was not to say interesting things, but to testify to the stage of the path undertaken by each one. The first desirable thing would have been to ensure that, as intellectuals, one could access a dimension of ecclesial life, a lively contact between the participants in order to obtain enrichment for all. He was of the opinion that it was not enough to refer to one's own predilections, even though everyone could boast of a wealth of personal interests. It was necessary to define oneself and move according to a spiritual, ecclesial rhythm, a defined order in which to find oneself. The liturgy served this purpose excellently. So, they had thought of starting a daily presentation regarding the liturgical calendar, with the celebration of the various saints and the various mysteries of the Lord. From there, one would start to find the bread that nourishes. The reflection then broadens on the concept of order, on what contemporary man follows, that is, the rational order. He reflects on the events of history, Nazism and communism, which present themselves as the denial of the great mysterious order of God. He thinks that God punishes us by leaving us at the mercy of the order of our mind alone, which inevitably leads us to disorder, to disaster. He is aware of living in a tragic moment, which he likes to define as the poverty of wealth, the extreme disorder of the modern rational order. Coming to Cernăuți is the consequence of having felt the insufficiency of the pre-established orders of the world, of feeling the need to assume another order, the ecclesial order, the order of God. This is the only purpose of their meeting, of their meditations: returning in a special way to the Church. He considered it regrettable that people lead a double life, the daily one according to their own commitments and activities and the one in the church, without the two actually being able to meet. He demonstrates that he knows the living conditions of Russian Orthodox exiles and emigrants in the West, whom he admires for the Christian testimony they give, so much so as to radiate their beauty outwards. He does not want to write literature, but to enter into true Christian life. It is interesting to observe that in his reflections he is well aware of the historical conditions of the moment. He is absolutely aware that in the Romanian Church the stage of seeing things spiritually has not been reached because, if that were the case, they would not simply be friends, but witnesses who live according to a certain style, the ecclesial style. In fact, the real difficulty that he finds in everyone is to be able to communicate well, that is, not only to communicate their thoughts to each other, but to find that adequate internal tone which allows the blossoming of thoughts, that is, arriving at the creation of a true ecclesial unity. He is convinced that we must arrive at an integral type of understanding and Cernăuți's meetings should serve this purpose. Addressing his monk and priest friends, he speaks of the tragedy of knowing things, but ultimately without knowing anything, without *knowing* in the authentic sense of the word. He was recalling what he had heard a monk from Athos say: life must become a liturgy. The philosopher Constantin Noica echoes this, adding that it was not necessary to create opposition between what they did in Cernăuți and what they did in the world, where each one came from: "We need to live in harmony with what we want to do here because then, returning to the world, the experience here must bear fruit there. Let us therefore speak gently and look at the world from which we have separated without hostility in thinking and speaking."

After Noica's intervention on *Pathos and Patmos*, Tudor recalls an episode experienced on Athos in a fierce discussion with Romanian monks on the question of the calendar. At the height of the discussion, an elderly monk came forward and said to him: "Give it up, brother, give it up!" "Here, this is what I thought: let us give up on each other to gain fullness as brothers in Christ." In one evening conversation with his philosopher friend, who was amazed at the strength with which he prayed in asking for help for the highest degrees of sanctity, his friend asked: "But isn't this pride?" He replied, "No, it's spiritual pathos!" Standing in true humility, it is the courage of the cross, it is the crucial dimension of humility, which is true courage. As the gospel says: Have courage: I have overcome the world (John 16:33). From this spiritual pathos we arrive at the place of revelation, Patmos, where we see clearly. And then we go further, we arrive at the prayer of the heart which, itself, is interior courage. And he reveals that he wrote something on the syntax of the cross to have a new thought on the problem of prayer of the heart.[66] The speaker's presentation with audience interjections shows quite well the tone and liveliness of the meetings because there is the sense of many people deep in thought, of people thinking with the Church, thinking with life, and with everyone focused on one sole understanding of life.

And when, in an afternoon meeting, again at Cernăuți, he wanted to comment on the prayer of the heart according to the method of Symeon the New Theologian, by which he showed he knew Hausherr's 1927 critical edition from the Oriental Institute of Rome, but starting from the manuscripts that he had found on Athos and which he himself translated, he dwelt further on the symbolic meaning of the cross as a paradoxical expression of living in fullness. He calls it the science of the ineffable, which is not logical, but experiential. It is in this context that he recognized—his precise words—his personal tragedy of being an intellectual. He had just related an old intuition of his about the tragic situation of the Romanian church. Taking the texts of the Fathers in hand, he said to himself: "The texts contradict each other, but can one saint contradict another saint?" Despite all the differences in approaches and expression, he noted that in all the patristic texts there exists an underlying unity, an identical general framework and experience and he said he was ready to direct all his effort precisely towards that fundamental orientation. Metropolitan Tit also intervened in the discussion, reminding him of the simplicity with which Jesus finally made his guidance count: "Unless you become like children, you will not enter the kingdom of heaven." And Tudor replied: "How easy it would be for me too... if I had this key to becoming a child in my hand!... Whoever has read the gospel feels that this profound way of living is a reality. Blessed are the poor in spirit, who are like children. But for me to become a child, without being one, is just not possible; I have to get busy, I have to commit myself, like Simeon the New Theologian." The metropolitan replied: "Clearly, you understand this quite well." And Tudor: "My tragedy is that I am an intellectual, and it is the tragedy of those who don't even make an effort."

[66] A volume would then be published, edited by Alexandru Dimcea, which collects the reflections and intuitions of Sandu Tudor, scattered among the handwritten notes that survived the dispersion of the *Securitate* search at the time of the 1958 trial, entitled *Taina sfinți cruci* (Caietele Preacuviosului Părinte Daniil de la Rarău, 3) (Bucharest: Christiana, 2001).

b) After the withdrawal from Cernăuți

The new staretz of Antim, Vasile Vasilachi (1944–1948), a dynamic and tireless administrator, with a profound theological preparation, promoted the renovation of the monastery, which was badly damaged by the terrible earthquake of 1940. He himself tells us about those years in his memoirs.[67] He set up a committee to oversee the work and find the necessary funds and material. It included generals Gheorghe Stratilescu, Gheorghe Lorgulescu, Ioan Tone, Traian Tetrat, the university professor Alexandru Mironescu and the writer Sandu Tudor, under the presidency of the same staretz and with Fr. Sofian Boghiu as secretary and treasurer. It also promoted artistic and musical research by establishing competitions for monks and lay people with related prizes in the fields of icon painting and musical composition. Here too, a committee presided over the selection of works and the related prizes. The painter Mac Constantinescu, professors Alexandru Mironescu and I. D. Stefanescu, together with Sandu Tudor, were part of this committee. Receiving prizes were Fr. Sofian Boghiu for icon painting, the best singers of the Byzantine music choir, and Paul Constantinescu, who had been called to lead the monastery choir, for the composition of oratorios for the Nativity of Jesus and Pascha.[68] Not only that, but there was the idea of annexing the nearby Pompilian Institute to transform it into a Higher School of Christian culture with monk tutors in various fields and a medical center where monks with medical degrees could work. The list of fathers and brothers of the monastic community of Antim says a lot about the level of devotion and competence that characterized it:

1. Archimandrite Haralambie Vasilachi, brother of the staretz, famous preacher and theologian, exarch of the monasteries of the archbishopric of Bucharest (died in Gherla prison in 1962)[69]

---

[67] Vasile Vasilachi (1909–2003), *De la Antim la Pocrov* (Cluj Napoca: Eikon, 2015), previously published, in 1984, by the Cuvântul Vieții editions, Detroit, Michigan, USA, where he had been sent in 1969. Sometimes his memoirs, written thirty or forty years after the events, are inaccurate or particularly subjective. For example, he never mentions the figure of Fr. Ioann the Stranger, nor does he give Sandu Tudor credit for initiating and piloting the Burning Bush movement. But his testimony is absolutely precious for giving an overall picture.

[68] Paul Constantinescu is also the composer of a well-known canon for the Jesus Prayer. See Appendix, p. 287.

[69] Nicolae Steinhardt also mentions him, *Diario della felicità* (Bologna: Mulino, 1996), 130–34.

2 Archimandrite Benedict Ghiuș, graduated from Strasbourg, assistant to the chair of ascetics and mysticism at the Faculty of Theology, then assistant to Fr. Stăniloae

3 Archimandrite Sofian Boghiu, student at the Faculty of Theology and the Academy of Fine Arts, secretary and treasurer of the monastery

4 Archimandrite Felix Dubneac, student at the Faculty of Theology and the Academy of Fine Arts

5 Hieromonk Antonie Plămădeală (later Metropolitan of Transylvania)

6 Hierodeacon Roman Stanciu, student at the Faculty of Theology, Geography and Pharmacy (later vicar bishop of Bucharest)

7. Protosinghel Gherasim Cristea, student at the Faculty of Theology (later vicar bishop of Râmnicul Vâlcea)

8. Hierodeacon Tarasie Negru, student at the Faculty of Theology and Letters (Latin and Greek)

9. Hierodeacon Emilian Havrici, student at the Faculty of Theology and Letters

10 Protosinghel Veniamin Gavrilovici, student at the Faculty of Theology and director of the choir

11 Hierodeacon Celestin Grigorescu, student in medicine

12 Hierodeacon Irineu Cheorbeja, student in medicine

13 Hierodeacon Stelian Ciobotaru, student in medicine

14 Hierodeacon Emilian Lupu, student in medicine

15 Hierodeacon Efrem Hancu, master in the workshops of the Biblical Institute

16 Hierodeacon Neofit Nica, student at the Faculty of Theology

17 Brother Andrei Scrima, student in medicine and student at the Faculty of Theology

18. Protosinghel Petronie Tănase, student at the Faculty of Theology and Mathematics

19 Hieromonk Emilian Andrei, student at the Faculty of Theology

20 Hierodeacon Porfirie Frunza, student at the Faculty of Theology

21 Hieromonk Joasaph Ganea, student at the Faculty of Theology and at the Conservatory

22. Hieromonk Maxim Mereanu, student at the Faculty of Theology and Polytechnic

23 Archimandrite Iustinian Florea, student at the Faculty of Theology

24 Monk Pavel Leca, student at the Faculty of Theology

25 Protosinghel Severian Burancea, student at the Faculty of Theology

26 Protosinghel Urpasian Popa, student at the Faculty of Theology

27 Hieromonk Eraclie Tautu, student at the Faculty of Theology

28 Brother Valentin Vitkovski, chorister at the Romanian Opera

29 Brother Alexandru T., student of mathematics

30 Archimandrite Stefan Lucaciu, doctoral student in theology

31 Hieromonk Paul Bogdan, official at the Biblical Institute

32 Protosinghel Macarie Brabete, student at the Faculty of Theology

33 Hierodeacon Pimen Georgescu, student at the Faculty of Theology and Letters (Latin and Greek)

34 Archimandrite Bonifaciu Barancea, iconographer

35 Protosinghel Ghedeon Cosofret, student at the Faculty of Theology

36 Hieromonk Damian Stogu, assistant bursar

37 Hierodeacon Macarie Dorobantu, cantor

38 Brother Luca Boghiu, student at the seminary

39 Monk Agaton Negraru, responsible for preparing unleavened bread for the liturgy

40 Brother Petru Achitenei, student of the fine arts

41 Hierodeacon Antinoghen, deacon

42 Brother Sandu Tudor, writer

43 Protosinghel Nicodim Ionite, former hegumen of Antim

44 Protosinghel Paisie Prelipceanu, student at the Faculty of Theology and Museography

Dr. Marius Vasileanu (1964–),[70] who has carried out post-doctoral research on the phenomenon of the Burning Bush for decades and who coordinates the *Arhiva Rugului Aprins* collection of Eikon editions, noting how the majority of the monks at Antim had a good level of university education, often with two degrees, has wondered: Perhaps this has somehow

[70] See the articles by Marius Vasileanu, which appeared in *Ziarul Financiar*: *Modelul Mănăstirii Antim* (30 January 2014); *Sandu Tudor și "Idea unei școli noi teologica"* (20 February 2014); *Rugul Aprins, un simplu cenaclu?* (19 February 2015).

impeded the practice of prayer and monastic life? Many of them have become reference figures in the spiritual life of the Romanian Church. He thus underscores the particularity of the Antim experiment in that period. In a context not yet tainted by communist perversion, with the contribution of first-rate personalities, the monastery had managed to attract numerous men of culture from the capital where they could freely discuss and share the paths of personal research into the depths of Orthodox mystical tradition. Sandu Tudor is not the inspirer, but the driver, the coordinator, so much so that he sponsored where he could the formation of a monastery of intellectuals capable of countering the harmful influence of communist materialism, well rooted in the Orthodox mystical tradition. The experience of prayer-theology-culture is the model that Sandu Tudor and his friends, both monks and lay people, have left us as a legacy.

The testimonies of the participants confirm this. It is again the elder Vasilachi who recalls that, in what he terms the "spiritual oasis of the capital," famous writers from the country regularly came, as if to an altar of the spirit, to deepen the meaning and purpose of their creations, in an attempt to find new paths in the search for truth and beauty. The aim was to restore new vigor to the dignity of man, in communion with God, according to the responsibility of the lordship of creation entrusted to him by God from the beginning. Two types of meetings were held there, one more exclusive, on Thursday evening, and the other, open to all, on Sunday afternoon. Every Thursday evening the meeting was led by the person who had been invited to present their literary or scientific or philosophical or religious creation. The staretz recalls the presentation of the research on the martyrdom of John the Baptist by the writer Marin Sadoveanu, the presentation of the poetic compositions of Vasile Voiculescu, the philosophical reflection on the absolute Truth by his brother Haralambie who had just published the book entitled *The altar of Romanian spirituality*, the reasoning of strict Euclidean logic by Professor Anton Dumitriu, the results of laboratory analysis in the chemical field by Professor Alexandru Mironescu with his study on the limits of scientific knowledge, the discoveries in the patristic field of the writer Paul Sterian, the philosophical reflections of Mircea Vulcanescu, and the sharing of the spiritual battles of the soul that Sandu Tudor illustrated with an overbearing charm. He also mentions his intervention in presenting some chapters from a book he was writing on spiritual healing from all kinds of afflictions. Above all, he recalls Sandu Tudor's clarity and depth of knowledge in the field of spirituality, both Christian and non-Christian, of the contemporary world. In these meetings, inevitably rather reserved for a narrow circle of participants, there was an atmosphere of joy in research, in the exercise of a critical spirit in the literary, theological and philosophical fields, according to each individual's propensities, in the atmosphere of a fervent Orthodox monastic community, dedicated to prayer and capable of creating the desire for an experience of prayer in everyone. So much so that one could say that in the monastery room where the meetings were held, one grew spiritually, wanting to share God's gifts to the glory of the Church and the people, with an open and good heart towards all humanity.

For the general public of the capital, however, for those who took part in the liturgical offices at the Antim monastery, public conferences on religious themes were held every Sunday afternoon. These meetings were led by Archimandrite Haralambie, Alexandru Mironescu, Sandu Tudor and the same people mentioned above and many others, including the young Andrei Scrima who already stood out for his intelligence and sagacity. The conferences were followed by public debate. In particular, these conferences were attended by various professors of theology such as Gheorghe Savin, Dumitru Stăniloae, Metropolitan Tit Simedrea and other bishops, as well as engineers, doctors, some army generals, and many students and faithful from Bucharest. Staretz Vasilachi recalls that the library room was always packed, as were the adjacent corridors. The spiritual interest that the conferences aroused was great, with many questions from writers and professors, in particular from Olga Greceanu, iconographer and mosaicist. The space at Antim was experienced as a real spiritual center (*vatra duhovniceasca*) where everyone could draw on the light of the Orthodox mystical tradition and monastery life. The testimonies of the staretz are completed by those of other participants, such as those of the future metropolitan of Transylvania, Antonie Plămadeală, and those of Dr. Nicolae Nicolau, leader of the group of students, both very young frequenters of Antim, together with those of Fr. Roman Braga.[71]

In addition to the names already mentioned for the lecturers, among the religious, we should add those of Fr. Felix Dubneac, who later emigrated to the USA, Fr. Petronie Tănase, future hegumen of the Prodromou skete on Athos, Fr. Sofian Boghiu, "peaceful and pacifying, confessor and essential reference for Antim,"[72] and Fr. Arsenie Papacioc, one of the last great spiritual fathers of the country. Without being part of the group, also in attendance were the writer Valeriu Anania, future Bishop Bartholomew, a group from Cluj, and especially the theologian Father Dumitru Stăniloae, known at the time for his translations of the *Philokalia*. Among the lay people were professors Alexandru Elian, a Byzantine scholar, Virgil Stancovici, Stefan Todirascu of the Faculty of Law, Barbu Slatineanu, and Paul Sterian, an old friend of Sandu Tudor since the time of the formation of the Association of Romanian Christian Students in 1928, together with the philosopher Mircea Vulcănescu, the architect Joja, Eugen Ionescu and Alexandru Elian himself. There were also the literary critic Tudor Vianu, scientists such as Dan Barbilian, mathematician and poet Ion Barbu (his pseudonym), Octav Onicescu, also a mathematician, Mihai Neculce, doctors such as I. Plăcințeanu, Valentin Poenaru, epistemologist and logician Anton Dumitriu, architect Constantin Joja, generals Gheorghe Stratilescu, Gheorghe Iorgulescu, and Constantin Manolache. Numerous students attended, among whom we find the names of Andrei Scrima, Roman Braga, Nicolae Bordașiu, Nicolae Nicolau, Gheorghe Văsîi, Șerban Mironescu (son of Alexandru Mironescu), Nicolae Rădulescu, Grigore Dan Pistol, Gheorghe Dabija, and Emanoil

[71] Antonie Plămădeală, *Rugul Aprins*; Nicolae Nicolau, *Rugul aprins al Maicii Domnului, Din documentele rezistenței*, no. 4 (Arhiva Asociatiei foștilor deținuți politici din România, 1992), 22–39; Roman Braga, *Ogni monaco ha un suo segreto con Dio*. Prof. Nicolau was a young doctor, an exceptional leader of the group of students who attended Antim, arrested in 1950 and sentenced to twenty years of forced labor, released like all political prisoners in 1964. Dr. Nicolae Nicolau defines Sandu Tudor as the animator of the entire group, a catalyst, a living expression of the purifying power of faith, a journalist, poet, and fearsome polemicist, capable of converting his argumentative energy into an explication of biblical truth.

[72] Scrima, *L'accompagnamento spirituale*, 164.

Mihăilescu (the last of the Burning Bush group to be arrested and who gave a beautiful testimony).[73]

The meetings at Antim had taken place since 1945 in a small group of participants, all friends or acquaintances of Sandu Tudor who, with the consent of the elder Vasilachi, had launched the idea. The experience was then consolidated and grew, so much so that he made an official request to the Patriarch to organize public sessions in the monastery. On 12 February 1946 Sandu Tudor signed a request to obtain the patriarchal blessing for the conferences/talks in the Antim monastery, which had already begun to be held on Sunday afternoons the previous year, after participation in the liturgical offices. This is what the cover letter stated:

> Since the past year, in the holy monastery of Antim, a spiritual activity has been started, for a deeper research and experience of Orthodox doctrine and faith, under the patronage of the staretz, Father Archimandrite Vasile Vasilachi. Every Sunday, a group of clerics and lay people take part in the liturgical offices and, in the afternoon, sessions are held which are edifying and deepen the Orthodox mystical life. Today, we take a further step, establishing ourselves as an association, with legal recognition, under the name Burning Bush of the Mother of God. For the good progress of our activity and the joy of the bond with this holy monastery, the only monastic place in the heart of capital, we come to your Reverend Eminence to ask you in all deference to grant us your assent and impart your paternal blessing.[74]

This is followed by the signatures of Alexandru Mironescu, Anton Dumitriu, Vasile Voiculescu, Gheorghe Dabija, Paul Sterian and Sandu Tudor.

A series of contributing factors added to the prestige of the monastery: the Biblical Institute had resumed its activities with its publications and the diffusion of texts for the faithful, the liturgical offices were celebrated by the community with care, taking up the consolidated monastic tradition, within the walls of the monastery was found a friendship of a large group of Orthodox intellectuals, the damage to the monastic buildings caused by the 1940 earthquake continued to be repaired, and

[73] *Organizatia Rugul Aprins, Din documentele rezistenței*, no. 4, 40–55.

[74] Cf. Daniil Sandu Tudor, *Taina Rugului Aprins. Scrieri și documente inedite*, 92–93.

numerous faithful came to seek peace and knowledge by rediscovering the treasures of the Orthodox mystical tradition. But the event that changed everything was the arrival of Father Ioann Kulygin, the Stranger.[75] Alexandru Mironescu, a close friend of Sandu Tudor, recalls with moving words the meeting that took place in Cernica in 1945. In his memoirs he places the meeting in a path that he had already been following for some time, together with his friend Tudor, who had spoken to him for the first time of the prayer of the heart, which had opened a world to him. He had participated in the Cernăuți meeting in 1943, in the midst of the war, and had been quite struck by that experience which had translated for all the participants, who would then cultivate friendship in the following years, into an overwhelming desire to live the path of a spiritual life. It was like finding themselves in the wake of the ancient fathers, with the same thirst, the same ardor and the same vision. He had understood the all-encompassing reality of spiritual values and above all the fact that the *nervum rerum* of those values, as he himself defines it, is precisely prayer. Scientist that he was, he recognized that those values involved a secret point of support, the famous standpoint of Archimedes, the vital point that pulsated like a heart at the center of the spiritual universe, a point that unites the fundamental principle of freedom with

[75] See above, p. 43, note 9. Andrei Scrima, in his *L'accompagnamento spirituale*, 169–91, had underscored the importance of this meeting and, on pages 29–118, had gone to great lengths to present the letter that Fr. Ioann had addressed to Antim's friends in the autumn of 1946, giving a subtle interpretation. Here I intend to exploit instead the description that Alexandru Mironescu (1903–1973) left us in his *Calea inimii. Eseuri in duhul Rugului Aprins*, foreword by Virgil Cândea (Bucharest: Anastasia, 1998). The title is an editorial choice for a series of Mironescu's writings assembled here and submitted by Mironescu's daughter, Ileana Mironescu Sandu. The first essay reports the letter of Fr. Ioann, in a version slightly different from that reported by Scrima, while the second essay is entitled "Calea către inima mea," which suggested the title for the collection. His testimony is particularly precious because it was written in 1947, although published in 1998, while all the other testimonies, adduced by the various participants, were written many years after the facts. Mironescu's is the sincere description of a spiritual itinerary followed with conviction and tenacity, not by a monk or by someone like the famous Russian pilgrim, free from the temptations of modern culture, but by a university student who proceeds and overcomes with all the weight of his scientific training and a passion for philosophy, literature and art. Mironescu's abbreviated testimony is also reported in *Cuviosul Ioan cel Străin (din arhiva Rugului Aprins)*, ed. Gheorghe Vasilescu, afterword by Sofian Boghiu (Bucharest: Anastasia, 1999), 105–14.

the maximum of rigor. He rediscovered the fathers' insistence on attention in prayer. Among other things, he recalls that years earlier he had been impressed by reading *The Secret Path* by the English writer Paul Brunton,[76] for the fact that a man like him, not a priest, not a monk, not a saint, not given to prayer as was the Russian pilgrim, spoke of the secret center of man's interiority. The meeting in Cernica with Fr. Ioann happened as if by chance. He had gone with Tudor and Fr. Benedict Ghiuș to the monastery to find a friend who in the end they did not find. They participated in the liturgical offices (they seem to recall that it was Pentecost Sunday) and in their uncertainty about whether to stay a little longer or go home, found themselves invited by their companion, Fr. Nicodim Bujor, to visit Fr. Ioann. None of them knew him. Emotions ran high. He came from the famous Optina Hermitage, where Dostoevsky had also stayed, where Tolstoy would have liked to come, facts that they knew well as men of culture. A providential coincidence: what divine Providence brought that man from so far away for them to meet him? They immediately recognized that they needed such a man, a great spiritual man who could have the right answers to their questions. He spoke to them about his vicissitudes, about prayer, in a simple, luminous way, with the help of a translator, Fr. Leontie. They experienced a highly charged atmosphere of spiritual communication (they called it *sorbatoreasca incandescență*, an incandescent participation in joy) and they marveled at the sense of communion that could be experienced. Fr. Ioann spoke for several hours. He revealed a life experience unknown to them.

The meeting was, for Mironescu, something totally new and, for many of the things he heard, he needed time to fully understand. He often spoke about this meeting with his friends, noting how the wonder grew over time due to the profound knowledge that Fr. Ioann had of life and men. On an interior personal level, he wondered about the meaning of prayer of the heart, whether it was really useful, whether it could be practiced without danger of illusion, etc.

---

[76] Paul Brunton (Raphael Hurst, 1898–1981), was an author of spiritual books who introduced the spirituality of India to the West in a theosophical key. The book that Mironescu cites is titled *The Secret Path. A technique of spiritual self-discovery for the modern world* (London: Rider & Co., 1934).

COMMENT: Such a volcanic event does not suddenly solidify in any particular way.

Over time he understood, like all his other friends, that Fr. Ioann was a great personality, who embodied an ancient and authentic tradition that he learned and practiced in a monastery, living a spiritual life that Mironescu could not even imagine. What was found in the patristic writings was all a confirmation of what Fr. Ioann spoke and taught. And he concludes his testimony by saying that the simplest and most natural things, such as prayer, are the most difficult to achieve. He felt taken by the hand like a son by his father: "Behold, this is the road that leads to your heart." Fr. Ioann didn't teach him how to play Beethoven's symphonies, but how to pick up and hold the bow. It was the key and the beginning of true knowledge. The prayer of the heart thus became the creative work through which to come into possession of what one truly is. Entering into yourself, where you meet, in a vital way, your humanity, with the profound image of man, of the Man who you are and for whom Christ became incarnate.

The meeting affected the three friends so deeply that Sandu Tudor did not delay in inviting Fr. Ioann to the meetings at Antim and his presence would play a leading role in the formation of the Burning Bush group. Sandu Tudor himself would become the spiritual son of Fr. Ioann and would receive a blessing from him for practicing the Jesus Prayer:

> The blessing for my son and spiritual follower, beloved in God, Sandu Tudor, in prayerful memory, from the spiritual father, protopriest Ioann Kulygin, disciple and spiritual follower, since the year 1906, of the startsy of the contemplative life of the monastery and hermitage of Optina, who are followers of Paisius Velichkovsky, of the hieroschimonks Joseph, Barsanuphius, Anatole, Nectarius, of the protopriest Theodot and of the hermits of the monasteries of the Caucasus mountains (25 March 1946, Cernica Monastery).[77]

Fr. Ioann was fully aware that his coming was governed by God's providence, as he declared in the letter he addressed to his Antim brothers and friends in the autumn of 1946, shortly before being arrested by the Soviets for treason:

[77] *Cuviosul Ioan cel Străin (din arhiva Rugului Aprins)*, ed. Gheorghe Vasilescu, afterword by Sofian Boghiu (Bucharest: Anastasia, 1999), 47.

> I strongly testify to the work of providence which is accomplished and does not cease to be accomplished in me.... Blessed are those who have not doubted me, your unworthy father and elder, who find myself among you as a dispatched stranger.... Since the time of my youth, the sweet energy of providence has graciously worked in my heart and, on the path of salvation, has given me the grace-bearing blessing of spiritual Inheritance. At the same time it gave me the gift of a spiritual father in whom grace operated, filling my existence. But, above all, it gave me, throughout my pilgrimage, the unmediated grace of the spirit of strength and understanding. I have spoken to you aloud many times about all this and I will undoubtedly give you even other particular teachings.... And so the Lord has given me what is called the charismatic tradition of spiritual inheritance, and at the same time the grace to guide the lives of men to salvation.... Yes, I bless the Lord who, on the threshold of adulthood, wanted to bring together in one—in the inner chamber of my young heart—all the abundance of gifts by which I live and which renew me still, and which sufferings and my life's twists and turns have failed to disperse; but with care and fear I have guarded this abundance, trying not to let it diminish. On the contrary, I can testify, in the *parrhesia* of the Spirit, without any deception, that I too, miserable and unworthy as I am, despite my weakness, have made known the true gift of God's prevenient love to many of those who have sought it with sincerity.[78]

It would be on the wave of the grace of this unexpected encounter that, in the summer of 1946, Sandu Tudor organized for the group of intellectuals, religious and students, who attended Antim's Sunday meetings, a prolonged excursion to the Govora monastery[79] under the guidance of the elder Antonie Barbalunga. Daily meetings were held there on the deepening of the patristic-philokalic tradition of the Eastern Churches. Next it was decided to establish an association with legal status and

[78] Scrima, *L'accompagnamento spirituale*, 30–32.

[79] Govora is one of the oldest Romanian monasteries, in Oltenia, in the municipality of Mihăești, Vrancea district, 18 km from the capital Râmnicu Vâlcea. It dates back to the fifteenth century and was subsequently expanded and consolidated first by Matei Basarab and then by Constantin Brâncoveanu. Matei Basarab himself had the first printing press in Wallachia installed in the monastery in which, in 1640, the so-called *Pravila de la Govora*, the first written code of laws in Romania, was printed. Antim Ivireanul, founder of the "All Saints" monastery, in Bucharest, was also staretz of Govora. The monastery was transformed into a female monastery in 1959.

with permission to hold public lectures aimed at sharing the experience of the Orthodox Church with the explicit authorization of the competent authorities in an ecclesial structure. Here in the monastery of Govora for the first time, in front of the fathers Benedict Ghiuș, Sofian Boghiu, Adrian Făgețeanu (his faithful disciple, who will follow him in all his travels), Felix Dubneac and the lay people Andrei Scrima, Valeriu Străinu and Stancovici Virgil, he expressed the idea of creating a monastery with intellectual monks to prepare them for the struggle to fight against materialist concepts.[80] The association was registered as a religious association in September 1946 at the Ilfov court, in Bucharest, by Sandu Tudor, Sofian Boghiu and Alexandru Mironescu, an association that the political authorities, with the mandatory consent of the patriarch, dissolved in 1948. The name "Association of the Burning Bush of the Mother of God" derived from the fact that Fr. Ioann had brought with him the icon of the Burning Bush of the Mother of God, and, with its mysteries, explained the path of prayer of the heart. The icon would then be bequeathed to Sandu Tudor. As demonstrated by Professor Nicolau, the establishment of the "Burning Bush of the Mother of God" had as its ultimate aim the creation of an interior climate that allowed the practice of prayer of the heart. That prayer, so simple in its statement and so difficult to practice even in monasteries and hermitages far from the world, became the ultimate reason for the activity of this group of men of the twentieth century, citizens of Bucharest, each engaged in their own professional activity, in particularly difficult times due to the materialist oppression of communism which was extending its noxious influence throughout Romanian society.[81]

The external, public form of these intentions was expressed with Sunday conferences for apologetic-mystical purposes in the Antim library room, followed by public debate. There was

[80] We owe this information to Fr. Adrian Făgețeanu in *File I 211015*, vol. 3, Arhivele CNSAS, f. 61–62, cited in the article by Mihail Stanciu, of the Aristotle University of Thessaloniki: *Părintele hieroschimonah Daniil Sandu Tudor - o viață de mărturisire și martiriu pentru Hristos*, 17 November 2017, posted on the Internet Archive website and accompanied by precious archive documents: https://archive.org/details/parintele-ieroschimonah-daniil-sandu-tudor-o-viata-de-marturisire-si-martiriu-pentru-hristos. Cf. Marius Oprea, *Adevărata călătorie a lui Zahei. V. Voiculescu și taina Rugului Aprins*, 51–53.

[81] Nicolae Nicolau, *Rugul Aprins al Maicii Domnului, Din documentele rezistenței*, no. 4 (Arhiva Asociației foștilor deținuți politici din România, 1992), 30–31.

no shortage of interventions by agents provocateurs, sent by the political authorities, to justify the public nature of the meetings. Fr. Benedict Ghiuș describes the meetings, which were increasingly attended by a large audience, to be structured as follows: Sandu Tudor opened the session with a word of teaching, prayers were then recited and then the designated lecturer on religious themes spoke, this being established previously and made known to the public, followed by a debate where anyone could interject. The texts of those addresses which revolved around the concern for the interior life of man have not reached us, but many remember the titles, which bear witness to the prevailing interest in the Eastern spiritual tradition, the hesychast tradition in particular. The conference that started the group's meetings, presented by Sandu Tudor himself, was entitled "The journey to the place of the heart." Well-remembered are the talks of Alexandru Mironescu: "The discovery of oneself"; of Fr. Benedict Ghiuș: "The interior life in the light of the Liturgy"; of Paul Sterian: "The martyrdom of Saint John the Baptist" and "The life of the Holy Martyr Anastasia"; and many others: "The invisible war of Paisius the Great of Egypt," "Hesychasm," "Jesus, the Incarnate Word," "Original sin," "The stage and the altar," "The prayer of the heart," "Exegesis of the cursed fig tree," "Portraits of some great hesychasts."[82] Topics of a more general cultural scope were also presented, as was, for example, a whole series of conferences given by the writer Ion Marin Sadoveanu on ancient theater and medieval mystery plays, in which the author spoke of the sacred rhythms that favored prayer even in the non-Christian world, conferences which seem to have made a great impression among the participants judging by the fact that everyone remembers them.

One cannot help but notice that the effort of the intellectuals who met in Antim reveals the possibility of accessing the meaning and practice of hesychast prayer as a way for modern man, without abandoning their condition as intellectuals, without leaving the world, without shying away from the task specific to understanding the phenomenon beyond

[82] Cf. Alexandru Dimcea, "Prefata," Ieroschimonahul Daniil Tudor (Sandu Tudor), *Scrieri* 1 (Bucharest: Ed. Christiana, 1999), 11; Antonie Plamădeală, *Rugul Aprins*, 119.

the cage of rationalism.[83] From a typological point of view, the intellectuals of Antim were of a peculiar type, at the crossroads between a certain sense of tradition and a freedom of creative research, also highly conscious of their duty to discover the profound spiritual contents of Christianity, to offer us a chance to survive as a people faced with the aggression of an aberrant modernity. Then there is the quality of the Antim experience, which is exceptional: In a non-institutionalized context, where hierarchical relationships do not apply, where a new fraternity between monks and lay people is rediscovered, without established programs, but with the premonition of the richness and liveliness of the Orthodox tradition, a sort of pre-established harmony was created between the typically monastic aspect and the secular-intellectual one. Although Fr. Roman Braga contrasts, in a certain sense, the position of the intellectuals of Antim with the practical, unreflecting stance of the Cernica monks; in reality he is merely pointing to the opposition that marks the difficult relationship between tradition and culture in the eastern space of Christianity.[84] The Antim group assumed a very important value because it represented an attempt made by educated laypeople to overcome this fracture, to start a dialogue between the two terms of the equation with the aim of adopting the contents of the Eastern spiritual tradition beyond the picturesque and popular devotion, in the context of a culture open to the wider world. However, on the part of the ecclesiastical institution, the fruitfulness of the experience was not grasped and, with the arrival of communism, everything remained at a standstill and any dialogue became impossible. One can only suppose that, in the face of the aggression of history, the difficult problem of the relations of the institution of the Church with the world had to be put aside in favor of the main objective: the assimilation of the contents of the Orthodox mystical tradition to help man to survive. The same concern also explains the absence of confessional controversy in the group's discussions, even though there were many fearsome

[83] Cf. Ioan I. Ică, "Il 'Roveto ardente': una fioritura dell'ideale esicasta all'alba del comunismo in Romania" ["The "Burning Bush": a flowering of the hesychast ideal at the dawn of communism in Romania], *Il monachesimo tra eredità e aperture*, ed. Maciej Bielawski and Daniel Hombergen (Roma: Studia anselmiana, 2004), 476–79; A. Scrima, *L'accompagnamento spirituale*, 146–47.

[84] Roman Braga, *Ogni monaco ha un suo segreto*, 58.

polemicists among the participants. The rivalries between the various confessions themselves subsided. A curious example of this is reported by Cristian Vasile. A Greek-Catholic monk, Agenor Danciul, a spiritual son of Monsignor Vladimir Ghika,[85] invited his teacher to participate in a meeting of the Burning Bush group at Antim. Sandu Tudor gave a lecture about the Orthodox view on the forgiveness of sins. He commented on texts by Gregory Palamas. Monsignor Ghika intervened to rectify an incorrect statement by the speaker. The speaker reacted angrily but Monsignor Ghika did not give in and they decided to meet on another occasion to address the topic. The meeting would take place later, and a friendship full of mutual respect would develop between the two, Orthodox Tudor and Catholic Ghika, a respect that would translate into communion when they, like many others, religious and lay, Orthodox and Catholic, would spend their time in communist prisons.[86]

It should also be added, as I have indicated previously, that the interest in the Christian tradition on the part of some of these intellectuals came from esotericism, but Sandu Tudor with his intelligence managed to purify it from all Guénonian residues and orient it towards an entirely Orthodox sense. This is certainly not the least of his merits.

In January 1947 Fr. Ioann Kulygin was repatriated. The following year, before Sandu Tudor was tonsured a monk with the name of Agaton in September, a change of leadership in Antim was decreed in April with the new policy of the communist party for control of the Church. Antim's new staretz, Valerian Zaharia, a former legionnaire co-opted by the communist authorities, is believed to be responsible for the dissolution of the group. Fr. Vasilachi and his brother Haralambie, fervent supporters of the Burning Bush, were dismissed. Once he became bishop of Oradea, in 1955, Valerian Zaharia visited the monasteries saying to the monks: "You young people, why do you stay here in prayer and in solitude? This was true in the time of Stephen the Great. Now times have changed. Why don't you modernize? Why don't

[85] On the extraordinary figure of Monsignor Vladimir Ghika (1873–1954), prince and priest, see *Le catacombe della Romania. Testimonianze dalle carceri comuniste, 1945-1964* [The catacombs of Romania. Testimonies from communist prisons, 1945–1964] (Milano: Rediviva editions, 2014), 79–100.

[86] Cristian Vasile, *Biserica Ortodoxă Română în primul communist deceniu* (Curtea Veche, 2005; Elefant.ro, 2013) 168–69.

you go to work?" It is clear that, even if the communication of the suspension of the conferences at Antim was made by him, the decision itself was made by Patriarch Iustinian Marina, as his contemporaries recall in their memoirs.[87] Meetings would continue for a few years in a reduced form, in a friendly and private way, in the Plumbuita monastery, and in Bucharest, where Fr. Sofian Boghiu was appointed hegumen.

To concisely define the experience of those years at Antim, the image used by Fr. Roman Braga in his memoirs is the most appropriate: a mystical volcano! The Burning Bush in Romania galvanized a reaction of the intellectual *elites* in a moment of epochal crisis. When communism was transforming everyone into an anonymous mass, prey to fear, without their own conscience and without responsibility, at Antim, man, looking for himself, encountered God.[88]

5. TRIAL AND PRISON

After two years of prison in Jilava and forced labor at the Danube-Black Sea Canal on charges of activity hostile to the state between 1950 and 1952, Sandu Tudor arrived in Slatina, Moldova, where, under the guidance of another great figure of Romanian monasticism, Fr. Cleopa Ilie, a great monastic fraternity was flourishing.[89] Fr. Cleopa did not take into account the

[87] Cf. Marius Oprea, *Adevărata călătorie a lui Zahei. V. Voiculescu și taina Rugului Aprins*, 54–57.

[88] Ibid., 132.

[89] Fr. Ilie Cleopa (1912–1998) is perhaps the most renowned and best-known Orthodox monastic figure in Romania. As a teenager, together with his two older brothers, he took the sheep to pasture near the Cozancea skete, where Paisie, whose disciple he would become, had retired in solitude. In 1929 he asked to enter Sihăstria, then governed by the hegumen Ioanichie Moroi, a severe man of Athonite style, who had been able to restore spiritual vigor to the monastery. From 1930 to 1942, out of obedience, he was in charge of the monastery's sheepfold. He was a shepherd. While he grazed the sheep, he devoured the books that he had managed to obtain at the Neamț monastery and, being gifted with a prodigious memory, he memorized everything. He did not know then that this assignment, in addition to helping him on the path of prayer and reading during the long times spent in solitude with his sheep, would also save his life later. Continuously wandering in the mountains, he knew all the paths and when, wanted by the police, he was warned to flee, there was no safer refuge for him than the mountains. In 1945 he was ordained a priest and appointed hegumen of Sihăstria, after the death of Fr. Ioanichie Moroi. In 1948 he had his first problems with the regime and retreated to the forest for six months. Then, through the intervention

suspicions that then surrounded Sandu Tudor for his past life and consecrated Fr. Agaton as a schemamonk with the name of Daniil, appointing him, in 1954, as staretz of the Rarău skete, dependent on the Sihăstria monastery. Here, far from controversy and on the margins of ecclesiastical and social life, he spent perhaps his most luminous years. There are several interesting testimonies from this period—first of all, about his ascetic life and the way he led the community. A disciple of his, Fr. Ioan Neagoe, the future *staretz* of the Rarău skete after the fall of communism, recalls that Fr. Daniil emphasized incessant prayer above all other monastic activities:

> This was one of the recommendations given to us by Fr. Daniil: In the Rarău monastery we never worked for a full hour. For half an hour you worked, for half an hour you had to either read or pray. Each monk had a prayer rosary on his arm and a small woolen bag in which he was obliged to place a prayer book. Shepherd monks could clearly be seen at the top of the mountain, kneeling among the sheep, with palms clasped in prayer, and so too did the staretz, dressed modestly, like a simple monk. Prayer, prayer, incessant prayer—this was his only recommendation![90]

Metropolitan Antonie Plămădeală reports in his memoirs that, at Rarău, Fr. Daniil continued to give him "lessons." He remembers some scenes with Fr. Daniil who went out to preach to the faithful gathered in church, holding the book he was reading at the time, with his typical green underlining, and would begin by saying: consider what Claudel says, or Shakespeare or Bernanos or another great writer, and for half an hour or an hour he commented on the text. If the ascetic labors of a saint came to mind, he began to talk about them and wept, bringing everyone to tears. At the time he was his disciple and Fr. Daniil

---

of Patriarch Justinian, he settled in Slatina, where he moved with about thirty monks from Sihastria. The monastery became, in the few years of life before it was closed and the community dispersed, a true spiritual center, a "spiritual academy," under whose influence other monasteries also flourished again: Putna, Moldovița, Rișca, and of course Sihăstria and Sihla. Between 1958 and 1964, when one arrest followed another, the most prominent men were imprisoned, with the exception of Fr. Cleopa who, for the third time and, this time, for five consecutive years, took refuge in total solitude in the forests around Neamț. Of those years the famous staretz would say: they were my university years, the university of prayer.

[90] Testimony reported by Marius Vasileanu, in *Ziarul financiar*, 2 December 2011.

allowed himself to be questioned: "Father, I listened to you in the celebration. You gave a very interesting sermon, but a university level one. I think that the farmers and elderly women who come up to Rarău from the valley with their knapsacks didn't understand a thing of what you said." And he replied: "I know. Do you think I need them to understand me? Haven't you seen them weep? It is more than enough."[91]

However, nostalgia for the friends of the Antim group caused him to make several forays into the capital, to the house of his friend Alexandru Mironescu (where he would later be arrested on the night between 13 and 14 June 1958) or to the Plumbuita monastery, or stopping in the Patriarchal Library to read his beloved hesychast texts. Fr. Cleopa also descended into Bucharest together with Fr. Arsenie Papacioc, the one who would later share the cell in Aiud prison with Fr. Daniil once they were both convicted in the 1958 trial. It is interesting to note that with them too, as at Antim about ten years earlier, the same climate of spiritual emotions was recreated in response to the words and testimony of a staretz speaking of the hesychast tradition and of the prayer of the heart in a completely natural way.[92]

The *Securitate*, however, kept an eye on them and by September 1956 had opened a file against Fr. Daniil de la Rarău's activities on suspicion of legionary activity under religious cover. 1958 marks a turning point in the activity of the political police in Romania. The tightening of repression, paradoxically at the same time as the withdrawal of Soviet troops from Romania, had basically three causes: 1) the Romanian communist authorities wanted to demonstrate to Moscow that they were capable of keeping the situation under control on their own; 2) in order to maintain power without the support of the Red Army, with the memory of the 1956 revolt in Hungary still vivid, they chose to intensify repressive practices in the purest Stalinist manner; 3) they needed to support the process of collectivization of agriculture by preventing any movement of peasant revolt as in the years 1949–1951. The two great trials, the one against the Burning Bush group and the one called Noica-Pillat against the philosopher Constantin Noica and his

[91] Antonie Plămădeală, *Rugul Aprins*, 88–89.

[92] As Nicolae Steinhardt recalls in his *Diario della felicità*, 197–98, regarding the meeting in early 1955 in Bucharest.

sympathizers, were not accidental. In a secret police report at that time, it is noted that in 1958, 4,083 counter-revolutionary individuals were convicted by judicial bodies, 2,080 of which were for conspiracy against the social order, as subversive and terrorist organizations. In all, 182 subversive organizations and groups were dissolved, including the Burning Bush group and the Noica philosopher's group. In the period between July 1 and August 8, in 1958 alone, 1,103 arrests were carried out across the country, for the most absurd reasons.[93]

The trial against the Burning Bush group, on charges of "Crime of conspiracy against the social order and against the working class and the revolutionary movement," art. 209, par. 1 of the Penal Code, opened on 29 October 1958 and with a public session on 8 November 1958. The Military Tribunal of the Second Military Region, fasc. no. 2164/958, sentence no. 125,[94] issued the sentence for the 16 members registered in the dossier "The Teodorescu Alexandru group and others." They were cited in this order: Teodorescu Alexandru (hieroschemamonk Daniil de la Rarău), Făgețeanu Alexandru (Fr. Adrian), Ghiuș Vasile Benedict, Braga Roman, Boghiu Serghie Sofian, Dubneac Felix, Papacioc Anghel Arsenie, Mironescu Alexandru, Văsîi Gheorghe, Mironescu Șerban (son of Alexandru), Rădulescu Nicolae, Pistol Grigore Dan, Dabija Gheorghe, Voiculescu Vasile, Stăniloae Dumitru, Mihăilescu Emanoil. The reasoning of the political police against churchmen and those who were interested in the religious tradition of Orthodoxy, in its perverse malignity, was simple: You are a legionary because you are a theologian and being a theologian you are anti-communist, therefore being anti-communist means being a legionary. Since several participants of the Burning Bush group had a legionary past, without ever participating in subversive actions or political propaganda and in any case when still quite young, before they entered the monastery, the accusation was always the same: mystical-legionary

[93] Cf. Marius Oprea, *Adevărata călătorie a lui Zahei. V. Voiculescu și taina Rugului Aprins*, 20–24.

[94] Criminal proceeding no. 202, traced back to the Archives of the Ministry of Justice, is today at the National Council for the Study of the Archives of the Securitate and includes criminal sentences, investigations and appeals by members of the group and has ten volumes. The proceedings of the trial were published by Ioana Diaconescu, *"Rugul Aprins." Studii și documente despre exterminare și supravietuire* (Bucharest: Fundația Academia Civică, 2018).

conspiracy. When asked by the inquisitor officer, with various tortures to extort the truth, about the meetings at the Antim monastery, which the police suspected were legionary propaganda meetings, the accused could only answer: our meetings were spiritual meetings. From the point of view of the communist authorities, the practice of hesychast prayer represented a danger, judged to be subversive with respect to the political and social commitments of citizens. Not for nothing, in the indictment against the Burning Bush group, the prosecution documents report: "The prayer of the heart had and has [*sic*] a hostile character, given the fact that the practitioner is required to comply with the condition of breaking with every political and professional activity, in order to have all the time just for prayer, which certainly leads to a total mysticism."[95]

Two singular testimonies deserve to be mentioned, those of Fr. Roman Braga and Emanoil Mihăilescu, the last of the group to be arrested. Fr. Roman recalls:

> It was practically a parody of a trial, behind closed doors.... The room was full of the wives of the Securitate officers called in to spit on us and insult us. Then they said to us: Don't you see? If we free you now, people will lynch you. At the trial, the prosecutor accused us of having intended to have the representatives of the new regime burned at the stake, alluding to the name of the Burning Bush association. Then we were accused of meeting to comment on texts hostile to the regime written by Basil the Great, John Climacus and Gregory of Nyssa.... In the end, when the conviction and sentence were pronounced for each one (25 years for Sandu Tudor, 20 for Mironescu, etc.) they added: Now, whoever wants can say a final word. Father Stăniloae stood up, but Mironescu pulled him down: Shut up, father, can't you see that it's useless, that everything is just a show.... Shut up, father, it will happen as God wants! He possessed an extraordinary calmness. He realized that everything was a farce, that it was hardly a real trial. It would have been absurd to contradict and demonstrate that Saint Basil had not written texts hostile to the communist regime! However, Father Staniloae wanted to give his own justification: "I didn't engage in politics—as if they hadn't known!—all I wanted to do was offer theological knowledge to Romanian priests, so that the Romanian priest knows..."

[95] Marius Oprea, *Adevărata călătorie a lui Zahei. V. Voiculescu și taina Rugului Aprins*, 38–39.

> Sandu Tudor interrupted him: "But that's why you're here, father, don't you understand? Because you wanted to offer theological knowledge to students and priests." Sandu Tudor was sitting on the bench in front of him.[96]

Emanoil Mihăilescu recalls that he was a fifth-year architecture student. Three other faculty friends, who attended Antim with him, had already been arrested since June. He had escaped a search at his parents' house because he was staying with relatives in the province. Having returned to Bucharest to attend his final year of architecture, he was arrested and forced to get into a police car, asked to put on a pair of dark glasses—it is the first memory of all those arrested in that period—heading to the Uranus prison, site of the first interrogations. He was the fifteenth of a group of sixteen people, which the investigators had christened the "Burning Bush Organization," a name deduced from the akathist composed by Sandu Tudor in honor of the Mother of God. Fr. Daniil was the central figure of the group and was seen in this investigation as the leader of the group. The other religious were well-known figures in the Romanian Orthodox world. During the interrogations, the investigators attempted to pass off the group as right-wing, stigmatizing it as a legionary organization, that was obvious. When Mihăilescu, the last of the group, was arrested, the investigation was coming to an end. His interrogation actually consisted of placing in his hands the voluminous dossier with the extorted statements of the suspects, and asking him to sign off on the truth thus concocted. He recalls in particular that they had shown him a packet with many newspaper clippings from before the war with articles written by Sandu Tudor against Stalin's crimes, against communism—vitriolic articles. But he exonerated Tudor from belonging to the legionary movement, defending his line of pure Christian-Orthodox militancy. During the trial Tudor behaved with dignity, never defending himself but defending the young people of the group, for whom he felt responsible. As for the sentences served, he sadly recalls that the men received hard years in prison in exchange for

[96] Roman Braga, *Ogni monaco ha un suo segreto con Dio*, 74–75. On Fr. Stăniloae see also the testimony about him collected by Mihai Rădulescu, *Consemnari despre Rugul Aprins dintr-o convorbire cu p. Dumitru Stăniloae. Din documentele rezistenței*, no. 4, 56–58.

the ranks earned by investigators and military prosecutors. He then goes on to introduce one by one the convicts of the group, whom he would never see again in the various prisons where he was held, with the exception of Gheorghe Văsîi, also an architecture student, whom he met in Gherla and remembered as the tireless animator of a student group.

He confirmed that Sandu Tudor had been under surveillance by the *Securitate* since the 1946–1948 period at Antim because he was considered an inspiration and supporter of a spiritual school with the ancient philokalic teachings at its center, an activity which he continued until the end. In the years 1955–1958, when Fr. Daniil would go down to Bucharest, staying at a friend's house or in Plumbuita, Mihăilescu, together with a group of students from the various faculties, would come to listen to his lectures. Many of them discovered in those meetings the revelation of a spiritual dimension of life, leading them to delve into a reading of hesychast texts. Not only that, but for some of them it was a real initiation into the prayer of Jesus. Taking into account the intellectual poverty of the time, the climate of suspicion and terror that hovered over the capital due to the omnipresence of the political police, those moments appeared to them as the grace of the possibility of another life. In the absence of Fr. Daniil, they went to Plumbuita in a group, on Sundays, to listen to the sermons of Fr. Sofian Boghiu and, to a more limited extent, those of Fr. Benedict Ghiuș in his cell at the patriarchate. In the house of Alexandru Mironescu, when Fr. Daniil was hosted there, real literary cenacles were held. Here he remembers hearing the poet Vasile Voiculescu read his compositions for the first time. Everything that was done in Fr. Valeriu Anania's small apartment at the Metropolia, even listening to symphonic music or traditional concerts, had the flavor of rebellion against the suffocating communist oppression. Aware of the church's compromises with the communist power, he was keen to underscore that many priests and monks, contemptuous of the danger, had tried to keep the torch of faith alive in the world of youth, especially the university. They knew that among them there were also informants from the *Securitate*, but men like Fr. Daniil certainly cannot be said to have behaved with caution.[97]

[97] Emanoil Mihilescu, *Organizatia Rugul Aprins, Din documentele rezistenței,* no. 4, 40–55.

After conviction, the defendants of the Burning Bush group were interned in various prisons: Malmaison, Jilava, Gherla, but above all, Aiud. The philosopher Mircea Vulcanescu died there in 1952, whose last words sounded like the testament of a martyr: "Do not avenge us!" Aiud had become a major extermination center for the religious and intellectual elite, in which, as the survivors testify, one could only resist with faith in God and prayer. Among the intellectuals who were moved to Aiud were the philosophers Petre Țuțea and Mircea Vulcănescu, the poets Radu Gyr and Vasile Voiculescu, Nichifor Crainic, Valeriu Gafencu, Fr. Dumitru Stăniloae, Fr. Gheorghe Calciu-Dumitreasa, Fr. Iustin Pârvu, the future metropolitan Anania Bartolomeu, Fr. Arsenie Papacioc, Fr. Daniil and many others. A few hundred meters from the penitentiary was the infamous Râpa Robilor (Prisoners' Cliff) named for the final stage of the journey made every night by a cart that left the prison, loaded with the corpses of those who had died in the cells, thrown into the municipal pits, and covered with earth and rubbish. This is the fate that befell Fr. Daniil, after four years of torture and beatings, who died on the night between 16 and 17 November 1962, at Aiud's Zarcă.[98] The inmates called him "Saint Daniil"; he was among the few prisoners who wore chains for the entire period of their detention. This is testified by the former prisoner of Suceava, Teofil Dumbraveanu, who, through a letter addressed to Metropolitan Antonie Plămădeală, wrote:

> As soon as he went out the door, towards the cemetery, they inserted an iron spear into his heart, to see if he was still alive or dead, as in the classic martyrologies. At the Zarcă of Aiud, among the prisoners, the memory of 'Saint Daniil' has always lingered. Later, young men digging trenches in the prison found a skeleton with its feet chained. They believed that this was the prisoner *Saint Daniil.*[99]

We have little evidence of the last years of Fr. Daniil's life at Aiud. His cellmate was Fr. Arsenie Papacioc. They had known each other for a long time; they had very different temperaments: the first, intransigent and fussy, the second, sweet and tolerant. Fr. Papacioc recalls:

[98] *Zarcă* was a total isolation cell, where the prisoner could only sleep standing up.

[99] Cf. Antonie Plămădeală, *Rugul Aprins*, 179–81.

> I lived in a monastery with him and I was in a cell with him. When we were assigned to Zarcă, a prison within a prison, where they only let us out for about ten minutes a month, where an extermination regime was in force and where the Lord helped me get out alive, we were together. They fed us only a mush of polenta, but a single spoonful, not two. Since we were both monks, we shared the same apprenticeship. We would take a spoonful, he would take another and in the end a little would remain at the bottom of the mess tin. I said: You continue to take (I respected him, because we had known each other since the time at Antim, when his name was Agathon), you continue to take, so at least we wouldn't argue anymore.

Fr. Daniil believed until the end that God would help him through this terrible ordeal and, even if he could not survive the years in the concentration camp, he would always remain faithful and uncompromising before God. His spiritual father, Fr. Cleopa, stated: "In the damp, cold and dark cell of the prison, tortured and hungry, the hieroschimonk Daniil reached the high degrees of the Prayer of the Heart.... His heart was always in a state of vigilance, because he trembled at the thought that he might give in, even for a little, out of weakness." He remained uncompromising in his faith. A curious episode reported by Fr. Papacioc says a lot about Fr. Daniil. Seriously ill, assisted by Fr. Papacioc in the cell before he was transferred to the infirmary, he refused to receive communion thinking that the sacred canons were not being respected. Fr. Daniil then told him that he had a short time to live. "Well"—replied Fr. Papacioc—"if you have a short time to live, why not take communion?" And Fr. Daniil: "But how can I be sure that it is really the Eucharistic bread?" "It is actually the Eucharistic bread," I replied. "I received it from a guard. With difficulty, but he sent it to me. They don't control the guards. Only I could give communion to those who were in the cell with me." It was the dried Eucharistic bread, as is given to the sick. I had it in a pocket for Holy Communion. "The guard gave it to me duly packaged. I put it in my chest pocket. A priest brought it to us from the city." Father Daniil, a rigorous observer of the canons and incredulous as to the sanctity of those pieces of dry bread brought by a guard full of humanity, remained inflexible in his refusal.

Also Fr. Sofian Boghiu, who shared the same sentence to Aiud, remembers meeting Fr. Daniil just once and they both smiled at each other, without being able to say anything to each other. And he confirms: "Fr. Daniil became a martyr and arrived in the kingdom of God with the Prayer of the heart."[100]

Recently, in Romania, the 1958 trial was reopened by the Supreme Court of Justice at the request of Fr. Adrian Făgețeanu (1912–2011), who in 1995, from the monastery of Lainici where he had retired, went down to Bucharest to demand a review of the trial and the rehabilitation of the convicts of the Burning Bush group. The Court recognized that the 1958 trial of the Burning Bush group was a judicial farce. On 8 April 1996, the Prosecutor General of Romania legally annulled the conviction that had been imposed approximately forty years earlier.[101] The strange thing, however, was that the ruling of the Supreme Court of Justice partially rehabilitated the members of the group because it suspended the judgment on the criminal nature of the activity of those arrested, leaving the suspicion of guilt intact in the eyes of the state. He did not go into the merits of the motivation for the conviction, suggesting that their behavior could be considered as a legionary plot. The absurd thing is that, in doing so, they have interpreted religious research, hesychast prayer, the mystical path, all rooted in tradition, as liable to be interpreted in an antisocial, anti-democratic key. So much so that the elderly Fr. Adrian Făgețeanu, the first of the Burning Bush group to be arrested, remarked: "In those days, men had wooden crosses and hearts of gold. Now, they have a cross of gold and a heart of wood."[102] His comment is particularly pointed because, when he was arrested and interrogated, the interrogating officer tore the cross he was carrying from his neck and threw it into the dustbin. And he bent down to pick it up without saying anything. Beaten, it was taken from him again. And he picked it up again. Again he was beaten but he did not give in and picked it up. So after eight or nine times, in the end, they let him keep it.

[100] On these testimonies, cf. Marius Oprea, *Adevărata călătorie a lui Zahei. V. Voiculescu și taina Rugului Aprins*, 112–14.

[101] The complete documents of the appeal for the annulment of the conviction against the Burning Bush group constitute vol. 11 of the previous dossier, in ten volumes, which collect the documents relating to the penitentiary documents, the investigation documents and the conduct of the 1958 trial. All the documents of the appeal are included in the volume by Ioana Diaconescu, *"Rugul Aprins," Studii și documente despre exterminare și supraviețuire* (Bucharest: Fundația Academia Civică, 2018).

[102] Marius Oprea, *Adevărata călătorie a lui Zahei. V. Voiculescu și taina Rugului Aprins*, 131.

6. A POSSIBLE PORTRAIT

When faced with Sandu Tudor, one cannot remain indifferent. What is striking was his impossible character and the simultaneous fascination with which he was listened to. A man of great character, but with an impetuous temperament, he had a style of speech that bordered on brutality, was prone to invective, could not bear to be contradicted, was intransigent but never banal, a vitriolic polemicist: all traits that characterized his youth and his appearance in the literary arena of the capital, but which did not disappear with his entry into the monastery. For those who did not know him well, Sandu Tudor was always a source of scandal, always offering a pretext for denigration. His longtime friend Alexandru Mironescu confirms this by saying that yes, he was a difficult man, sometimes very difficult, hard to bear, unpleasant, but without hypocrisy. For those who could tolerate him, he became an invaluable friend, a wonderful man, a person of rare spiritual delicacy, always original. Mironescu often repeated to him, affectionately: "My dear friend, you would be unbearable if you weren't extraordinary." Andrei Scrima describes him like this: "His excessive temper, which sometimes manifested itself in eruptions of verbal violence, actually hid an exceptional sensitivity, very close to the 'fragility' of someone who is capable of true compassion, of someone who is conscious, at the same time, of the price of every man: the more humble, the more respectable.... At the same time, he brought with him, into the Antim circle, a charisma of long experience 'in the world': the charisma of the creative and tenacious organizer."[103]

And Antonie Plămădeală remembers that wherever he was, it was difficult for others to speak; he was always critical of anyone and anything, but he had an upright spirit and managed to attract many people into his circle.[104]

His level of culture was well known. In the time of Antim he possessed perhaps the richest library, some 8,000 volumes, of any man of letters in the capital. However, he was unable to speak systematically about a topic; he made constant references to authors and works; he enriched his words with continuous quotations and provocations, so much so that a

[103] Scrima, *L'accompagnamento spirituale*, 129.

[104] Plămădeală, *Rugul Aprins*, 25 and 34.

friend once said: What a haphazard library you are! Yet he had a way of speaking that was enchanting. His "impulsive graphomania" was characteristic of him. He took notes everywhere, even during liturgical celebrations; he thought by writing. He left numerous notebooks which, for the most part, ended up in the hands of Antonie Plămădeală, who had had Fr. Daniil as godfather at his monastic tonsure and who had listened to him many times in Rarău. From sifting through all those documents he realized that Fr. Daniil was a man with a solid spiritual structure, internally organized in a precise way, even if he never managed to be systematic in his speech. A more critical note, however, comes from the testimony of Bartolomeo Anania, archbishop of Cluj, who was never part of the Burning Bush group.

He then worked at the patriarchate library and lived next to Fr. Benedict Ghiuș, whom Fr. Daniil, in his forays to Bucharest from Rarău, came to visit. On these occasions he met Fr. Daniil, whom he made fun of for his mania, for showing off his robe in the streets of the capital, and for his talkative disposition. "If a hermit is required to say seven words a day, he said seventy a minute and another seven hundred to answer a question. He would ask to borrow books and then forget to bring them back.... He read enormously and spoke colossally; I later discovered that he wrote immensely, probably being among those who cannot think except with a pen in their hand. He was a fierce interlocutor: he defended opinions ruthlessly, intolerantly and was not ashamed to accompany arguments with abusive invectives." The last image he remembers is that of a Fr. Daniil, angry, hemmed in by his own reasoning, unable to apologize. It had happened in Aiud where they were both locked up together with three hundred others in the section for TB patients. At a certain point Fr. Daniil and another person got into an argument about a cultural topic. The discussion became heated, Fr. Daniil got furious and hurled insults at his interlocutor. A few days passed and Bartolomeo Anania tried to appease Fr. Daniil, who refused to give in even though the other person was sorry and had apologized to him. After a short time Anania received the news that, in another part of the penitentiary, where Fr. Daniil had been transferred, he had died. Fr. Daniil was unable to apologize directly, but his name is certainly written in the heavens because he died as a martyr.[105]

A counterbalance to the intransigence and angularity of his character was his great thirst for the absolute, his faith and his spiritual research, in particular of the hesychast tradition. Fr. Sofian Boghiu remembers meeting Sandu Tudor, together with Fr. Gala Galaction, in Cernica in 1933, when he was a student at the monastic seminary. Tudor had returned from Athos a few years before and had been invited to speak to the students. He spoke with enthusiasm of the Athonite experience, of the spiritual climate on the Holy Mountain and above all, in great detail, of the practice of the Jesus Prayer, inviting students to combine this holy hesychast practice with their regular prayers. Bartolomeo Anania remembers that, on a train journey with Sandu Tudor, Anania admired how Tudor spoke to him with competence and enthusiasm about the hesychast experience of Basil of Poiana Mărului, who flourished in the territory of the Romanian Principalities in the eighteenth century. The Jesus Prayer had conquered him, even though he would struggle for many years before reaching the point where the prayer itself descended into his heart and burned like the fire of the Burning Bush that burns without being consumed. However, the fact remains that fundamental to the Burning Bush group, of which Sandu Tudor was the animator and organizer, was the prayer of Jesus, discovered in the wake of the Romanian hesychast tradition, with the decisive and fundamental contribution of the Russian monk, Fr. Ioann Kulygin. A recollection of Fr. Arsenie Papacioc illustrates well Fr. Daniil's angularity of character and his thirst for the absolute. He had just taken up residence in his cell, in the bell tower of Antim, filled with his books. He asked Fr. Arsenie who had come to visit him: "Father Arsenie, do you weep?" And Fr. Arsenie replied: "And do you?" "—I weep!—He is not Orthodox [who does not weep]!" And Fr. Arsenie told him, "Father, if I had half a tear, I would stand before God with great boldness, but I don't even have that." [Fr. Daniil] ended the discussion, but he

[105] An unfortunate controversy arose between Bartolomeo Anania and Sandu Tudor, as can be seen from the testimonies following Tudor's death. Both went through the infamous re-education process, a communist form of coercive persuasion. Bartolomeu Anania, a former sympathizer of the Iron Guard, accused Sandu Tudor of supporting the use of re-education methods against stubborn fascists, perhaps because Tudor said that the legionaries should be ashamed of having stained the cross of Christ with criminal actions.

let the whole monastery know. And since then, as Fr. Arsenie remembers, that name stuck with me "Arsenie, man of God."

Toward the end of his life, Sandu Tudor, recalled the years before his monastic decision:

> "I too have lived a scattered life, loving, hating, desiring one or another of human and worldly things. Between one and another of these things I had flashes of inspiration, I wrote, I reflected, then everything got boring and I wanted something unique and sublime."[106]

It was his friend Alexandru Mironescu who described his profound faith in God with some significant, rather mysterious anecdotes from his life. On an excursion to Predeal, a city north of Bucharest, in front of the enchanting panorama of the mountains in the area, he thought: "How can I thank you, Lord, for such a day?" and suddenly an unseen hand reached out and a voice was heard: "Be merciful." Sandu Tudor put his hand in his pocket and, with all the money he had and with tears in his eyes, he thanked God, satisfied. In his generosity, he sold his car, his two apartments, and contributed significantly to the restoration of Antim's buildings even before becoming a monk.

In 1936 Sandu Tudor obtained his tour-plane pilot's license and the following year, had a bad accident. It is not clear whether he was flying for pleasure (with his personal plane, as some sources say) or as an exercise for reservists on behalf of the Ministry of Aviation. The plane lost altitude due to a botched maneuver and crashed into the ground, but the pilot escaped unharmed. With his characteristic determination, he showed up at the airfield the next day to take the same route again and repeat the same maneuver, this time correctly, to overcome his fear. But the thing he confided to his friend Mironescu was his interior experience: he found himself face to face with the angel of death and the spontaneous, heartfelt prayer of Jesus rose to his lips, for which he felt graced—just as it happened to him on another occasion, during the war, when he was director of the Motorcycle-Mechanization technical school in Bucharest. This time, he had severely reprimanded a non-commissioned officer, and in the evening he decided to

---

[106] These are sentences from a letter written in 1956 at Rarău to a young poet from Câmpulung Moldovenesc. Quoted by Marius Oprea, *Adevărata călătorie a lui Zahei. V. Voiculescu și taina Rugului Aprins*, 89.

move his bed from one wall to the other, as well as the icon of the Burning Bush that he always carried with him. During the night he was awakened by gunshots from his window, aimed at the corner where the bed had previously been, thus escaping death. He experienced it as a providence helping and guiding him, until it led him to his monastic choice, to which he had felt attracted since the months spent on Athos. Mironescu reports a conversation with Sandu Tudor, who at that time had been at Rarău for several years, which summarizes well the fiery human and spiritual temperament of Fr. Daniil, absolutely aware of the tragedy of the times he was living in:

> Christianity is the tragic aspect of supreme joy, the tragedy of divinization. Man is not led to God from without. God is, and could not be, anything but supreme Humility. He is within us in all his Eucharistic fullness. The kingdom of heaven is within us with its tri-hypostatic presence. This means drinking all the apocalyptic bitterness of supreme joy, the bitterness of the seven cups. This means, until the end of the ages, that we overcome through weakness and, enlightened, complete the torments and sufferings of Christ. This means that, to overcome the pains of sin, precariousness and death, a supreme, tremendous abasement in everything is necessary. God himself works with the power of weakness, which is stronger than men: for this reason, he chose the foolish things of the world, to shame the wise ones; the weak things of the world, to shame the strong; things below, despised, even those that are not, so that those above may be humiliated. The Lord himself, and it could only be like this, works with a delicate presence, like a lack, like an absence.... Tremendous is the path of Christian joy and its victory, because first one will have to see the abomination of desolation in the holy place. Holiness will not fail because of this, but will gain even more splendor.... God's great creative freedom always allows the paradox of all miracles. For this reason, especially after the Incarnation, he wants men to be led by non-men, sinners to be sanctified by sinners, and his chosen ones—the Church and the Saints—to be subjected to such equivocal guides and sometimes far beyond any possible permission. The great drama of true and holy Orthodoxy is the jarring lack of spiritual guides and ministers of the Church. The Holy Spirit takes the place of everyone... so that no flesh becomes proud or boasts before God![107]

[107] All three testimonies of A. Mironescu, B. Anania and S. Boghiu are found in Daniil Sandu Tudor, *Taina Rugului Aprins. Scrieri și documente inedite*, 127–49.

Virgil Maxim (1922–1997), one of the "prison saints," recognized Sandu Tudor as a martyr for Christ. He met him in his first imprisonment in Jilava and the Canal in the years 1950–1952 and then in Aiud in the years 1958–1962. He remembers that in Jilava, when Sandu Tudor was well, he conversed with the inmates, instilling hope in everyone in the fear of God. He explained passages of the Scriptures to them starting from the Fathers and above all he spoke about hesychast prayer. Tudor had humbly confessed to him that he had not been a good young man, nor a serious man, and that only God had saved him from the devil's deception: "When you hear bad things said about me, believe them, because I have been a great sinner." In Aiud, when the torturers tried to extort compromising statements against the Church and its ministers from the prisoners, Fr. Daniil asked for paper and ink and wrote a long indictment against the materialist conception of communism and the actions of the government, while waiting to be called to testify.[108]

We have the same testimony from Andrei Scrima, who describes him as a man who refused any compromise—"...in prison, weakened, subjected to physical and moral pressure to sign nationalist, patriotic compromises, advantageous for the sad regime of the time, he trembled at the mere thought of being able simply give in out of weakness. Death found him in this state of resistance."[109]

[108] Virgil Maxim, *Imn pentru crucea purtata* (Antim, 2002), 257–58.
[109] Scrima, *L'accompagnamento spirituale*, 153, note 12.

Romanian Hesychast Tradition[1]

In modern times, among Western Christians, it seems that the prayer of Jesus is viewed in relation to the *Philokalia*, a collection of patristic texts between the fourth and fifteenth centuries. The image that most have in mind is the figure of the Russian pilgrim, who travels through the immense spaces of the Russian lands reciting the Jesus Prayer and carrying in his bag a single, voluminous book, the *Dobrotoljubie*, the Slavonic version of the *Philokalia.*[2] The Jesus Prayer is then combined with the guidance of an expert spiritual father, as highlighted by Doina Uricariu, poet and essayist, editor of the recent edition of the *Filocalia de la Prodromul*,[3] at the conclusion

---

[1] This chapter essentially reiterates research and conclusions that I have already presented in various studies in past years. In particular: "La scuola filocalica di Paisij Velichkovskij e la Filocalia di Nicodemo Aghiorita. Un confronto," in T. Spidlik, et al., *Amore del bello. Studi sulla Filocalia* (Bose: Qiqajon, 1991), 179–207; "La tradizione teologico-spirituale dell'ortodossia romena," in Adriano Roccucci, ed., *Chiese e culture nell'Est europeo. Prospettive di dialogo* (Milano: Paoline, 2007), 101–138; "Paisij Velickovsky e il contributo delle terre romene alla storia della spiritualità ortodossa," in Luciano Vaccario, ed., *Storia religiosa dello spazio romeno*, under the direction of Cesare Alzati, vol. 2 (Milano: Centro Ambrosiano, 2016), 515–36.

[2] Aleksej Pentkovsky, ed., *The Pilgrim's Tale* (New York & Mahwah: Paulist Press, 1999). Paisij Velickovsky, ed., *Dobrotoljubie* (Moscow: 1793). This is a folio of 721 pages, in three parts, including 15 of the 36 authors of the Greek edition. Between the years 1797 and 1800 was the addition of a fourth part of 466 pages, including 9 other authors. Subsequent editions present the four parts in a single volume: 2nd ed. 1822, 3rd 1832, 4th 1840, 5th 1851, 6th 1857. In 1990, in Bucharest, the editio princeps of 1793 plus the fourth part was reprinted, in anastatic copies, in a folio of 1187 pages, edited by Dan Zamfirescu.

[3] Called "Filocalia de la Prodromul" from the initiative of the Romanian monks of the Athonite monastery to collect the ancient Romanian versions of the Philokalic texts. The work of transcribing the texts, typed and gathered into a single voluminous tome of over 1600 pages, was completed in 1922. The current edition, in two volumes (New York: Universalia Books, 2001), presents that tome again. The texts cover the entire Greek *Philokalia* of 1782 with the addition of some texts: Life of St. Nephon of Constantinople (excerpts), Dimitri of Rostov (excerpts from the title: *Spiritual doctrine of the inner man*), Basil of Poiana Mărului (Introduction to Philotheus of Sinai, Introduction to Gregory of Sinai), Paisius Velickovsky (On the prayer of Jesus), John Chrysostom (excerpts from his letters to monks), Nil Sorsky (his work and the introduction

of her labors: "May the Lord give everyone understanding! You for your part, together with everyone who desires to live according to God, do you seek through what we have said to learn as it were from its fringe the texture of the golden and spiritual garment of blessed obedience; and in this way do all you can, as we have already explained, to find a reliable and fully qualified teacher."[4]

An initial warning is needed. The Christian tradition is not an esotericism with its lines of descent from masters to disciples, as, for example, in Sufism, but rather the realization of the Christian mystery, always susceptible to being reborn from the sacramental life and the spiritual understanding of the scriptures.[5] When there are no masters, tradition refers to the scriptures and the Fathers, within a profound sacramental life, by the observance of the commandments, with humility and confidence. In the modern era, think of Nil Sorsky (1433–1508) and Paisius Velichkovsky (1722–1794),[6] who present themselves as self-taught or, better, "theodidacts," instructed by God. This is commonplace in the Christian spiritual tradition—the complaint about the lack of experienced teachers and all the new

to his writings by Basil of Poiana Mărului), and John of Kronstadt (some thoughts). Already before the Greek edition of the *Philokalia* (Venice: 1782) and the Slavonic edition of Paisius (*Dobrotoljubie*, Moscow: 1793), Romanians had access to a Romanian *Filocalia* called "Filocalia de la Dragomira" since 1769 (ms. rom. 2597 of the B.A.R.), written by the well-known copyist Rafail of Dragomira, where in 1763 the Paisian community from Athos had settled, including several authors of the same Greek *Philokalia* plus the *Introductions* of Basil of Poiana Mărului to Gregory of Sinai and Philotheus of Sinai, as well as the work of Nil Sorsky (1433–1508) .

[4] St. Kallistos and St. Ignatios Xanthopoulos, *On the Life of Stillness and the Monastic State: 100 Texts*, chap. 15, in *The Philokalia*, trans. G. E. H. Palmer, P. Sherrard & K. Ware, vol. 5 (London: Faber, 2023), 33.

[5] In this sense, the attempts to understand the hesychast experience in an esoteric key, as if it were a variant of a spiritual experience that is also found in other traditions, such as, for example, in the Sufism of the Muslim tradition, do not account for its mystery and give rise to misunderstandings. Cf. Enrico Montanari, *La fatica del cuore. Saggio sull'ascesi esicasta* [The labor of the heart. Essay on hesychast asceticism] (Milano: Jaca Book, 2003), 81–179.

[6] See Paisij Velickovsky, *Autobiografia di uno starec*. Introduction, translation and notes by the community of the Contemplative Brothers of Jesus (Abbazia di Praglia: Scritti monastici, 1988), republished by Qiqajon editions (Bose: 1998); E. Citterio, "La dottrina spirituale dello starec Paisij. Radiografia di una comunità" in N. Kauchtschischwili, et al., *Paisij, lo starec* (Bose: Qiqajon, 1997), 55–82; E. Citterio, "La fecondità della sua eredità: una santità come fermento di umanità," in *Il monachesimo tra eredità e aperture*, ed. Maciej Bielawski and Daniel Hombergen (Roma: Studia Anselmiana, 2004), 459–69.

seasons of re-flowering, which, even though they begin with certain personalities, are not simply the continuation of previous ones. There is always talk, in various periods, of a movement of renewal, of rebirth. Everything refers to the typical ecclesial and spiritual context of the Christian experience, where "The abasement of God allows the elevation of man and his 'deification' (*theosis*): assuming the entire humanity of man in his flesh and vivifying it with his resurrection, Christ allows him to participate in divine life; and only by conforming to him, with the help of the gift of the Holy Spirit, does man achieve both likeness to God and the fullness of his own humanity."[7]

THE ROMANIAN HESYCHAST TRADITION

In the same historical period (13th–14th century) in which the formula of the Jesus Prayer was defined in the East and its practice spread with the theological-spiritual vision that supported it (Gregory Palamas, 1296–1359; Gregory of Sinai, 1275–1346), in the West we witness a revival of the invocation of the name of Jesus. Let us think of the blessed Giovanni Colombini (1304–1367), founder of the Gesuati, so called for the habit of often repeating the name of Jesus and going through the city streets, in groups, shouting his name: "[L]et us not sleep; let us proclaim the blessed Name of Christ by day and night, in the streets and market-places: let us go to hell, if need be, to proclaim It there and do It honor: the world goes there because it does not remember It: let us go there to proclaim and publish It: may the most holy Name of Christ live for ever: let not tongues be weary or hearts satiated with proclaiming Christ crucified."[8] Along with this experience of repeating the name *Jesus Christus*, out loud, more than a thousand times a day, let us also consider the experience of giving the name of Jesus to the soul in the female convents of Germany in the fourteenth and fifteenth centuries.[9]

Here it is not a matter of retracing the history of the particular form of prayer, commonly called the Jesus Prayer, which has

[7] From the preface by Enzo Bianchi in Antonio Rigo, *Mistici bizantini*, IX.

[8] Feo Belcari, *The Life of B. Giov. Colombini* (London: R. Washbourne, 1874), 44.

[9] See Bernard McGinn, *The Flowering of Mysticism. Men and Women in the New Mysticism (1200–1350)* (New York: Crossroad, 1998), where the distinctive experience of Margaret Ebner is related (308–14).

its roots in the dawn of the monastic movement in the Egyptian desert, rather, it would be rightly defined as a monastic creation.[10] Here I would just like to trace the path that Fr. Daniil and the regular Burning Bush participants discovered and followed.

In his course on mystical theology, the first of its kind held at the Faculty of Orthodox Theology of the University of Bucharest in the years 1935–36, the well-known theologian, poet and publicist Nichifor Crainic (1889–1972) had dwelt on the presentation of the prayer of Jesus, which he had grasped as the essence of that vast spiritual movement which was called, in the Romanian tradition, "Paisianism." Fr. Irénée Hausherr, of the Pontifical Oriental Institute of Rome, had relaunched interest in the prayer of the heart also in the West with his research: *La méthode d'oraison hésychaste* (OC IX, 1927). When Crainic took up the topic again for the magazine *Gândirea* (XVII, 1938), he added a text on the power of the name of Jesus taken from the "Lives of the Saints," January 1, the feast of the circumcision and the bestowal of the name of Jesus.[11] That text is also taken from the *Filocalia de la Prodromul*, volume II (pages 532–34). I reproduce it here in full because it clearly summarizes how, for the tradition of the Eastern churches, the value of Jesus's prayer is rooted in the veneration of the Name of Jesus itself. The text is introduced in this way: "After the anonymous Master had narrated the cause for which our Lord God and Savior Jesus Christ endured circumcision on the eighth day, continuing, he also added the following notes about this divine Name of Jesus":

> "It is at circumcision that they gave the Name Jesus to the Blessed Child, a name brought from heaven by the archangel Gabriel when he announced His conception to the most pure Virgin Mary, before he took shape in her womb, before she said: 'Behold the handmaid of the Lord: let it be done to me according to your word' (Luke 1:38). With those words of hers, the Word of God immediately became Body, taking up residence in her most pure and holy womb. Hence this holy Name

[10] I will limit myself to citing the entry "Jésus (prière à)" in the *Dictionnaire de spiritualité*, 8 (Paris: Beauchesne, 1974), col. 1126–1150; A. Rigo, "La preghiera di Gesù," in *Parola, Spirito e Vita* 25 (1992), 245–91; Schimonaco Ilarione, *Sulle montagne del Caucaso*, afterword by Adalberto Mainardi (Bose: Qigajon, 2019), 415–57.

[11] Nichifor Crainic, *Cursurile de mistică. I. Teologie mistică. II. Mistica germană, mystica* (Sibiu: Deisis, 2010), 385–93.

Jesus, whom the angel had announced before his conception, was given to the Anointed of the Lord in His circumcision, according to the promise that the same angel had conveyed to Joseph when appearing to him in his sleep and telling him: 'you shall call his name Jesus, for he will save his people from their sins' (Matt. 1:21). And again, the holy apostle Peter gives this testimony on the name Jesus: 'And there is salvation in no one else, for there is no other name under heaven given among men by which we must be saved' (Acts 4:12). This Name Jesus, the Savior, before the ages was kept in the council of the Trinity, was written and until now preserved for our redemption; like a pearl of great price, for the ransom of humanity, from the heavenly coffers it was brought and through Joseph it was given so that it might be known that all the unknown and mysterious secrets of Science of God have manifested themselves in this Name. This Name has shone like a Sun upon the world, as the prophet reports: 'who can endure the day of his coming, and who can stand when he appears? For he is like a refiner's fire and like fullers' soap.... For you who fear my name, the sun of justice will rise with healing in its wings' (Mal. 3:2, 4:2). Like a sweet-smelling Myrrh it filled the world with fragrance. 'Myrrh poured out,' [scripture] says, 'is your Name' (Song of Sol. 1:2) [the ancient versions say: out-poured perfume, later interpreted by the Fathers as referring to the Passion of Jesus], the perfume of his Name is not stored in a vase, but is poured out. Because as long as the perfume is kept in a vase, its fragrance does not spread, but when it is poured out, the fragrance immediately fills the air.

The power of the Name Jesus was not known, since it was kept in the divine council before the ages, as in a covered vessel. But after this Name was poured from heaven to earth, immediately like a fragrance of myrrh, it filled the world with the perfume of Grace at the shedding of the child's blood at the moment of circumcision. So that 'every tongue proclaims: "Jesus Christ is Lord!" to the glory of God the Father' (Phil. 2:11). The power of the Name Jesus was shown, because this wonderful Name has amazed the angels, cheered men, and terrified the demons, because even the demons believe and tremble and the Underworld trembles only before this Name, the powers of the Underworld are overturned, the lord of darkness is annihilated, his power is lost, the darkness of the diabolical idols is dispelled: behold, the light of blessing shines and illuminates every man who comes into the world: 'so that at the name of Jesus every knee should bend in heaven, on earth, and under the earth' (Phil. 2:10). This Name of Jesus is a weapon to be used against those who attack us, as St.

John Climacus says: 'flog your enemies with the name of Jesus, since there is no stronger weapon in heaven or on earth.'[12] This most precious Name, oh how desirable it is! As the Song says: 'His speech is most sweet, and he is altogether desirable. This is my beloved and this is my friend, O daughters of Jerusalem' (Song of Sol. 5:16). This most holy Name of Jesus, how lovable it is for those who are united with Jesus, for those who serve him out of love for him. Jesus in the mind, Jesus on the tongue: 'For with the heart one believes to obtain righteousness, and with the mouth one professes faith to obtain salvation' (Rom. 10:10). Whether walking, sitting or doing anything else, have Jesus before your eyes as the Apostle says: 'For I decided to know nothing among you except Jesus Christ' (1 Cor. 2:2), because, for whoever clings to Jesus, it is enlightenment for the mind, beauty for the soul, health for the body, joy for the heart, help in sorrows, joy in afflictions, healing in illnesses, defense and hope of salvation in all trials, and only for the one who loves him and is dear to him, reward and salvation, gratification.

The unpronounceable Name of God was written on a gold plate that the High Priest wore on his head (see Exod. 28:36). Now the divine Name of Jesus is written with the blood shed at his circumcision and is not written on golden metal but spiritually in the hearts and mouths of the servants of Jesus as for the one about whom it is said: 'he is the instrument [vessel] that I have chosen for myself, that he may bear my name' (Acts 9:15). Like a very sweet drink, his sweet Name of Jesus wants to be carried in a vessel, because it is truly sweet for those who taste it with love, to whom it is said in the Psalms: 'O taste and see that the Lord is good' (Ps. 34:8). For those who have tasted the Prophet cries out: 'I love thee, O Lord, my strength' (Ps. 18:1). And, having tasted, the holy apostle Peter: 'Lo, we have left everything and followed you' (Matt. 19:27). Because: 'Lord, to whom shall we go? You have the words of eternal life' (John 6:68). With this sweetness the holy martyrs rendered even bitter torments sweet and were unafraid of even the bitterest death: 'Who shall separate us from the love of Christ? Shall tribulation, or distress, or persecution, or famine, or nakedness, or peril, or sword? ... neither death nor life' (Rom. 8:35, 38). 'For love is strong as death' (Song of Sol. 8:6). In what kind of vessel does this unspeakable sweetness of the Name of Jesus like to be carried? Surely in a golden vessel 'so that the genuineness of your faith, more

[12] John Climacus, *The Ladder of Divine Ascent*, trans. C. Luibheid and N. Russell (London: SPCK, 1982), Step 21, 200.

precious than gold which though perishable is tested by fire, may redound to praise and glory and honor when Jesus Christ is revealed' (1 Pet. 1:7), as with precious stones it is enriched by the wounds suffered for Jesus: 'I bear on my body the marks of the Lord Jesus' (Gal 6:17)—sweetness needs a vessel of this kind. In a vessel like this the Name of Jesus wishes to be carried. It is not in vain that Jesus receives the Name when he sheds blood at his circumcision, indicating: the vessel that will bear his Name will be red with blood. Thus, after the Lord had acquired the vessel chosen for his Name in the apostle Paul, there is immediately added: 'and I will show him how many things he must suffer for my name's sake' (Acts 9:16). My vessel must be bloodied, wounded, and so the Name of Jesus is written, with the red ink of one's blood, with the sufferings and torments of those 'who resisted to the point of shedding their blood in the fight against sin' (see Heb. 12:4).

We greet Thee with love, O sweetest Name of Jesus! We zealously adore Thy most holy name, O sweetest Jesus, even in all the sufferings endured. We praise Thy powerful Name, Jesus the Savior, we prostrate ourselves to the blood shed in circumcision, O Child devoid of malice and supreme Lord. And we pray to Thy great goodness, through Thy most holy name and through Thy most precious shed blood and through Thy most pure Mother who gave birth to Thee without corruption, so that you may spread your most rich mercy upon us, so that our hearts may be softened by Thee, Jesus, so that Thou protect us and shelter us on every side with Thy Name Jesus, so that Thou sign us and seal us, your servants, with this Name of Jesus, so that in the age to come we may be recognized as Thine and, with the angels, glorify and hymn Thy most honorable and most holy Name of Jesus unto ages of ages. Amen."

PAISIUS VELICHKOVSKY'S MOVEMENT

Now, in the Romanian tradition, the revival and renewal of the practice of the Jesus Prayer manifested itself in the eighteenth century. In that period, unlike other countries in which the culture of the Orthodox faith had its wings clipped due to the anti-ecclesiastical policy of the tsars or the Turkish domination in Greece and the Balkans, the territories of the Romanian principalities became as if the center of Orthodoxy, where the eastern patristic tradition remained alive.[13] We witness a

[13] Concerning this, in his *Sfințenia—împlinirea umanului (Curs de teologie mystică) (1935-1936)* (Iasi: Ed. Mitropoliei Moldovei si Bucovinei, 1993), chap. XVI,

phenomenon of osmosis between the Romanian territories and the Russian lands, the Ukrainian lands in particular. At the end of the seventeenth century, with the multiplication of restrictive measures against monasticism in Russia, in the line of a policy of control of ecclesiastical property and due to a policy of uniatism pursued by the Poles in Ukraine, there was a flow of Russian-Ukrainian monastic emigration towards the Romanian territories, where the princes were outstanding in their zeal to support the church and monasticism. The character who would profoundly mark the Romanian monastic and ecclesial tradition would be that very Paisius Velichkovsky, of whom Sandu Tudor was a great admirer and with whom, through Sandu Tudor, the frequenters of the Burning Bush would become acquainted.

When the young Paisius, in search of the living tradition of his fathers, emigrated from Ukraine, his native land, and arrived in the Romanian lands in 1743, he had already been preceded by an entire generation of his compatriots, who, in the climate of high Orthodox culture of the Romanian environment, were able to bring to maturity the seeds of their own genius and spirituality. The hermitages visited by Paisius, namely Dălhăuți, Traișteni and Cîrnul, were all under the influence of the staretz Basil of Poiana Mărului, who also had emigrated from Ukraine and had now become a point of reference for everyone. In those communities that deferred to him, the hesychast practice was combined with the study of the Fathers, whose texts the scriptorium of Poiana Mărului, the hermitage founded by Basil in 1733, was responsible for copying and disseminating in both the Slavonic and Romanian languages. Uniquely in the history of Romanian hesychasm, Basil had founded a sort of confederation of over ten hesycasteries linked to Poiana Mărului. It was not on Athos, where he also resided for seventeen years, from 1746 to 1763, that Paisius Velichkovsky first breathed the air of the hesychast tradition. Athos was only the ideal reference and repository of the patristic writings that he would take care to explore with tireless zeal. Paisius discovered this model of life, this living example of the hesychast tradition, and made it flourish again on a large scale in the Romanian

"Rugăciunea lui Iisus, esența Paisianismului," Nichifor Crainic rightly argues that the eighteenth was the golden century of Romanian Orthodoxy (150).

principalities in his monasteries of Dragomirna, Secu and Neamț in Moldavia, giving life to all that powerful spiritual movement historians would call *Paisianism*. A biographer of his summarizes the experience of the three years spent in the hermitages of Muntenia thus:

> From those fathers he understood what true obedience is, from which true humility is born, in which one comes to let one's will and one's personal opinion die, even towards all the things of this world, a fact which constitutes the beginning and interminable end of true monastic work, and what is attention and true peace of mind, attentive prayer carried out above all in the heart.[14]

The introduction to the biography of Paisius Velichkovsky by Gregorio Dascălul is interesting.[15] It outlines a historical overview of the development of monasticism starting with the Fathers of the Egyptian deserts: Anthony, Macarius, Pachomius; continues with the Fathers of the deserts of Palestine: Euthymius, Saba and Theodosius; and then with the flourishing of monasteries in Constantinople and Athos. From here monasticism then spread to Russia with Anthony and Theodosius of the Caves. It arrived next in Wallachia and Moldavia, "quiet Orthodox regions, when fervent princes had erected the holy monasteries which adorn these places like the stars in the sky," and then was the arrival of this blessed elder Paisius:

> "I will instead show how and when, with the coming of this blessed staretz and the establishment of this great community, according to the benevolent providence of the Most High, a work was started which now has no parallel in all of Orthodoxy, so that a divine work like this may also be known to posterity, to the glory of God and for their benefit."[16]

[14] Cf. Isaac Dascălul, *Biografia inedita dello starec Paisij il Grande*, ed. D. Zamfirescu, in *Revista fundației Drăgan*, nos. 3–4 (1987), 498.

[15] Grigorie Dascălul (1765–1834), was tonsured a monk in Neamț by Paisij in 1790, until 1802 in Bucharest at the school of St. Saba, again in Neamț between 1802 and 1819, then in Căldărușani, and from 1823 metropolitan of Ungrovalachia. He had received from Paisius the obedience to dedicate himself to the translation of patristic texts. His biography of Staretz Paisius, which bears the title *Povestire din parte a vietii prea cuviosului părintelui nostru Paisie*, is included in the volume *Adunare a cuvintelor celor pentru ascultare* (Neamț: 1817). See *Cuviosul Paisie de la Neamț (Velicicovski), Autobiografia și Viețile unui starec, urmate de Așezăminte si alte texte*, ed. Ioan I. Ică, Jr., 2nd ed. (Sibiu: Deisis, 2002), 333–51.

[16] *Cuvinte despre ascultare*, ed. Virgil Cândea (Bucharest: Anastasia, 1997), 172.

Since the Paisian community continued to grow and there were never enough cells for the monks, Prince Constantine Moruzi intervened, ordering Paisius to move to the largest monastery in the region, that of Neamț. He gave the following reason for his decree: "This monastery was granted to your community not only for your foundation, but also so that it becomes the model for other monasteries, according to your order of life."[17] The prince's decision had been unintentionally brought about by Paisius himself because the monastery of Secu had turned to him for grants to build another four large buildings for the needs of their growing community. He needed a tailor's shop, a shoemaker's shop, a weaver's shop and an environment for teaching the Greek language to young monks to enable them to translate spiritual books. This interesting detail, which we deduce from a letter of Paisius himself,[18] is provided by the fact that the space for teaching the Greek language was reserved for Fr. Ilarion, a Romanian schooled at the St. Saba Academy in Bucharest. He entered the Paisian community in Dragomirna and became, together with the older Macarie, also a Romanian, the community's Greek expert, and Paisius's trusted man in the work of translating patristic texts. Paisus's first disciples at Athos were all Romanians, and his first teachers in terms of translations from the Greek were all Romanians. Likewise the Romanian ecclesiastical and civil authorities surely deserve credit for having offered him the most suitable structures in order to make the most of the spiritual and cultural charge carried by his work. Thus he had found, in the Romanian lands and tradition, the ideal terrain for its development.

With Paisius—and this is a real revolution!—the "common life," an incomparable school of true obedience, with which humility flourishes, came to be the true place of hesychast

[17] Ibid., 183.

[18] This is the letter written to the disciples Ambrose, Athanasius and Theophanes, who left for Russia in 1777, wherein Paisius describes the events relating to the move from Secu to Neamț which took place in 1779. The text can be seen in Sf. Paisie de la Neamț, *Cuvinte și scrisori duhovnicești,* ed. Valentina Pelin, vol. 1 (Chișinău: Tipografia centrală, 1998), 84–98. Other letters by Paisius on the spiritual life can be read in Paisij Velickovsky, *La preghiera del cuore e Lettere scelte sulla vita spirituale* [The Prayer of the Heart and Selected Letters on the Spiritual Life], ed. Fr. Michele Di Monte (Eremo degli Angeli-Vendrogno: Monasterium, 2019).

practice, without which one would end up misunderstanding it. Now, Paisius's true strength lay in putting the key into his disciples' hands to understand from the inside what he urged them to practice. In this context, the assiduous and loving reading of the scriptures and the Fathers receives all its meaning together with the practices of the daily confession of thoughts and the prayer of Jesus. Scrutinizing the scriptures and the patristic writings day and night is Paisius's response to the lack of experienced guides. Such a serious and demanding response as the study of patristic texts, combined with the effort to translate them into Church Slavonic and Romanian, had gradually become the main activity of our staretz—the foundation, the strong point of his work, an activity by which he found his most effective support in Romania. However, what remains most impressive in the consciousness of his disciples would not be the result of this immense work of correcting and translating patristic texts, but rather the purpose and spiritual vitality with which this task was accomplished. The great importance and diffusion enjoyed in the Slavic world by the *Dobrotoljubie*, the Slavonic version of the *Philokalia* published in Moscow in 1793, eleven years after the Greek edition in Venice, is well known. None of the five known biographies of Paisius, composed by his disciples some twenty years after his death, mention it. Yet, they all unanimously stress the extraordinary fruitfulness of the work of correction and translation of the patristic texts by their staretz, a work which constitutes the most direct context of that monastic renewal which so impressed contemporaries.

With Paisius, a charismatic guide and man of profound spiritual experience, monastic life recovered its life as a passionate ideal capable of forging men and communities to the point of shaping the entire ecclesial life. Paisius introduced the lifeblood of hesychastic spirituality into the life of the monastery.[19] The rediscovery of scripture and the Fathers went hand in hand with the rediscovery of the Jesus Prayer. Having these as the basis for cenobitic life, with all the consequences that followed in the organization of community life and personal

---

[19] Cf. Ioan I. Ică, Jr., "Lo starec Paisij Velickovskij e la preghiera del cuore," in AA. VV., *La preghiera di Gesù nella spiritualità russa del XIX*. Proceedings of the 12th International Ecumenical Conference on Orthodox Spirituality, Russian section, Bose, 16–18 September 2004 (Bose: Qiqajon, 2005), 71–104.

asceticism, is the essence of great renewal brought by Paisius. In Dragomirna his main occupation consisted precisely in the "service of the word"—an expression used by his disciples!—that is, in preparing the evening instructions for the community where he read and explained the texts that he was translating together with his closest collaborators, all of them Romanians. The introduction of those evening instructions, in which the themes of inner warfare were addressed on the basis of the exegesis of scripture and the teaching of the Fathers, earned Paisius the title of the *golden mouth* of Moldavia. The young Paisius had already witnessed these practices in the hermitages of Wallachia in the years 1743–1746. He took them up, regulated them and animated them on the basis of all that work of translating and correcting patristic texts that he was organizing. Starting in 1769, in Dragomirna, the monk Rafail was able to collect in a voluminous anthology of 626 pages a series of texts on the Jesus Prayer, the result of ancient and new Romanian translations, including the authors of the famous *Philokalia*, plus two modern authors, namely the work of Nil Sorsky and the elder Basil of Poiana Mărului.

The most conspicuous part in the work of translating patristic texts was carried out by Romanian translators. In one of his letters Paisius writes:

> I began my work . . . in this way: I placed for my instruction and guidance the translation of the Patristic books into the Moldavian language which was made by our beloved brethren Hieromonk Macarius and Hilarion the Didascalos from the ancient Greek into their own Moldavian language; they are skilled in the translation of books and are learned men. Brother Macarius translated a part of them while still on the Holy Mountain of Athos, and a part in Dragomirna; likewise also, the honorable Didascalos, Father Hilarion, translated a part of them in our community. Accounting their translation to be true in all respects without any doubt, I began to correct the Patristic books . . .[20]

In Romania the Paisian spirit triumphed in the very organization of the church. First-rate ecclesiastical personalities

[20] Letter to Theodosius, in Schema-monk Metrophanes, *Blessed Paisius Velichkovski*, trans. Fr. Seraphim Rose (Platina, CA: Saint Herman of Alaska Brotherhood, 1976), 112.

imbued with that spirit, such as Benjamin Costachi, metropolitan of Moldavia and Gregory Dăscalul, tonsured a monk by Paisius himself, Paisius's biographer and future metropolitan of Wallachia, promoted and extended the renewal resulting from the work beyond the circle of Paisius's monasteries, both on a spiritual and a cultural level. They reorganized the monasteries, created schools, were fully committed to a vast activity of promoting translations and printing books (the installation of the printing press in Neamț was the work of Benjamin Costachi with the desire to spread the translation works of the Paisian community), revived ecclesiastical structures severely tested by the wars and the tsarist occupation of 1808–1812 and subsequently by the revolutionary uprisings of 1821. The cenobitic type of monasticism flourished again under the influence of the Paisian model, so much so that towards the mid-1800s almost all monasteries followed the *Rule* of Paisius.

In Wallachia his work was continued by one of his great disciples, the elder Gheorghe, originally from Transylvania. Passing through Bucharest on the way to Athos, after leaving Neamț in 1781, the staretz Gheorghe accepted the invitation of Metropolitan Gregory II to establish a monastic community similar to the Paisian one and chose to settle in a now abandoned hermitage on the outskirts of Bucharest, Cernica, soon transformed into a large monastery. In 1794 he was also entrusted with the leadership of the nearby large monastery of Căldărușani. In his *Testament*, a sort of rule of life for the communities that defer to him, he claimed three specific charisms for his teacher Paisius: the gift of prayer from the heart, the gift of leading a multitude of brothers, and the very rare gift of keeping brothers of various nationalities together. The elder Gheorghe did not believe he could attribute them to himself and therefore invited the brothers of his community to dedicate themselves to the prayer of Jesus, but not exclusively, at least until they had purified themselves of all passions; he limited the number of brothers in the community to one hundred and three (a number that would be greatly exceeded after him); he considered the possibility that the Romanian, Russian and Greek monks live separately, without decreasing their mutual love (but as long as he was alive the community remained united). His emphasis inclined rather to ascetic effort and the active life. The lifeblood, however, was derived from the Paisian spirit itself, even though, in Romanian literature, Cernica's tendency is normally indicated in a specific sense: Cernican spirituality. The most famous exponent of this spirituality would be Saint Callinicus, a monk in Cernica for forty-three years and then bishop of Rîmnic. Along with prayer and asceticism, he joined love for his community, which under his guidance reached up to three hundred and fifty brothers, with concern for the poor and pastoral activity. To him we owe the construction of the Frăsinei monastery where, on the Athonite model, he introduced severe rules of life (remember that, even today, Frăsinei is the only Romanian monastery where access to women remains forbidden, as in the Athonite monasteries). By freeing oneself from passions with asceticism, one can cultivate the virtues of meekness, humility and love which overcome selfishness, dedicating oneself to various activities without in the least impeding a fervent life of communion with God.[21]

In Russia the Paisian renewal slowly but steadily progressed until it merged into what would be called the great tradition of the startsy of Optina, the true center of irradiation of the Paisian heritage, with profound religious and literary cultural reverberations.[22] In Romania to the contrary, after a rapid upward path, a slow but sure decline followed. That specific context in which Paisius came to shape his experience, namely the fact of the large number of brothers who lived in a single community (as staretz of the monasteries of Secu and Neamț he had the guidance of about a thousand monks) and the fact that these brothers were of different origins and peoples (Romanians, Ukrainians, Russians, Bulgarians, Serbians, Greeks) did not stand the test of time. This is perhaps due to the changed historical circumstances that occurred at the end

21 Regarding the startsy Gheorghe and Callinicus of Cernica, see, Ioan I. Ică, Jr., ed., *Sfinti stareti Gheorghe și Calinic de la Cernica, Viețile, povățuirile, testamentele* [Saints Gheorghe and Callinicus of Cernica, Lives, teachings, wills] (Sibiu: Deisis, 2018).

22 Consult the perspective table about the Paisian diffusion, with its impressive list of disciples and monasteries under Paisius's influence, prepared by Chetverikov, but published only in the Romanian version by Bishop Nicodim: S. Cetverikov, *Paisie starețul Mânăstirii Neamțului din Moldova. Viața, invățătura și influența lui asupra Bisericii Ortodoxe* (Neamț: Mănăstirii Neamțului, 1933). Cf. V. Kotelnikov, *L'eremo di Optina e i Grandi della cultura russa* (Milano: Casa di Matriona, 1996).

of Paisius's life with Moldavia occupied by the Russian army, with the ecclesiastical tensions that had broken out between the respective churches, and with the onset of a new national, if not nationalistic, spirit.[23] Or perhaps this was due to a decreased internal tension of the Paisian community itself. This is hard to say. But the fact remains that, even if these two features were to disappear, the charm that attracted so many and aroused so much admiration had certainly disappeared.

In the perception of scholars, it is still a widespread habit to trace the fruits of the hesychast renewal in the Orthodox church of modern times to that movement which flourished within the Greek church, in particular on Athos, in the eighteenth century, with the edition of the Greek *Philokalia* in Venice in 1782, edited by Macarius of Corinth and Nicodemus the Hagiorite.[24] Yet, the ways in which the hesychast renewal was transmitted through Orthodox countries and touched, in the last century, also the Catholic world, can be traced back to another context, that of Paisius Velichkovsky and his Russian disciples, with the mediation of the Romanian environment and tradition. If we take the *Philokalia* as a symbol of that renewal, we cannot refer to it as a book on which to educate ourselves and learn to pray. Before being a book, the *Philokalia* was the daily experience of a community of brothers, with all the effectiveness that a living reality entails. In this sense the *Philokalia*, for Paisius and his disciples, does not only represent the deposit of the wisdom of a tradition, but the reverberation of an experience before everyone's eyes, at least for two generations. It is this spiritual vitality, which links monastic practice and fraternal life to the centrality of Christian revelation, and consists in God's giving grace to us in Christ (Eph. 4:32), which has produced so much fruit. All the teaching was based on the scriptures and the Fathers, read with loving concern and thoroughness, but only for the purpose of learning to be submissive to one another and growing in the spiritual intelligence of the mystery of God. And, if the practice of Jesus's prayer was privileged, this was

[23] See Ioan I. Ica, "La posterità romena dello 'starec' Paisij" in N. Kauchtschischwili, A.-Ai. N. Tachiaos, V. Pelin and AA. VV., *Paisij, lo starec. Atti del III Convegno ecumenico internazionale di spiritualità russa "Paisij Velickovskij e il suo movimento spirituale,"* ed. A. Mainardi (Bose: Qiqajon, 1997), 245–66.

[24] See my "Nicodemo Agiorita," in *La théologie bizantine et sa tradition,* II, ed. C. G. Conticello & V. Conticello (Turnhout: Brepols, 2002), 905–97.

because that practice was directly connected to the radicality of the mystery of the Christian revelation, that is, it led to the experience of God's gracious giving of Himself, in Christ, to the sinful heart, submissive to everyone.

TRADITION AND RENEWAL

It is interesting to note how tradition continually reinterprets itself according to an ever-renewed practice of prayer and the theology that supports it. When reading the hesychast texts one gets the impression that preference is given to hermetic and contemplative spirituality rather than to the liturgy, or to monasticism rather than the church. The vision of tradition, however, tends to "include," not to "separate," so when we dwell on the personal prayer of the hesychast, we do not mean to detach this from common liturgical practice. The text of the Xanthopouloi bears witness to this, who, addressing hesychasts, combined the practice of Jesus's prayer with liturgical prayer and the Eucharistic celebration.[25]

I report the example of an isolated chapter by Gregory Sinaita on submission and obedience, taken up by Basil of Poiana Mărului in his *Mirror of a True Hesychasm*,[26] because it is a passage that Sandu Tudor knew very well and which bore fruit on various occasions. Here is the text:

> Submission is servitude to Christ, angelic activity, fulfillment of the commandments. Obedience is eternal life, ladder of heaven, a short ascent, richness of crowns, work of angels, path of impassibility, path that leads to heaven. Submission is the mother of humility, obedience is the door of ascent. In fact, submission leads the disciple of Christ to God: it makes one a family member, unifies, frees from nature, severs relationships, cuts off attachments, frees from all carnal ties and passions, as a generator of love, as the mother of the flame of desire, and draws one close to God as a pure and immaculate sacrifice. Obedience carries out all the commandments, straightens everything, does everything and builds the soul in an invisible, unknown and

[25] *On the Life of Stillness and the Monastic State*, 91–93, in *The Philokalia*, vol. 5, 125–31.

[26] A. Rigo, *Il monaco, la chiesa e la liturgia. I capitoli sulle gerarchie di Gregorio il Sinaita* (Firenze: Edizioni del Galluzzo, 2005), 51. Cf. Vasile de la Poiana Mărului, *Introduceri în rugăciunea lui Iisus și isihasm* (Sibiu: Deisis, 2009); *Oglinda adevăratului isihasm*, 207–25. This is a summary of Basil's three introductions to Gregory of Sinai, Philotheus of Sinai, and Hesychius of Sinai.

> providential way, enriches and accumulates in a short time, makes it rise towards God, presents, crowns and beautifies it mystically. Submission in fact resembles a mother who has given birth to a child and offers her offspring, the renouncer, new and supercelestial things. Obedience resembles a nurse who suckles, makes her disciple grow and leads to maturity. Submission is in fact a heaven and obedience is the heaven of heaven as the most divine ascent. One is transported to the throne of grace by humility, the other by love. For this reason, whoever falls from submission is fallen from heaven and from God, as the more than divine Fathers have established.

Basil of Poiana Mărului's exhortation starts from the consideration that those who enter the monastic order have two possibilities to progress: that of observing the commandments and that of repenting. But since we always fail to comply with one commandment or another, the preferred path is that of repentance. And he gives an absolutely intelligent and very real explanation. He says that we are not willing to repent every day and every moment for all our shortcomings because we blame the brothers for our sins, we blame them on them, we put them on their shoulders. If we could remove this type of "justification" from ourselves, we would only accuse ourselves and repent and ask the Lord for forgiveness always in the secret of our inner man. The tension of that interior attention, which the Fathers call "sobriety," which does not give freedom of movement in the heart to any hidden word so as not to incur God's condemnation, is the fruit of continuous repentance. Quoting Deut. 15:9: "Take heed to yourself, lest the hidden word in your heart become a violation of the law," the explanation of Hesychius the Priest states: "The mere appearance of the thought of an action hateful to God is called a hidden word."[27] And again he insists on the fact that, if we do not blame our brothers for our anger or afflictions, but we accuse ourselves and ask for forgiveness, the Lord comes to meet us with his mercy. And this is the interior activity, the working of the mind in secret, with which we will arrive at being freed from passions in such a way as to incessantly invoke the Lord Jesus, having our memory fixed in God and being submissive to our brothers.[28]

[27] Hesychius the Priest, *To Theodulus*, I, 2, *Philokalia*, vol. 1, 230.

[28] Cf. Gregory the Sinaite, "On the Signs of Grace and Delusion," chap. 3, *Philokalia*, vol. 4, 259.

Everything is summarized in the formula: "without obedience and without renunciation of one's own will no one can see God." Since God's commandments can only be fulfilled through obedience and renunciation of one's own will, then one must act "with great intelligence," so as not to be submissive except for Christ and for no other purpose. In this sense, Gregory of Sinai's passage on submission and obedience is read as giving the fruitful context to submission for Christ, whereby being submissive to everything and everyone, in the name of Christ, means being made participant in the secret of God that Jesus reveals, to open us to the splendor of the love that derives from obedience. So obedience is superior to submission, but it is based on that. To grasp the spiritual dynamic that submission favors, it is necessary to reach the point of not accusing anyone of one's innumerable shortcomings, so much so as to live in continuous repentance and expectation of God's mercy: "Submission is in fact a heaven and obedience is the heaven of heaven as a most divine ascent. One transports to the throne of grace by humility, the other by love. For this reason, whoever falls from submission is fallen from heaven and from God, as the more than divine Fathers have established." It is precisely that continuous repentance while awaiting God's mercy, being submissive to everyone, which constitutes the soil from which the continuous prayer of the heart blossoms. Just as Abba Sisoes reiterated: "A brother said to Abba Sisoes: 'I am aware that the remembrance of God stays with me.' The old man said to him, 'It is no great thing to be with God in your thoughts, but it is a great thing to see yourself as inferior to all creatures. It is this, coupled with hard work, that leads to humility.'"[29]

Maximus the Confessor's commentary on the Our Father highlights this to the highest degree. The Our Father is a prayer that can be read from beginning to end and from end to beginning. Precisely by rereading the Our Father by going back from the bottom to the beginning, Maximus the Confessor has a brilliant intuition. Explaining the request "lead us not into temptation" he gives this interpretation:

[29] *Sayings of the Desert Fathers. Alphabetical Collection*, trans. B. Ward (Kalamazoo, MI: Cistercian Publications, 1975), Sigma 13, 214.

> Scripture reveals that those who have not perfectly forgiven those who fall and have not presented to God a heart free from sadness, made radiant by the light of reconciliation with their neighbor, will not obtain the grace of the good things for which they have prayed, and, by a just judgment, will be handed over to temptation and to the Evil One. In this way they will learn to purify themselves from sin, eliminating their complaints against others.... For it is said: If you do not forgive men their sins, neither will your heavenly Father forgive you. Thus we will not only receive forgiveness for the sins committed, but, moreover, we will overcome the law of sin, because we will not be allowed to experience it.[30]

We are led into temptation, we are tried by evil and the evil one until we forgive our debtors. The expression is very strong. It tells us that man, with a just judgment from God, will be put at the mercy of temptation and the evil one for the sole purpose of learning to purify himself from his sins by suppressing his accusation against others. If a man could fully withdraw his pointing finger, every accusation against another man, he would not suffer any temptation to evil. All our exposure to evil is only a function of us learning to never accuse anyone. We will not suffer temptation if we have the ability, to be assimilated little by little, of not accusing anyone because the heart will be meek and humble like that of Jesus, He who was indwelt by the Holy Spirit, and who could say: "Come to me, all of you who are weary and burdened, and I will give you rest. Take my yoke upon you and learn from me, who am meek and humble of heart, and you will find rest for your souls. For my yoke is easy and my burden is light" (Matt. 11:28–30).

The same intuition is expressed by St. Ephrem in his famous penitential prayer, which in the Byzantine tradition is recited nine times a day during Lent. His prayer does not end with the request for an abundance of charity but for repentance: "Yea, O Lord and King! Grant me to see my own errors and not to judge my brother; for blessed art Thou unto ages of ages. Amen." Seeing your own sins and not accusing your brother summarizes the power of holy fellowship: the humility of charity.

The ancient Fathers, unlike we moderns who are more

[30] Maximus Confessor, "On the Our Father," *Philokalia*, II, 310–11. I refer to my translation of Maximus's text: *La vita spirituale, i suoi segreti* (Bologna: EDB, 2005), 231, 78–79.

sentimental and much less radical, had no doubts about it. The main path is the path of repentance. In the systematic collection of the Sayings of the Desert Fathers, chapter ten, "On Discretion," we read: "A brother inquired of an elder, 'Am I being saved if I fast?' 'No,' said the elder. The brother said, 'Am I being saved if I flee from people?' 'No,' the elder told him. The brother said, 'If I practice love of the brethren, am I being saved?' The elder said, 'No. But to be saved is this: to endure blame of oneself and not to afflict one's brother in any situation, for God is merciful with a person like that.'"[31] This means living submissively from the perspective of obedience, this means rooting love in humility and humility in love, which is the very meaning of Jesus's prayer combined with incessant interior work, as I explained above.

CHARACTER OF ROMANIAN HESYCHASM IN MODERN TIMES

A very close and natural relationship binds monks and faithful to each other, they all breathe the same spiritual climate. Moldavia, in particular, where the largest monasteries in Romania are located and where Fr. Daniil lived the last years of his life in the hermitage of Rarău, in the Ceahlău mountains, preserves intact the traditional structure of the village of which the monastery represents the natural appendage and the unifying vital center. This fact still today constitutes one of the most striking and original characteristics of Romanian society, distinguishing itself from this point of view also from other Orthodox countries. When I think of Romanian hesychasm, I think above all of an attitude of the soul that distinguishes it. One anecdote seems particularly expressive to me. I heard it narrated by the famous elder of Sihăstria, Fr. Cleopa (1912–1998) about his brother Galaction: "One day Father Galaction asked this question to a hermit he had met by chance in the forest: 'Tell me, Father: when will the end of the world come?' And that holy man, sighing, replied: 'Do you want to know, Father Galaction? When there will be no longer any path between a man and his neighbor!'"[32]

---

[31] *The Book of the Elders. The Sayings of the Desert Fathers. The Systematic Collection.* X, 133, trans. J. Wortley (Collegeville, MN: Cistercian Publications, 2012), 175.

[32] See I. Bălan, *Pateric românesc* (Bucharest: Institutul biblic, 1980), 621.

When people aspire to live behind selfish barriers, close their hearts towards one another, when they forget love and mutual service, in a word, *communion*, life will be emptied of meaning, the world will have reached its end. The admirable expression of the anonymous *sihastru* thoroughly conveys perhaps the most salient feature of a way of understanding life, religious commitment and culture which has always characterized the spirituality of the Romanian people throughout its history.

It seems to me that I can recognize the source of these two characteristics that recall each other, one of a more internal type (life as communion), the other of a more socio-religious type (the close osmosis between the faithful and monastics), what the famous *Book of teaching of the Romanian prince Neagoe Basarab for his son Theodosius* called "dulceața lui Dumnezeu": "rădăcina bunătăților iasti dulceata lui Dumnezeu" ("the sweetness of God": "the root of goodness is the sweetness of God").[33] The complete passage reads: "Whoever makes himself a companion of the divine virtues will have imperishable life and existence, since the root of goodness is sweet intimacy with God." *Dulceața dumnezeiasca* involves a dimension, a timbre, which touches the very nature of the Romanian lands, the spirituality, the liturgical celebration itself and the singing, the people. It denotes a vision, it reveals a specific internal experience, one that matured in the climate of the hesychast tradition that deeply permeated the spiritual space of the East, particularly Romania, and which Sandu Tudor rediscovered and to which he bore witness.

During last century's long communist winter, it was monasticism that preserved the ideal, values and freedom of faith in Romania. Faced with the multitude of lay people, and priests and monks who had chosen the path of martyrdom, whose courage in their testimony is being rediscovered today,[34] the hier-

[33] In Romanian see *Învățăturile lui Neagoe Basarab către fiul său Theodosie* (Bucharest: Minerva, 1984), 125. In Italian see *Come vivere e praticare l'esichia. Libro di insegnamento del principe romeno Neagoe Basarab per suo figlio Teodosio*, translation, introductory study and notes by Adriana Mitescu, Bulzoni (Biblioteca di cultura, 480), (Rome, 1993), 69. The passage is taken from chap. V, "Discourse on the fear and love of God," preserved only in the Romanian version.

[34] See *Le catacombe della Romania. Testimonianze dalle carceri comuniste, 1945–1964* [The Catacombs of Romania. Testimonies from communist prisons, 1945–1964] (Milano: Rediviva, 2014); Violeta Popescu, *La Chiesa Ortodossa Romena dopo la Seconda Guerra Mondiale. Figure dell'Ortodossia romena nell'Occidente* (Milano: Rediviva, 2018).

archy had chosen a difficult and humiliating path—structural viability on the objective level—of personal compromise for the sake of maintaining ecclesiastical institutions (parishes, theological schools, monasteries). The very existence of the church was shielded behind a liturgical isolationism, tolerated as an unofficial social subculture, with the relative repression of any attempt at alternative social thought and the acceptance of the ideological monopoly of the Romanian communist party over the entire society. The price paid for the maintenance of this ecclesiastical space was high. It could be said that it consisted in the renunciation of the prophetic function of the Church as an institution and in the acceptance of the humiliating role of the Church as "servant" of the ideological objectives of the regime, even though the religious practice of believers was not affected. "Prophecy" had turned into servile propaganda, a political doctrine in religious language. The result was disastrous both from a moral point of view and above all from an intellectual and social point of view. The humiliation of the political subjugation of the hierarchy entailed, moreover, the aggravating circumstance of a certain intellectual perversion of the theological thought of the Church. Beyond violence to consciences, political calculation or careerist opportunism, compromise in the Romanian Orthodox Church was able to invest itself with a kind of theological infrastructure and a unique kind of ideological justification. We have arrived at the theorization of an ideological convergence between the spirituality and social doctrine of the Orthodox Church, on the one hand, and the Marxist social doctrine and practice, on the other, which goes by the name of "Social Apostolate"[35] and "Servant Church."[36] Both theological-ideological constructs were considered as normative in the theology and pastoral practice of the Orthodox Church in

[35] *Apostolat social* was the generic term for all the pastoral interventions of the patriarch Justinian Marina (1948–1977) published in twelve volumes between the years 1948–1975. A detailed and complete analysis, taking into account the context of the time, with its lights and shadows, is yet to be done.

[36] *Biserica slujitoare în Sfânta Scriptură, Sfânta Tradiție și în teologia contemporană* is the title of a doctoral thesis by the then patriarchal vicar bishop Antonie Plămădeală, prepared in a first version at Oxford (1968–1970) and then published in a more extensive Romanian version in the journal *Studii teologice* 24 (1972), nos. 5–8 and in an extract of 344 pages (an abridged edition was published at Sibiu in 1986).

the new socialist reality.[37] The mixture of popular Christianity with Marxist ideological populism and the captivity of thought led to an intellectual imprisonment of those who were oppressed and persecuted by the thinking of the communist persecutor, more devastating than the moral humiliation of compromise and collaborationism. The common substructure that prevented conflict between the hierarchy and the communist state was provided by nationalism and the 'popular' character of Christianity, whereby the Church was active in the State in the name of national unity, by virtue of the natural link between the interests of a Church of the people and the People's state. The Byzantine *symphonia* was transformed into a cosmocracy, under the control and total domination of the communist state over the Church which reluctantly accepted the humiliating function of propagating an oppressive and dehumanizing ideology. In a dialogue with Andrei Pleșu, Father Scrima recalled that, after 1964, the underlying argument prevailing in the rhetoric of the regime, and imposed on the church, went something like this: the head of state does everything he does in the name of the people, for the good of the people, in spiritual communion with the people. Consequently, the representatives of the people's Church find themselves carrying out their role for the unanimous good of the people.[38]

And yet, beyond this attitude accepted under duress and even justified in its mythological-political vision, the Church continued to be itself, to carry out its mission among the people. The Church found its true strength in monasticism, in its ability to bear witness to and support the faith of believers and be an energy reserve for not giving way to communist ideology.

In Romanian history, charismatic figures not only affected the renewal of spiritual life in the monastic communities to which they belonged, but also had a much broader impact. It was like this with Basil of Poiana Mărului, it was like this on a larger scale with Paisius Velichkovsky, it was like this with Gheorghe and Callinic of Cernica and it was also like this with the contemporary figures of Romanian monasticism. In

---

[37] Cf. *La théologie orthodoxe romaine des origines à nos jours* (Bucharest: Institut biblique et de mission orthodoxe, 1974), 9, 11, 285, 359–74.

[38] Cf. André Scrima, "Un test ultim al faptului religios," *Teme ecumenice* (Bucharest: Humanitas, 2004), 104–38, in particular 124.

its specific characteristics, the Burning Bush movement was situated both within the Romanian hesychast tradition and within a broader movement which can be defined as the reaction of believers to communist pressure. In the 1950s, at least four centers of spiritual irradiation in Romania could be identified around as many charismatic figures. There was Fr. Arsenie Boca (1910–1989), patron and spreader of the *Philokalia* together with Fr. Dumitru Stăniloae, first at the monastery of Sâmbăta de Sus (Judetul Brasov), then at Slatina, under surveillance by the Securitate and arrested several times; Fr. Ioan Iovan, in Vladimirești, along with Maica Veronica Gurău, a female community dispersed in 1955 and then recently reconstituted and still very lively today; and Fr. Cleopa of Slatina and Sihăstria in particular, from whose example, teaching, and spiritual power all Romanian Orthodoxy, both faithful and monks, drew strength and consolation in the dark times of communist oppression. The group that had formed around Fr. Cleopa in the 1950s was dispersed, but in turn the disciples, after their imprisonment, were credible witnesses of a spiritual life that strengthened the people and animated their church, now impeded and, in some ways, entangled in the coils of the regime (I can recall Fr. Petronie Tănase of the Prodromou monastery on Athos, Fr. Iachint Unciuleac of Putna, Fr. Arsenie Papacioc of the Santa Maria monastery of Techirghiol on the Black Sea and many others, not to mention the major female figures, more in the shade but no less present).

The fourth center is Antim, with Sandu Tudor and the Burning Bush movement. It is a very particular center of spiritual radiation. Some, like Bartolomeo Anania, bishop of Cluj, somewhat hastily and as if distancing themselves from it, had branded it as an affair of intellectuals, a movement restricted to the circle of Bucharest intellectuals, unlike the other centers that had had a national resonance. Not only that, but they had viewed Tudor's commitment to wanting to see the movement publicly recognized by both civil and religious authorities as a veiled attitude of submission to the regime.[39] What was Antim's defining characteristic? What role did it play

[39] See the somewhat condescending attitude of Bartolomeo Anania in his otherwise positive testimony on Fr. Daniil in *Daniil Sandu Tudor, Taina Rugului Aprins. Serieri și documente inedite* (Bucharest: Anastasia, 1999), 137–44.

in the tradition of the Romanian Church? It should be noted first of all that the awareness of the role and importance of the Antim movement arose in the Romanian Church forty years after the events, with the fall of communism. The testimonies of the time were replicated, the various participants returned to the events that profoundly marked their lives, and a debate, ongoing even today, was born.

It seems to me that the main characteristics of this historical prodigy can be summarized in three points. But first, Andrei Pleșu provides an illuminating overall judgment by presenting the first attempt at a hermeneutic elaboration of the events of that time, that of André Scrima, then one of the young participants in the meetings, who recognized himself as marked by that prodigious beginning:

> ...it was the unique meeting between intellectuals and clerics that took place in the Antim monastery around the 1950s. The Antim group was the last episode of a real conciliarity for our church in the years of the communist dictatorship. Great intellectuals and great monks lived together an experience of communication and 'communion,' with an incredible interior freedom, until the authorities decided to define this spirit in terms of the penal code.[40]

First point. It was a group of intellectuals in dialogue with the Orthodox monastic model. They were modern men, involved in the cultural debate of their time and with a personal formation from the most varied backgrounds (philosophical, scientific, artistic, religious), fascinated by the mystical tradition of the Church, in particular by the hesychast tradition of the prayer of the heart. Three figures combined to generate a movement that involved everyone. Sandu Tudor, in the role of a charismatic secular intellectual, arrived at the monastic choice with all the cultural baggage and liveliness that distinguished him, capable of attracting many other intellectuals, who like him were in search of a spiritual dimension of life in the wake of the luminous tradition of the Eastern Church. He arrived at Antim with his entire prestigious library. He involved his friends and colleagues, such as Alexandru Mironescu, a professor of physical chemistry at the University of Bucharest, and Vasilie

[40] Scrima, *L'accompagnamento spirituale*, 23.

Voiculescu, whose library, "a kind of cathedral, built with care, ordered almost by a well-balanced vertigo, offered us always new, enchanting discoveries."[41] On the monastic side, with a doctorate in theology from Strasbourg and a university assistant first to Nichifor Crainic and then to Fr. Dumitru Stăniloae, the amiable, sweet and profound figure of Fr. Benedict Ghiuș stands out. The entire Antim community found in him the essential reference for a climate of openness and benevolence towards seekers with different backgrounds and paths. Lastly, the figure of Fr. Ioann Kulygin, the Stranger, who became the spiritual guide of the group as if embodying in his person the values that both lay people and monks admired in the rediscovery of Orthodoxy's mystical tradition. If the driving force of the group was Sandu Tudor, the inner soul of the group was Fr. Ioann, with everyone recognizing in him that teaching of the Fathers whose splendor of truth they admired.

It was a group of intellectuals looking for a form of spiritual life that, in modernity, has no equivalent. The conviviality with which the meetings were held, the friendship between the participants, the freedom of thought in the exploration of the themes created by the climate of respect between the participants and the monks, everything favored a space for culture and spirituality that finally proceeded together, the one leavening the other. The Antim participants were simply intellectuals fascinated by the Orthodox tradition that they discovered and contributed to discovering, and upon which they dwelt, committing themselves to knowing it and adopting it in their respective lives. However, it was not a private group, since their search, born of friendship and the desire for knowledge, had a much broader reach. In addition to the closed meetings on Thursday evenings, Sunday afternoon meetings were open to all and participation was great. Many faithful and many students came. Everything took place without formalism, any listener able to interject. The event contrasted with the grayness that reigned in the country, which was now unable to think out loud due to communist ideological oppression, which was taking away every possible space of freedom and knowledge. The group did not fit into any type of organization, institution, or

[41] Ibid., 161.

pre-established model. The very special aspect of this meeting of intellectuals in a traditional monastic environment was seen in the convergence of intentions between lay people and monks, between prominent intellectual figures and prominent monastic figures. Anca Manolescu, author of a very interesting examination of study circles and spiritual friendship in ancient and modern Romania, had invited André Scrima to participate in a panel discussion on "Bucharest in the time of communism: resistance, normality, survival" in 2000 for the magazine *Martor*.[42] Unfortunately, his death in August 2000 prevented Scrima from reviewing his speech, which therefore remained unpublished. But in that speech he maintained that the only normality of life in that historical period was ensured by reading and discussion groups, informal groups of friends brought together by a common cultural and spiritual interest. Antim's case was special. At Antim there lived monks who were sensitive and open to the spiritual search of other people of different origins and backgrounds, and these other people found in Antim the welcoming atmosphere of the Church in the brightness of its liturgical theology, so much so that Scrima writes: "Beyond the traditionalists, no one placed barriers, no one underscored differences, no one expressed refusal or contempt towards our way of remaining involved in tradition."[43] In short, it was a meeting between "cult and culture," living

[42] Cf. Anca Manolescu, *Modelul Antim, modelul Păltiniș. Cercuri de studiu și prietenie spirituală* (Bucharest: Humanitas, 2015). Anca Manolescu is the editor of the editions of Fr. André Scrima's texts at the Humanitas publishing house. The unpublished work mentioned bears the title: *Grupul de la Antim.* In addition to the texts and the library of Fr. Scrima, in the "André Scrima Archive" of the New Europe College in Bucharest there are also about fifty letters which testify to the friendly exchanges between Scrima and the participants of the Antim group. The two most sensational cases, among many, of the 1958 trials due to the regime's fury against Romanian intellectuals, both secular and religious, are those against the Burning Bush movement in Antim and against the entourage formed around the philosopher Constantin Noica (1909–1987) and which had seen the condemnation of men of the caliber of Alex Paleologu, Nicu Steinhardt, and Dinu Pillat. Noica, having been released from prison, retired in 1975 to Păltiniș, a small mountain village about thirty kilometers from Sibiu, where he lived under surveillance by a special guard of the Securitate, attracting talented young people around him for a renewal of culture. The testimony that would make known the importance of the figure and his formative work is from Gabriel Liceanu who wrote the *Jurnalul de la Păltiniș*, published in Bucharest in 1983 and translated into French in 1998.

[43] Ibid., 105.

the spiritual experience not by reducing mental exercise, by impeding acquaintance with literature and the arts as if such interests were territories forbidden to holiness, but, on the contrary, underscoring the possibility of drawing knowledge at ever deeper levels to experience the freshness of the evangelical invitation and the brightness of the tradition of the Church. It was like rediscovering the radiating force, the attractiveness of the Christian experience even for modern man, beyond any dogmatism, traditionalism or devotionalism. I believe I am conveying the profound feelings of the members of the movement through a reference to the troparion of the poem by Cosmas the monk, Ode 9, of the Holy Thursday Orthros: "Come, ye faithful, let us raise our minds on high and enjoy the Master's hospitality and the table of immortal life in the upper room; and let us hear the exalted teaching of the Word whom we magnify."[44]

Second point. It was within a universalistic purview. Absolutely significant of the atmosphere experienced in Antim is the episode recalled by Scrima in a conversation with Andrei Pleșu. "At the end of a Sunday conference with great participation by lay people"—declares Fr. André—"where there was also discussion about Jalal al-Din Rumi (1207–1273) and Ramakrishna (1836–1886), a monk stood up and said: 'Sorry. You quoted a Muslim. Someone else quoted a Hindu. So what's going on here?' Fr. Benedict Ghiuș answered very simply: 'If the Lord said that, at the end of time, he will gather all the sheep, how can I exclude them? How can I reject someone who speaks like this about him? How can I not listen to him?'"[45] This was a matter of returning to what belongs essentially to the profound dimension of religious men: attention towards others, the sense of freedom, the openness of one's intelligence and one's own sensitivity to be able to welcome, from the other, the fruit of intelligence and sensitivity bestowed under the same sky. Scrima also recalls:

> When, in 1946–1947, I had the opportunity to encounter Orthodoxy as a living spiritual tradition (around the one who was, in himself, 'Ioann the Stranger': what 'exotic' terminology!), it

[44] Mother Mary & Archimandrite K. Ware, trans., *The Lenten Triodion* (South Canaan, PA: St. Tikhon's Seminary Press, 1978/2002), 553.

[45] Scrima, *Teme ecumenice*: "Un test ultim al faptului religios," 114.

> appeared to be present in that 'center' which guarantees and entails a universal orientation: a center which is however 'inner' and 'outside the world.' There, discovering the true intellectual teaching of Orthodoxy (the apophthegms of the Desert Fathers, Gregory of Nyssa, Maximus the Confessor, Simeon the New Theologian, Gregory Palamas and others), the Eastern tradition came back 'into Its own'.... Personally, I understood that it was not foreign to my own research conducted up to that point.[46]

Such admissions I find shared by many of the participants in the Burning Bush meetings. This simple observation should still be added. In the first part of the twentieth century, the intersection between cult and culture, according to the beautiful expression of Andrei Pleșu, was already frequented. Significant voices—Nichifor Crainic, Nae Ionescu, Mircea Vulcănescu—had highlighted faith in the public space, adopted a new religious language, and prodded the church by criticizing a conformist devotion. The pitfall was the nationalist interest in attempting to outline a system of national values to give Romania an important place in Europe. The past and the Romanian religious tradition figured as materials to be used for the construction of that identity. Faith was perceived in the category of something of the people and the people's spirituality. An indigenous Christianity was dreamed of, an obligatorily Orthodox "Romanity" or an ethno-religious state, according to a movement of ideas and feelings that historians later called Orthodoxism. The Burning Bush movement followed other trajectories. There was no particular ethnic privileging, there was no guaranteed excellence. They recognized the problematic of spiritual creativity in modernity, but saw this through the lens of the creative power of Christianity acting in people. One of the most acute examples of this inner feeling can be found in Sandu Tudor's faithful friend, Alexandru Mironescu, who placed the human person at the center of his reflection in search of the ultimate meaning of things. The Christian way moves within the great human spiritual family, as the way to realize the longing of the human heart. He declares: "The awareness that I am a Christian gives me the fullness of belonging to the whole of humanity...made up of all men, of all cultures, of all eras, with all kinds of experiences and

46 Ibid., 134.

traditions...of everything that unites them and gives them an understanding, a purpose."[47]

Third point. Did the Burning Bush movement also have a social objective? In the participants' memoirs, the response is not unanimous. If for André Scrima the Antim movement was based on the desire for spiritual knowledge without intentional opposition to the sociopolitical regime of the time, for others, such as Antonie Plămadeală, Roman Braga, Adrian Făgețeanu, and for some historians, such as Gheorghe Enache, it corresponded to Sandu Tudor's intention to train young intellectuals with the aim of preparing a spiritual resistance to communism.[48] Even if it is true that between 1945 and 1948, in the period in which the meetings of Antim participants were held publicly and prior to the dissolution of the association and the prohibition of meetings, there is no trace of other purposes other than that of knowledge and rediscovery of the great tradition of the Orthodox Church, the urgency of forming consciences in view of an inevitable cultural and religious battle so as not to succumb to communist ideology is undeniable. The very notes written by Fr. Ioann the Stranger, who warned about the real intention of the regime which wanted to undermine the religious dimension in the souls of believers, bear witness to this. This is demonstrated by Sandu Tudor's concern to take particular care of the group of young people, a concern that he was ever mindful of until the end, so much so that he outlined an actual training program for those who intended to enter monastic life, which he saw as the only significant bastion for the very survival of faith and culture in Romania.

What is certain, however, is the non-participation in any political movement opposed to the regime, partly because resistance to the regime would have entailed violence, something for which Sandu Tudor had always reproached the legionary groups and from which he had always distanced himself, despite a certain affinity of thought. The accusations of his

[47] Cf. Anca Manolescu, *Modelul Antim, modelul Păltiniș. Cercuri de studiu și prietenie spirituală*, 111. See also Mironescu's commentary on Constantin Noica's essay, *Pagini despre sufletul românesc* (1944) in Alexandru Mironescu, *Calea inimii. Eseuri în duhul Rugului Aprins* (Bucharest: Anastasia, 1998), 135–54.

[48] See the question in Anca Manolescu, *Modelul Antim, modelul Păltiniș. Cercuri de studiu și prietenie spirituală*, 214–18.

belonging to the Legionaires brought against him by the *Securitate* in the various trials and especially in that of 1958 with the condemnation of the entire Antim group, are false and totally fabricated. The point is exactly this. Antim's approach enhances the spiritual dimension of consciences, and believes in the radiance and strength of religious commitment for the purification of hearts, keeping cultural commitment high in the ecclesial context together with the principle of the holiness of life, a holiness of life beyond any devotional and conformist patterning, beyond daily banality, the purview of which is accessed by prayer and, in particular, the prayer of the heart. This seems to me the true legacy of Antim, which I would now like to reflect upon.

The Prayer of the Heart[1]

> ...the Spirit comes to the aid of our weakness,
> because we do not know how to pray properly,
> but the Spirit himself prays in us
> with inexpressible groanings.
>
> (Rom 8:26)

In the book of Zohar we read this mysterious prediction:

> In messianic times God will build Jerusalem: God himself will build it. The first and second temples will be erected together: the first will be the mysterious, hidden temple located in highest heaven and the second temple, which will also be the work of God, will be visible to all. The city of Jerusalem itself is not yet built, as it is said: 'I myself—declares the Lord—will be to her a wall of fire round about...and I will be a glory within her' (Zech. 2:5). All this should have been accomplished at the time of the first Liberation, but it will not be accomplished until the end of days. As regards the sufferings of Israel, it is certain that Israel is the heart and that all the other peoples constitute the other members of the body. Like the body it cannot exist for a single moment without the heart, so the world cannot exist without Israel. Now, the heart is the most sensitive of all the limbs, the slightest suffering rebounds on it much more than on the other limbs. This is why Israel seems more tormented than all other peoples.[2]

---

[1] Among the multitude of notes that Fr. Daniil wrote on loose, unorganized sheets of paper, we find many of his reflections on prayer, particularly on what he calls 'sanctified prayer,' that is, the prayer to which one dedicates oneself by engaging in incessant repetition. Alexandru Dimcea took the trouble to collect and publish these manuscripts, left directly by Fr. Daniel with Fr. Niculae M. Popescu and other friends and subsequently placed in the Library of the Holy Synod at Bucharest. Four notebooks have been published so far: 1, *On the love of God*; 2, *On prayer*; 3, *On the mystery of the cross*; 4, *On Man*. I will particularly refer to the second notebook on sanctified prayer, republished with additions in 2008 (1st ed., 2000). The quotation in the epigraph is a passage from St. Paul according to the Romanian version cited by Sandu Tudor. It is from these texts that I have collected the reflections contained here.

[2] *Zohar*, III, 221a-b. The image of the heart as sky is used particularly in the Hasidic tradition. This saying is reported among the Hasidim: "This is how Rabbi Hanokh interpreted the words in the Scriptures: '...and the mountain burned with fire unto the heart of heaven' (Deut 4:11): 'The fire of Sinai burned

It seems to me that this prediction comes true in the heart of the one who prays, in the heart of the one who has chosen prayer as an interior occupation, in the heart of the one who with prayer has arrived at the king's chamber, where man finds all the splendor of his dignity. The hesychast tradition would say: with the mind in the heart. The completely original aspect of the experience of the Burning Bush movement is shown by the fact that its members came to share the contemplative breath of the great tradition of the church and to express the sense of the Christian vocation in history by following new paths and using new languages, in response to the expectations and questions of people today. They managed to highlight the secrets of the Fathers because they did not take anything for granted. They did not simply repeat what they read, but they used what they read to interpret and guide what they experienced. Not only that, but they managed to situate what they personally experienced within what is usually called a "conciliarity," an "ecclesiality" of being that the liturgy of the church exalts in its rites. As for prayer, I chose to basically follow the spiritual path of the leader of the Burning Bush, Sandu Tudor, who in everyone's eyes appeared to be the main inspirer of the movement. I have tried to grasp more the underlying dynamics than the detail of his teaching, more the elaboration of his path of prayer than the recommendations for the practice of prayer. I find the creativity and modernity expressed, capable of restoring liveliness to traditions, very noble traditions, but often experienced only as devotional practices.

Quoting St. Augustine: "How, then, do I seek You, O Lord? For when I seek You, my God, I seek a happy life,"[3] Sandu Tudor thinks of prayer as an expression of a yearning for a higher, richer life, as a powerful desire for life and for a more powerful, purer, more precious, happier life. He recalls the absoluteness of Jesus's statement: "I am the way, the truth and the life. No one comes to the Father except through me" (John 14:6). And he interprets this as Jesus saying: through me you do not simply come to God, but to God known in all his fullness, as far as is possible for man. God can be known

into the core of men until it made them a heavenly heart'" in Martin Buber, *Tales of the Hasidim*, trans. O. Marx (New York: Schocken Books, 1947 & 1975), 717.

[3] St. Augustine, *Confessions*, 10.20.

in nature, outside of us, in a thousand ways, but nature does not provide the certainty of holiness, nor of justice, nor of the love of God. It does not have the possibility of knowing him in truth, of discovering him as Father. I can come to know God through my consciousness, but it cannot give me the certainty or knowledge of the infinite love of God who is the Father. Only through Christ and his grace do I come to the full and unshakable, living discovery of God who is the Father, I come to live the same divine life which is the splendor of love through Him and in Him. One might even ask: is prayer part of this world? And he replies: as it helps me to survive down here, not to despair, to find solutions in every circumstance, certainly. But prayer is a discipline of advanced knowledge, because it does not refer only to this world. It is a discipline so vast that it cannot be fully discovered on this earth.

The scope of meaning for the practice of prayer therefore consists in the experience of incessant prayer of the mind in the heart elevating one to the dignity of union with God without mediation. With prayer man rediscovers the splendor of his dignity. It is the underlying longing that moves the heart to burn without burning out, to burn in a divine way, making use of every little motivation or moment of life. And here we come to the first, fundamental, statement on prayer shared by the Burning Bush movement: prayer is a means to knowledge, the most perfect means because it leads us to knowledge "face to face," to knowledge par excellence. This is prayer as ontological knowledge of the world, knowledge as the Lord says: "in spirit and truth"! However, this is about spiritual knowledge, knowledge understood as a co-birth, a birth in one another, a birth in a communion, a synodality (sobornicity). It is just such knowledge that is our divino-creaturely seal.[4]

[4] In this I see the similarity with a feature of Constantin Noica's thought who defines his search in this way: "I felt invested with the responsibility of consecrating myself. My doctoral thesis, *How something new is possible*, is what lies at the heart of the historical part of 'open concepts' and of the problem to which I have dedicated myself all my life, to the *intru*." See Gabriel Liiceanu, *Le journal de Paltinis, 1977–1981. Récit d'une formation spirituelle et philosophique* (Paris: La Découverte, 1999), ePub edition 2013, pos. 320 of 4288. *Intru* is an untranslatable Romanian preposition that expresses a dynamic interiority whose meaning is similar to the English "into" and which can be rendered with "in and towards." The dynamic value of thinking, always open to the new, remains underscored.

Sandu Tudor does not talk about prayer in general. He speaks of "sanctified prayer," the incessant prayer of the heart. It is a characteristic expression found quite often in his *Sfințita Rugăciune* writings. Not simply "holy prayer," but prayer which has risen to the state of purity of the heart which pours itself out before its Lord, enjoying his forgiving love. In the Canon of Prayer that he wrote in 1952 in Sihăstria, Moldavia, after being consecrated as a monk of the great habit with the name of Daniil and dedicated to his friends of the heart, Fr. Benedict Ghiuș, Fr. Sofian Boghiu, Fr. Petroniu Tănase and the young André Scrima, he beseeches:

> "Cover me, O Good and Holy One, in the meek shadow of the Spirit, with that divine knowledge, with that unblemished, elevated feeling, with that luminous and abundant spiritual reconciliation, in which, like very clear crystals, in full transparency, the creatures of all the worlds shine again, as within a clear atmosphere, gathered together within me."

And a little further:

> "Edify me in the dignity of the vision of your wonders, those which obtain for us forgiveness and transfiguration and healing from every evil, so that, wide-open, my healed eyes, with all joy, might dare to behold the glory of thy Face, to see it as a reflection of your mercy."[5]

It is extraordinary to approach prayer with an understanding of its most characteristic and powerful movement: humility, which prayer of the heart demands and achieves to the highest degree. Humility, which concerns the whole of man's being in his freedom to know, feel and act. An apotheosis of humility, capable of introducing integral, organic, living thinking. The internal structure of prayer grows and is based on the Trinitarian faith, on the unification of spiritual knowing, spiritual feeling, and spiritual action in a transfigured heart. First the humility of the mind, which opens itself to welcoming the revelation of the Holy Trinity, not simply as a dogmatic fact, but as the real and living fact that structures one's heart in its longings and nostalgias. Then, the humility of feeling, of sentiment, which opens to the sensation of the real and immediate

[5] Daniil de la Rarău, *Sfințita Rugăciune, Caietele 2* (Bucharest: Editura Christiana, 2008), 195–96.

presence of God as a personal experience of the mystery of the Incarnation and the Eucharist. Finally, the humility of the work at hand, which concerns the purification of the will in its desire for communion with God, beyond any selfish and worldly interest. It is the creative struggle of prayer, beyond any psychological process, when tears will introduce us to the life of God that begins to burn in the heart of man.

At the Antim meetings the question of the relationship between faith and knowledge was often reflected upon. Christian gnosis, true gnosis, was often discussed. Salvation has to do with knowledge, but a prayerful knowledge, an experiential knowledge.[6] In the early centuries, faith was a path to lofty knowledge, according to the experience that adherence to the Truth is the way by which Christ saves us. And he, the Truth, in approaching which man is reshaped, rediscovers his dignity, grows in capacity for vision and familiarity with the same living Truth which is his person. Now, the revelation of the Truth, which is Jesus, belongs to the Father and to know Jesus is to enter into the relationship that binds the Son to the Father. Man is called to participate in this relationship by grace. This is the mystery of prayer. For this reason, when in the Christian experience we talk about knowledge, we always mean a knowledge capable of introducing us into divine life or, better, capable of welcoming into ourselves divine life activated by the Spirit. Sandu Tudor speaks of creative knowledge, of knowing in a living, creative way, as of a perennial birth from above. Jesus says: "Truly, truly, I say to you, unless one is born of water and the Spirit, he cannot enter the kingdom of God. That which is born of the flesh is flesh, and that which is born of the Spirit is spirit. Do not be surprised if I told you: you must be born from above. The wind blows where it wants and you hear its voice, but you do not know where it comes from or where it is going: so is everyone who is born of the Spirit" (John 3:5–8). Living knowledge is in fact man's divine privilege, and the fulfillment of our ability to create.[7]

[6] The question is well focused in Anca Manolescu's study, *Modelul Antim, modelul Păltiniș. Cercuri de studiu și prietenie spirituală*, 257–90.

[7] Vasile Voiculescu expresses the same perception in his poetic compositions, in symbiosis with the intensity of his prayer. For him prayer is the "angelic space" in which man becomes himself. The man, who "imagines having

Starting from these considerations, Sandu Tudor asks himself two essential questions: what does it really mean to create? Is modern man capable of praying? To the first question he responded with a quote from Rainer Maria Rilke, taken from *Letters to a Young Poet.* He quotes from memory the passage in which Rilke invites the young writer, who had sent him one of his compositions for an opinion, to treat everything that passes through his heart as material for poetic creation because creating means first of all creating oneself.[8] Prayer puts our creative power into action. But is modern man still capable of such an attitude? Sandu Tudor specifies: modern man has lost his poetic, lyrical capacity, so he is unfit to decipher the world in a symbolic key, closed as he is in a functional and abstract

---

discovered prayer, the only living being in the world who prays," realizes that in fact "the definition of this man would not be *homo politicus*, or *homo faber*, but *homo adorans*. Prayer is a universal and eternal act.... Whoever has touched God finds the whole world within himself.... Prayer becomes another existence. A new, superior being is created in us, in which substance and essence become identified, contradictions dissolve, birth and death fall away; immutable, permanence remains: eternal truth, infinite love, incessant beauty. Seeing and feeling the world like this means seeing God face to face." See Gheorghe Ionascu, "Vasile Voiculescu, il poeta della preghiera," chap. 3 in *Il Roveto ardente* (Viterbo: Tagete, 2008).

[8] Here is the original passage: "If your daily life seems poor, do not blame it; blame yourself, tell yourself that you are not poet enough to call forth its riches; for to the creator there is no poverty and no poor indifferent place. And even if you were in some prison the walls of which let none of the sounds of the world come to your senses—would you not then still have your childhood, that precious, kingly possession, that treasure-house of memories? Turn your attention thither. Try to raise the submerged sensations of that ample past; your personality will grow more firm, your solitude will widen and will become a dusky dwelling past which the noise of others goes by far away. And if out of this turning inward, out of this absorption into your own world verses come, then it will not occur to you to ask anyone whether they are good verses. Nor will you try to interest magazines in your poems: for you will see in them your fond natural possession, a fragment and a voice of your life. A work of art is good if it has sprung from necessity. In this nature of its origin lies the judgment of it: there is no other. Therefore, my dear sir, I know no advice for you save this: to go into yourself and test the deeps in which your life takes rise; at its source you will find the answer to the question whether you must create. Accept it, just as it sounds, without inquiring into it. Perhaps it will tum out that you are called to be an artist. Then take that destiny upon yourself and bear it, its burden and its greatness, without ever asking what recompense might come from outside. For the creator must be a world for himself and find everything in himself and in Nature to whom he has attached himself." *Letters to a Young Poet*, rev. ed., trans. M. D. H. Norton (New York & London: W. W. Norton, 1954), 19–21.

rationality that has dried him up. Modern man completely ignores the reality of the ineffable, he rejects it in the very organization of his inner world. Consequently, since prayer is an infinite recognition of the Ineffable, indeed, the knowledge of the Ineffable beyond one's natural capabilities, modern man cannot enter into prayer without totally renouncing himself, without accepting to pass through this regenerating death in the Spirit. There is no direct path to God for modern man. We must let death bury death and be reborn to the vital senses of prayer. In essence, Tudor invites us to recognize this: we have lost contact with the vital energies of the heart, so much so that knowledge for us always refers to a secondary product, to abstract knowledge. In other words, the lyrical sense of truth has been lost. We no longer know what prayer is because we no longer know poetry, we no longer know that praise, that singing, which is the absolute recognition of the truth. Modern man distrusts lyricism, considers it deceptive. He has lost the doxological sense of knowledge, he no longer knows the true "orthodoxy" that is a great doxology, a just giving of glory, a song of gratitude. And without the rediscovery of the truth contained in the poetry of life it will be impossible to discover what it means to pray and how one should pray.

Tudor is passionate about the topic. He asks himself: where does the difficulty in praying come from for modern people? He himself, like all his literary colleagues, scientists and artists in the group, experienced this difficulty. He argues like this: if a modern person is faced with the question of what is the origin of the prayer of the heart, he cannot help but be disappointed by the answer of the ancient Fathers. And the same happens when faced with the symbolic logic of the patristic interpretation of the Gospels. Modern people move with a historical mentality, they seek causes and effects, they want to be honest about the facts, they investigate the evolution in the formation of texts, they specify, define, contextualize. For example, if we ask ourselves: is there a beginning for hesychast prayer? Can we trace who first practiced it? Tradition surprisingly responds: the prayer of the heart is the prayer of Adam in the earthly paradise before sin; it is the prayer of the Mother of God introduced into the Holy of Holies when she was a small child; it is the prayer experienced by the disciples on Tabor at the transfiguration of Jesus; it is the prayer that came from the hearts of the apostles when the risen Jesus breathed on them his creating Spirit. But are we, accustomed to an abstract way of reasoning, still capable of truly understanding the work of the Spirit, of understanding Christianity according to the faith of our Fathers?[9] In response, Sandu Tudor relates an extraordinary passage from Theognostus, an unknown philokalic author of the thirteenth century:

> I shall tell you something strange at which you are not to be startled. A mystery is accomplished secretly between the soul and God in the higher reaches of perfect purity, love and faith. When a man is completely reconciled to God he is united with Him through unceasing prayer and contemplation. Such was Elijah's state when he closed the heavens, causing a drought [cf. 1 Kgs. 17:1], and burnt the sacrifice with fire from heaven [cf. 1 Kgs. 18:36–38]. In such a state Moses divided the sea [cf. Exod. 14:21] and defeated Amalek by stretching out his arms [cf. Exod. 17:11–13]. In such a state Jonah was saved from the whale and from the deep (cf. Jonah 2:1–10). For the person found worthy of this mystery compels our most compassionate God to do whatever he wants. Even when still in the flesh, he has passed beyond the limits of corruption and mortality, and he awaits death as if it were an everyday sleep that pleasurably brings him to the fulfillment of his hopes.

The passage recalls this other one:

> I shall tell you something strange, but do not be surprised by it. Should you fail to attain dispassion because of the predispositions dominating you, but at the time of your death be in the depths of humility, you will be exalted above the clouds no less than the man who is dispassionate. For even if the treasure of those who are dispassionate consists of every virtue, the precious stone of humility is more valuable than them all: it brings about not only propitiation with the

[9] There is an expression in the letter to the Hebrews that is very illuminating. Believers in Christ are defined as those who, having been baptized and having approached the Eucharistic table, are made participants in the Holy Spirit who opens hearts to the understanding of the scriptures and welcome the Kingdom that comes: "Those, in fact, who having once been enlightened and having tasted the heavenly gift, have become partakers of the Holy Spirit and have tasted the good word of God and the wonders of the world to come" (Hebrews 6:4–5). The Greek term δυνάμεις does not only mean "wonders" but also alludes to the "energies," to the power of the coming Kingdom. It is the dimension that is lacking in the Christian experience of modern people.

> Creator, but also entry with the elect into the bridal chamber of His kingdom.[10]

The powerful logic of the Fathers' understanding of the mystery of the revelation of Jesus, which in prayer becomes accessible to the soul, is illustrated with one of those flashes of insight now and again displayed by Tudor.[11] On the principle that everything found in scripture is for the transfiguration of daily life into a divine life, it combines the great moments of the life of Jesus with the life of each one of us in order to rediscover the daily value of the Transfiguration, on the path to the transformation and fulfillment of our being. He considers the eight great moments of the Savior's life: annunciation, birth, baptism, transfiguration, crucifixion, resurrection, ascension, and descent of the Holy Spirit. This is the octave of the mystery of God's humility for our salvation. By superimposing the first four moments on the other four, a perfect polar correspondence is obtained which illuminates the mystery of our salvation: the annunciation corresponds to the crucifixion, birth to the resurrection, baptism to the ascension, and the transfiguration to the descent of the Holy Spirit. It is the mystery of the cross that constitutes the angel's announcement; it is the resurrection that allows us to be reborn from above; it is the ascension to heaven that reveals the adoption as sons by introducing us into the kingdom; it is the descent of the Holy Spirit that allows us to transfigure ourselves in the divine light. These are all steps that define the mystery of prayer, which cannot help but tend to become incessant prayer through a daily existence in grace. For man this involves sharing, as far as possible, the same aptness for enlightenment as the humanity of Jesus, sharing in the sensation of the light of God's holiness which is the radiance of love for all. A sign of this is a joy in afflictions suffered for Christ according to the words of Jesus in the Gospel: "These things I have spoken to you, that my joy may be in you, and that your joy may be full" (John 15:11). Evidently, this is not a question of trying

---

[10] Theognostus, *On the Practice of the Virtues, Contemplation and the Priesthood*, nos. 69 and 62, *Philokalia*, vol. 2, 375 and 373. See the critical edition of his work in Antonio Rigo, ed., *Da Teognosto alla Filocalia (XIII-XVIII secolo). Testi e autori* (Bari: Edizioni di Pagina, 2016), 99–162.

[11] Cf. Daniil de la Rarău, *Sinfita Rugaciune*, 138.

to understand what Jesus did, but of accessing what Jesus achieved for us. This is Tudor's response.

And when the discussion directly concerns the prayer of the heart or the prayer of Jesus, Tudor asks himself: what can we say we know? Very little, if we rely on written testimonies. If there are no saints to show us through their holy way of life, it is difficult to access it. It does not do much to want to know with your head. In this sense Tudor, who had explored the libraries of many monasteries, who had rediscovered the richness of a once lively tradition, who had cherished the desire for prayer for many years before taking it on as a reason for living, knew that he lived in difficult times, due as well to the lack of experienced guides in the church. All that remained, as he said, was to "follow the trail of the lost gold." This does not simply mean: let us go back to the texts of tradition, but: let us go back to sharing the dynamics of the understanding of the Fathers expressed in those texts. This seems to me to be precisely the answer to the difficulty of modern people in living the faith and dedicating themselves to prayer. And when he finds himself before the figure of a man who presents himself as a living embodiment of the teachings of the Fathers, Fr. Ioann the Stranger, we understand all of Tudor's amazement and his full surrender to that teaching.

PRAYER AND ITS PARADOXES

I believe that the best way to grasp the depth of the experience of prayer of the heart is to approach it through the evident paradoxes that it entails and that Sandu Tudor highlights. First of all, regarding the method, the technique.

a) The Method of Prayer

—*A prayer very simple to perform, very complicated to carry out.* Despite what numerous hesychast texts, especially medieval ones, say—that one can learn the prayer of Jesus easily and above all that it quickly bears fruit—prayer instead requires infinite patience, continuous interior violence, precise discipline.[12] And why? Because man has lost with sin and the consequent

[12] See my talk "La preghiera e la pratica della preghiera. A proposito di alcuni autori esicasti minori," in *L'Athos e l'esicasmo*, ed. Antonio Manzella (Firenza: Nerbini, 2016), 59–82.

expulsion from paradise that which was Adam's very own activity in paradise, namely, pure prayer, that is, he has lost the joy of self-control in the heart. Thoughts and desires naturally move everywhere except towards God, and to bring them back to the Lord requires a great effort, a long and painful struggle. In essence—here is another paradox—the violence that man exercises on himself—"the kingdom of heaven suffers violence and the violent take it by force" (Matt. 11:12)—has as its aim victory over every form of violence that stirs in the divided heart. That violence is aimed at obtaining rest from every other form of violence that generated sin, that violence which makes us use everything and everyone for our glory. This is where all the agitation that torments and upsets us comes from. Only in this way can we obtain what the Fathers call *hesychia* of the heart, where the peace achieved is accompanied by the dynamics of a love that no longer has impediments. I would add this comment: it is not a quiet peace, it is a paradoxical and effervescent peace, experienced as an anguish of love for all, so that everyone finally might know the love of God and God is exalted by all as the Father of mercies. As for Jesus: "I have come to cast fire on the earth, and would that it were already kindled! I have a baptism to be baptized with; and how I am constrained until it is accomplished!" (Luke 12:49–50).

—*A monotonous, yet spontaneous prayer.* A repetitive, yet superabundant prayer. If it is true that a word repeated out of habit is empty, it is not always true that a habit only expresses emptiness. The sun rises every day while I may not even get up every morning. If the sun rises regularly every morning it is because it is never tired of doing so, while, if I do not get up in the morning it is because I am tired. Tudor means that habit, the repetitiveness of the same action, is not always caused by a lack of vitality, but can derive from a superabundance of life. Never being tired of doing something means enjoying that thing constantly. The example of children and liturgical prayer is very expressive. When the child listens to a story that he likes, he will always like to hear it told and always in the same way, without variations. Whenever something done pleases him, he will repeatedly insist: again, again![13] In

[13] The same observation is valid in the Jewish tradition too. A Hasidic saying tells us: "Said the maggid to Rabbi Zusya, his disciple: 'I cannot teach you

the Eucharistic liturgy the deacon invites us several times: again and again let us pray to the Lord! Repetition then is full of life, it is superabundant with life. However, we get there step by step. And the absolutely original thing, which an experience of long practice reveals, is the observation that the passage from an oppressive habit to a vital habit occurs as if by an explosion, in a prophetic way. Without revelation there is no prayer. And the same crisis, due to fatigue from the sense of formalism and uselessness that assails a person praying, demands a qualitative leap. However, this is not an epilogue as a result of the tenacity of effort, but a beginning. Childish repetitiveness is abandoned to access another stage of childhood, the spiritual one, where spontaneity wells up with vitality. The paradox lies in the fact that, once again, on a much deeper level, prayer becomes the perception of an acute feeling of fragility and dependence and, at the same time, the discovery of an inexhaustible source of life. It is not for nothing that the Gospel tells us: "Truly I say to you, unless you turn and become like children, you will never enter the kingdom of heaven. Whoever makes himself as small as this child, he is the greatest in the kingdom of heaven" (Matt. 18:3–4).[14] And this is because, beyond the words, the heart feels the presence that radiates from the Name invoked, the heart warms. It activates what Tudor calls the "cherubic wheel" which bears us upwards. The pall of the monotony of words is broken to reveal, as if enclosed therein, the permanent fire of holiness and love, all the more ardent, the words remain ever the same, without the soul ever feeling a need to change them. The starting point, however, always remains that of feeling the lack of, the hunger and thirst for God. Those who have not suffered this hunger and thirst will never be able to pray with ardor.

—*Prayer has its technique, but the technique alone is unable to give rise to prayer.* Stated more generally, this is the problem of

---

the ten principles of service [to God]. But a little child and a thief can show you what they are. From the child you can learn three things: He is merry for no particular reason; never for a moment is he idle; when he needs something, he demands it vigorously'"; in Martin Buber, *Tales of the Hasidim,* 134.

[14] Tudor does not point this out, but this is all the more true if we translate the Gospel text literally. The verb translated as "to make oneself small," literally means "humiliate oneself." And this is much more in tune with spiritual childhood, with the experience of prayer of the heart.

asceticism in spiritual life: it is absolutely necessary, without in itself ensuring good fruit. Tudor coins his own terminology to make it clear that any type of effort in prayer, regularity, use of the body or discipline of the mind, if it does not participate in the mystery of the cross, does not produce any spiritual fruit. Remembering the motto of the Carthusian order "*stat crux dum volvitur orbis*" ("The cross stays fixed while the world turns"), he places the mystery of the cross as a symbolic understanding of the entire spiritual journey and of prayer itself. Everything is conceived in "crucial" terms. The oppositions that man is continually registering in his life (body and soul, freedom and grace, asceticism and prayer, self-denial and spiritual realization, etc.) must be experienced at the point of intersection of the two terms in the manner of a cross. For example, he takes up the invitation that Jesus makes to the three disciples in Gethsemane: "Watch and pray, so as not to enter into temptation. The spirit is willing, but the flesh is weak" (Matt. 26:41). Between vigil and prayer there is a fundamental antithesis, a "crucial" contrast. Vigil and prayer must go together perfectly to bear the fruit of the victorious cross of a continuous resurrection. Only in this mysterious agreement can asceticism, which is our vigilance, our deep interior attention, be beneficial to us, can it bear fruit. Asceticism for asceticism's sake is not a savior; only spiritual asceticism, spiritually rich asceticism, pneumatic asceticism. *Pneumatic* is a term often used by Tudor: pneumatic asceticism, pneumatic freedom, pneumatic science, pneumatic style, pneumatic struggle. Not to mention pneumatic metapsychology. This is because a real dictatorship can be exercised over prayer starting from our freedom or our will, preventing prayer from blossoming in the heart.[15] The sobriety about which the Fathers speak is not simply the attention of the mind, but a spiritual lucidity, the opposite of what a drunk experiences who cannot distinguish anything clearly and staggers on the street. The pneumatic dimension of ascetic commitment and of every corporal or mental technique for entering into prayer is what allows us to enjoy its fruits. It is a victory over oneself to the point of interior transparency in the awareness of the

[15] In this regard, Tudor criticizes the Ignatian method of spiritual exercises, without actually knowing its spiritual strength, thinking of it only as a sort of meditative activity, however intense.

work of grace, when our effort moves in synergy with the power of the Spirit in a continuous going beyond ourselves, to the point of living in full communion with God. The direction of movement is important in this process. It goes from the center to the surface and not from the surface to the center. In other words, what matters is to activate the inner man so that the outer man moves within his orbit. When Tudor talks about the "pneumatic" he alludes to this internal movement. It would be the meaning of purifying thoughts and not simply actions, of reaching the roots of the heart and not simply avoiding evil, of opening oneself to the love of God and not simply striving for the heavenly prize, touching the kingdom and not simply conquering virtue. What the Paschal liturgy sings: "he conquered death by death."

The most precise statement that justifies his explanation is reported as the basis of all hesychast theology that no true ascetic can ignore as to the foundation of spiritual longing: "In this lies love: not as though we loved God, but that he loved us" along with the following: "and sent his Son to be the expiation for our sins. Beloved, if God so loved us, we also ought to love one another. No one has ever seen God; if we love one another, God abides in us and his love is perfected in us. By this we know that we abide in him and he in us, because he has given us of his own Spirit" (1 John 4:10–13). The "pneumatic" disposition is the one that inaugurates every effort, every commitment, every longing for the experience of that love, with prayer the ideal tool to give us access to that experience. That experience blossoms from the secret and mysterious depths of our being and all our desire is aimed at letting ourselves be touched by it, at knowing it and following it to enjoy its fruits. So much so that all the teaching of the Hesychast Fathers resolves itself into affording us a wondrous and pure encounter with that love.

b) The Mystery of Prayer

With respect to the very nature of prayer, to the mystery it entails, we have understood how the emphasis is placed entirely on humility. Reading Tudor's writings on the prayer of the heart, on the prayer of Jesus, we could interpret them based on this question: why did the tradition of the Eastern Churches give preference to this very simple and complex prayer? What did our Fathers see in celebrating and practicing it with such assiduity over the centuries, even though there have always been few who have been able to live and teach it in the fullness of its mystery?

I could reduce the basic observations to three, which are also paradoxical:

1) The place of the heart and self-denial. The first paradox is that of the underlying internal dynamics. Prayer is the most personal thing there is and, at the same time, the most common. Tudor even speaks of one becoming a stranger, a foreigner (he uses the same term by which Father Ioann Kulygin is called, "the Stranger"). For man, it is at once both a movement of singularization and universalization. Entering the secret chamber, closing the door, collecting oneself within in our most hidden place means, in reality, obtaining the opposite: by placing ourselves in the center (in the spiritual terminology "center," "depths," and "secret place" refer to the same reality), prayer finds itself placed at the most open point of man, before God and the world. It is man's essentially open point to reality, beyond any boundary imposed from without, what we call the heart.[16] For Tudor it is the spiritual center, man's heart of grace, invisible and free from sin. It is the supernatural heart of man, his holy place or, as we often like to say in philosophical language, the ontological place or, said even better, without confusing the spiritual order with the abstract dimension, the pneumatic place, the place through which we enter into the spiritual world, the place or altar of the Holy Spirit.

Evidently, the condition for arriving at this encroachment which simultaneously extends to the divine and the human is the free consent to self-denial, to the denial of the old man, to the abandonment of the worldly to take on the spiritual. It is with sin that man has confined himself to himself, separating himself from God and the world, and by which he is

[16] The heart is not simply the most interior or deepest point of the person, but an open border, the place for the encounter with the Other, the open point of our psychic structure. This is the interpretation of the Orthodox tradition by the Russian poet Olga Sedakova, "The Light of Life. Some Remarks on the Russian Orthodox Perception," in *La Nuova Europa* 2 (2009), 23–41 [Eng. trans. online: https://www.olgasedakova.com › eng].

as if closed off to the truth. Entering the crucial dimension of prayer means rediscovering the freedom of being from any marginalization. In this sense the problem of true prayer is the union of the mind and the heart. Stated more specifically, it is the humility of a mind brought to the center of our being, to the holiest place, where enlightenment flows from the adoring invocation of the Lord's Name of glory. If the whole tradition defines the path of prayer as bringing the mind into the heart, this means that it is not a question of learning to pray with the mind and the heart, but of the meeting of mind and heart. As if to say: we do not pray with the soul, with the body, nor do we pray by ourselves, but the Spirit prays in us. So much so that this movement of prayer is not temporary or occasional, however prolonged, but is incessant. As tradition emphasizes: learning to pray means doing without prayer. We only know how to pray imperfectly, according to certain times and in a certain space; we in fact do not know how to pray. This is why the great effort of prayer is to let the Spirit pray in us as in a perennial liturgy of praise: with the mind as a celebrant worthy of its service and the heart as the most pure altar. The dignity of the mind and the purity of the altar refer to the victory over thoughts and passions; to withdraw from the world and open oneself to God is to see and offer the world in the light of God's holiness. If I may comment in my own words, I would add that the remarkable aspect of this teaching is typically evangelical. Self-denial, self-disavowal is not a renunciatory act, but a creative one. It is not simply a matter of taking something away, but of allowing something to blossom, to come to light. The purity that the Fathers speak of does not have to do with a subtraction, with a purification, but with a renewed vitality, with a full life, with a return to the vital roots of the heart where man returns to the powerful sensation of love of God who surpasses everything and brings everything together. Here St. Francis of Assisi and St. Isaac the Syrian should be our unsurpassed teachers.

2) Repentance is the most radical path to charity. This second observation arises directly from the first. And it answers the question: Can our effort really procure that dignity of mind and purity of heart that make us capable of God's love? This is a process, which Tudor calls "spiritualization," whereby praying means learning to spiritualize oneself, that is, to live life entirely in the light of the Spirit. What allows us to return to living in the splendor of creation made in the image and likeness of God and move in the light of the Spirit? The unanimous response of tradition, condensed in fidelity to the practice of Jesus's prayer over the centuries, is only one: repentance. As I recalled above regarding the text of Basil of Poiana Mărului, to which Sandu Tudor often refers, it is continuous repentance in waiting for God's mercy, being submissive to everyone, which constitutes the soil from which continuous prayer of the heart blossoms. The truer the awareness of our being sinners before God, the more burning the repentance becomes and the more lively the love for God and others. In reality, it is not our efforts that overcome evil; it is the strength of repentance that burns our passions and every evil thought. Just as Abba Sisoes repeated:

> A brother said to Abba Sisoes, "I am aware that the remembrance of God stays with me." The old man said to him, "It is no great thing to be with God in your thoughts, but it is a great thing to see yourself as inferior to all creatures. It is this, coupled with hard work, that leads to humility."[17]

To this should be added another saying:

> Abba Agathon said, "If I could meet a leper, give him my body and take his, I should be very happy." That indeed is perfect charity.[18]

What repentance achieves, since it makes everyone stand lower without claiming anything for themselves, is the condition for experiencing total solidarity with the humanity of all. In other words, it situates us where the experience of God's love is lived in full solidarity with everyone. Here we have the realization of the universal Church, of ecumenical communion—as Tudor calls it—of the union and unity of all in Christ. The tension of prayer then becomes that of broadening the field of intercession more and more, to perceive in a real way and to concretely assist other people, our fellow human beings, in their suffering. It becomes the prayer of knowing love. Our prayers will no longer be just words. In them the love

[17] *The Sayings of the Desert Fathers, Alphabetical Collection* (Sisoes 13), 214.
[18] Ibid. (Agathon, 26), 24.

of Christ will be felt, no longer hindered by anything within us. Continuous, ardent, supplicating repentance will ensure the passage from the secret depths of the heart to the totality of life. Love welcomes and esteems man as man, as he is, with the lights and shadows that characterize him, it surrounds him in its warm embrace of light and joy, as he is, in his good and bad traits. He does not want it from the beginning as should be the case, but starting from who he is, it urges him higher. Love does not love sin and wickedness, but loves the person in man, who is our neighbor, who is the very image and likeness of God in us. It is the supreme victory against individualism. The prayer of Jesus leads the person who practices it to live as capable of communion with everyone and everything, as a realized Church.

3) The ascent is a descent. The sole hesychast technique of prayer can be summarized in the principle of the incarnation. Only those who go down can go up. This is the explanation of the movement we have explained in the previous point. Man, who is dispersed externally in his senses, divided within himself and contradictory in his tensions, entrenched in the affirmation of himself towards others, cannot reach unity unless he descends. Here, Christ's example is being followed exactly, he who, with the incarnation, lowered himself and then ascended the cross, in reality descending to the point of losing every figure of beauty, handed over to men who did whatever they wanted with him, but thus making God's love for men shine, in the most absolute intimacy with the Father and the Holy Spirit. The movement of descending alludes to the realization of man as a being of communion, rediscovering the similarity with God as a spiritual man, in antithesis to the unconditional search for himself which instead characterizes carnal man. The "descent" presupposes that man can place himself where the love of God can shine in all its brightness and the Spirit can act in all his unitive power. It is perhaps the least explainable paradox of man's spiritual journey, which instead always aspires to go higher, to ascend. One of the most recurring and lucid thoughts in Sandu Tudor's texts is precisely the idea of prayer as a descent into the mystery of humanity, down into the recesses of the heart where evil lurks and acts deviously, and yet to find there, having cast aside every pretense and justification, the sources of holiness, which is Christ in ourselves. For this reason, like all tradition, he speaks of the energies of baptism that are activated and allowed to flourish. In practice, prayer is only a means, a ladder, so that we can become worthy again of expressing that holiness that already lives within us. Sometimes Tudor uses the image of the secret angel who is released within us, alluding to the ancient conception that men, as we ask in the Lord's Prayer, become on earth like the angels in heaven, that is, that the kingdom of God shines in men vanquished by communion with their God and with all humanity. The access door through which the mind can descend into the heart is given by tears, by crying over oneself as Evagrius says, whose chapters on prayer Tudor translated in 1946: "First pray for the gift of tears, so that through sorrowing you may tame what is savage in your soul. And having confessed your transgressions to the Lord, you will obtain forgiveness from Him."[19] This is the door that must constantly remain open.

THE MYSTERY OF PRAYER IN REFERENCE TO TRADITION

The approach of Tudor's thought stands out in all its freshness if one keeps in mind its four fundamental references: the prayer of the Our Father, the Beatitudes, the priestly prayer of Jesus, and the prayer of St. Ephrem. On the basis of this absolute principle: prayer arises from prayer. And he refers to the Gospels where he notes how they never tell us how to pray; there is no presentation of a method of prayer. Only in the Gospel of Luke is there a hint of a teaching when Jesus utters the Our Father prayer (Luke 11:1–4). The Lord, who was emerging from a moment of prayer, gave the disciples only a prayer as a teaching on prayer. As in music: to learn a melody, you have to sing it, repeat it while singing it. And Tudor does not fail to underscore this: to learn prayer you must pray in sweetness and harmony. It is the fundamentally philokalic meaning of every prayer that derives from the teaching of Jesus. Thus the prayer of the Our Father is the model prayer, the source prayer, which includes everything that can be said about the method of every good prayer. The teaching on prayer occurs through prayer.

[19] *Philokalia*, vol. 1, 58, *Discourse on prayer*, no. 5. Formerly attributed to Nilus the Ascetic. Cf. Évagre le Pontique, *Chapitres sur la prière* (Paris: Cerf, 2017), 223.

But if we ask ourselves what the direct connection is between the prayer of the Our Father and the Jesus Prayer, then the comment by Maximus the Confessor comes into play, which Tudor refers to and which we spoke of in the previous chapter.[20] Only by going back from the bottom to the beginning of the Our Father prayer can we grasp the fundamental connection between being freed from evil and the confession of God as Father. All the questions of prayer are addressed to God. But just one is addressed to us, that of forgiveness. It is the only request in the Gospel narrative that is echoed in a subsequent admonition from Jesus: "For if you forgive others their sins, your Father who is in heaven will forgive you too; but if you do not forgive others, neither will your Father forgive your sins" (Matt. 6:14–15). Why so much insistence on forgiveness? Because forgiveness is the essential characteristic of Jesus's humanity in his revelation of the Father. It is the seal of his life: "Father, forgive them, for they know not what they do" (Luke 23:34). And it is his promise to those who repent: "And he said: 'Jesus, remember me when you come into your kingdom.' He answered him: 'Truly I say to you, today you will be with me in paradise'" (Luke 23:42–43).

The love of the Father is the love of mercy. If I forgive my brother it means that I have been freed from the power of evil and I can fully recognize him as a son of the same Father, like me. If I do not forgive, evil secretly works in me and I end up denying God as Father. Thus, if I acknowledge myself as a sinner, it means that I no longer have any reason to assert my own rights or to assert rights against my brother because I remain totally within the petition to be accepted into God's forgiveness, that is, within the revelation of God who is the Father. The Jesus Prayer, which favors this awareness of being a sinner, predisposes us to the discovery of the Father's face, rich in mercy, a mercy which, shared with everyone and in any instance, will provide proof of the truth of the encounter with God and of the fruitfulness of prayer itself.

The other evangelical text that Tudor connects directly to Jesus's prayer is the passage of the Beatitudes. For him the series of beatitudes constitute the stages in the development of the prayer of the heart. They are based on the principle that

[20] Supra, pp. 131–32, n. 30.

the evangelical teachings are not formulations of ideals, but spiritual paths, deduced from the humanity of Jesus who lives the mystery of union with the Father, in solidarity with us, in a complete way. His intuition on the technique of hesychast prayer which consists in a movement of incarnation is always valid: man takes on the humanity of Jesus to the point of forming a single body with him in his being moved by the Holy Spirit, to show the greatness of love of the Father for all. It is worth quoting his comment in full:

> Humble as the earth: like Jacob who sleeps on a holy place. I wait with the external senses brought back into my interior. In this attitude of recollection in the most extreme poverty of my spirit. With the most disparate thoughts as if in the middle of the night I arrive within myself, in the kingdom of heaven that is within me. Blessed are the poor in spirit.... Humility is the threshold of prayer of the heart: the condition of spiritual life. 1. Blessed are those who mourn... this is the whole question of repentance and the theology of tears without which there is no interior life nor activity of the Holy Spirit; this is the baptism of the Spirit, the second baptism. 2. Blessed are the meek... this is the problem of victory over the passions, of spiritual impassibility. Only in this way will we be able to dominate our earth, our body on its dark side. 3. Blessed are those who hunger and thirst for justice... 'justice' has been rendered by tradition as integrity, holiness. Man, when he finds himself purified within himself, desires Grace in all its forms of sharing and communion. Daily bread is twofold: after the Body and Blood of Christ, the Eucharistic communion, we have the communion or eating of the Word, of the Name of Jesus. And we will be satisfied according to the power of both. 4. Blessed are the merciful.... Communicated with spiritual gifts, it is necessary that we enter into external actions, that we act with spiritual riches, so that we too can receive mercy. Otherwise we will remain impoverished and be cast out. 5. Blessed are the pure of heart... purity is entering the deepest part of the heart. The discovery of our holy place, the place of the heart, is the discovery of the presence of the Lord in us. 6. Blessed are the peacemakers.... The peacemaker is only he who has found peace, *hesychia*, through the prayer of the heart. You cannot give peace to others if you do not have peace in yourself, if you do not have the Sabbath rest of the future age. 7. Blessed are those persecuted for righteousness' sake.... The struggle, the temptation, the adversities, the persecution that we suffer to remain in innocence and in faithfulness to our dignity, make us for eternity possessors of the Kingdom

> of Heaven, of all the heavens, of the heavens of our heart and those of the future age in the fullness of everything in God. 8. Blessed are you when they insult you.... Martyrdom, in every form, in oppression and injustice, for Christ and for His Name is the supreme blessing. It happens for those who long for Christ. In particular, we remember every outrage in which those who live in the peace of the Lord rejoice and especially who pray the Jesus Prayer, who glorify in their hearts and always invoke the glorious Name of the Lord. Beyond these eight steps of the ladder, the threshold of humility must be added as well as the closing of the beatitudes: Rejoice...this is how they persecuted the prophets who were before you. The fulfillment of the prayer of the heart exposes one to martyrdom and prophetic testimony.[21]

By way of comment, I will simply say that the less we seek glory for ourselves, the more we see the glory of God, which is love for us. Thus, at the level of our inner feelings, the more someone divests himself of himself, the more he fills himself with God, with the extraordinary consequence that, by filling himself with God, he remains absorbed in his love for everyone. At this point, the spiritual man is no longer centered on himself but acquires a capacity for "empathy," for benevolence for everything and everyone, finding himself regenerated in his deepest feelings. He has a sense of the coming kingdom of God. The most obvious consequence will be that in our neighbor, in others, we learn to recognize that same Spirit that dwells in our hearts. This recognition, which expands our consciousness, ensures that the other person acquires his own identity in our eyes, emerging with his true self and not as an artificial extension of ourselves. This is truly an exploration of the mystery of humanity as communion.

It is worth reporting a suggestion from André Chouraqui (1917–2007), the French translator of the Bible, who honors the original Hebrew version. Even in the translation of the New Testament he tries to maintain the Jewish eloquence that Jesus would have used. He translates the Greek term μακάριοι, not with *bienheureux*, an indeclinable noun in French, but with *en marche*, with the idea of evoking the righteousness of those who walk on a path that leads straight to God. He reports in a note the only parallel passage of the Old Testament, 1 Kings 10:8, when

[21] Daniil de la Rarău, *Sfințita Rugăciune*, 150–52.

the Queen of Sheba, visiting King Solomon, remains speechless before the magnificence of the sovereign and proclaims: "Blessed (*En marche*) your servants who are always in your presence and can enjoy your wisdom." It is the whole meaning of the beatitudes: being able to be in the presence of Jesus and enjoy his wisdom in walking along the paths he traces. And joy is given by the fact that when one arrives at the goal one is filled with joy.[22] But the gateway always remains the second beatitude, which in relation to the path outlined by the series of beatitudes, is the first: "Blessed are those who mourn..." The gateway to the inner man is knowing how to cry over one's sins. This is exactly what the Jesus Prayer tends to achieve for the person praying.

Another evangelical connection with the prayer of the heart is the passage from John 17 which relates the high priestly prayer of Jesus.[23] Tudor dwells on the interpretation of this text in relation to prayer, referring it to the mystery of the union between the Father and the Son in which the believer participates. He explains how the spiritual man, through love, unites with the Lord in three ways: according to his nature, according to the gifts of grace and in the fullness of glory. We can be united in a mediated way, in an immediate way, and in an indivisible way. The first way is the union that occurs with the practice of the commandments and virtues, dying to sin and every disorderly movement of nature. The second way, which is available to few, is to die completely to oneself when all one's intellectual and affective powers are reunited in God and moved by him for holy action. The third way is when man becomes one spirit with the Lord, one with him. Jesus's priestly prayer is interwoven with three questions/promises: he asks that we be united with him (John 17:24: "Father, I desire that they also, whom thou hast given me, may be with me where I am, to behold my glory, which thou hast given me in thy love for me before the foundation of the world"); he asks that we be united among ourselves and that all of us are united with him (John 17:21: "that they may all be one; even as thou, Father, are in me and I in thee, that they also may be in us, so that

[22] See *La Bible*, trans. and intro. André Chouraqui (Paris: Desclée de Brouwer, 1989), 637, 1883.
[23] See André Scrima, *L'évangile de Jean. Un commentaire* (Paris: Cerf, 2017), 288–306.

the world may believe that thou hast sent me"); and he asks that we be consummated in love like him and the Father in unity (John 17:22: "And the glory which thou hast given me I have given to them, that they may be one, even as we are one"). The issue is that we can have something like a perception of the divine, of the Absolute. This sensation blossoms when all our senses are gathered in the heart, where we can obtain the perception that every thought, every feeling, every intuition, every interior movement has its root in God, as a discovery of the divine law of life. It is a discovery which Tudor recalls as the prerogative of the simple believing man, citing Dostoevsky's speech upon Pushkin's death. Speaking of Dostoevsky, in the novel *The Brothers Karamazov*, the words of the elder Zosima sound very pertinent to Tudor's intuition:

> Much on earth is concealed from us, but in place of it we have been granted a secret, mysterious sense of our living bond with the other world, with the higher heavenly world, and the roots of our thoughts and feelings are not here but in other worlds. That is why philosophers say it is impossible on earth to conceive the essence of things. God took seeds from other worlds and sowed them on this earth, and raised up his garden; and everything that could sprout sprouted, but it lives and grows only through its sense of being in touch with other mysterious worlds; if this sense is weakened or destroyed in you, that which has grown up in you dies. Then you become indifferent to life, and even come to hate it. So I think.[24]

The Russian monks, whom Dostoevsky had in mind, would not have expressed things in this way, but the substance of what is declared by the elder Zosima is this: if we do not live in the sensation of the Kingdom that is within us, which has come to us in the person of Jesus, life remains fearful. Even Tudor does not express things in this way, but the substance of what he says is the same.

And I will also quote a passage by Isaac the Syrian, an author very dear to Tudor:

> "Implant in me the astringent of Thy love, that being drawn away by fervent love for Thee I may come forth from this

[24] Part 2, Book 6: "The Russian Monk, 3 (g). On Prayer, Love and the Touching of Other Worlds," trans. R. Pevear & L. Volokhonsky (New York: Vintage Books, 1990), 320.

world. Awake in me understanding of Thy humility, wherewith Thou didst sojourn in the world in the tenement composed of our members which by the mediation of the Holy Virgin Thou didst bear, that with this continual and unfailing recollection, I may accept the humility of my nature with delight."[25]

However, I found the best comment on Tudor's words in a passage by André Scrima, who had a veneration for Fr. Daniil, in the explanation of a verse of the passage which records the priestly prayer of Jesus: "This is eternal life: that they may know thee, the only true God, and Jesus Christ, whom thou hast sent" (John 17:3). Scrima writes:

> Every word here is worthy of being examined, meditated on, assimilated: 'you are the only true God.' There are therefore gods that are not true. At issue here are not the idols of pagans that existed in the world at the time of the chosen people, but rather the fact that within man himself there is a negative force that invents false gods and it is this that is the cause of all those gods and their origin. Man basically has a tendency to adore himself, to adore himself and project this tendency outwards, towards others, as a mirror for himself, and venerates kings for example (in primitive times) or ideas which become internal idols for him and this without him generally becoming aware of it, such as dominating others with money, with intelligence, with a haughty attitude towards them, isolating and distinguishing himself from them, etc. Wanting to be adored is a tendency we all have. We are not yet liberated, healed from the disease of idols. True healing is the knowledge of the only true God through Jesus Christ. Jesus is the only way forward for our healing. Throughout his life on earth, Jesus absolutely did not seek glory for himself, he did not seek his own glory even though it was before the creation of the world. As for us, we seek our glory from our brothers and this against our brothers.... We endeavor to have our brothers glorify us! This is something that makes people both laugh at us and weep for us. We still do not know the only true God.[26]

Man is made for this supreme knowledge, the knowledge of the only true God and of the one he sent, Jesus Christ, made to be assumed into the same divine life which is love for us. This is the natural outcome of the prayer of the heart.

[25] Saint Isaac the Syrian, Homily 36, *Ascetical Homilies*, trans. Holy Transfiguration Monastery (Boston: Holy Transfiguration Monastery, 1984), 161.
[26] Scrima, *L'évangile de Jean. Un commentaire*, 292–93.

Tudor sees the same intuition expressed in the penitential prayer of St. Ephrem, which he says contains the essence of Christianity. It is the prayer that the Byzantine tradition has recited nine times a day during Lent.[27] The prayer does not close with a request for charity but for repentance:

> O Lord and Master of my life. Take from me a spirit of sloth, despondency, lust for power, and idle talk. But give rather the spirit of purity, humility, patience and love to Thy servant. Yea, O Lord and King, grant me to see my own transgressions and not to judge my brother, for blessed art Thou unto ages of ages. Amen.

Tudor, as a poet, reads and hears the prayer of St. Ephrem as a song more powerful than a prose text, a song that has entered the liturgical prayer of the church. The liturgical order itself is concerned with establishing the rules for reciting this prayer: deep prostrations with the forehead touching the ground, with profound humility, fear of God and with tears, to be recited in church and in one's cell. The simplicity of the prayer comes from the depths of experience. Due to its conciseness and precision of words, like a mathematical formula, it should be combined with the Our Father prayer and the evangelical beatitudes. It is the creed of penance. It is not just a request but a trail guide, and Tudor provides a brief explanation.

The sequence of four bad dispositions is contrasted with that of four good ones, emphasizing that the progression of the struggle becomes increasingly more difficult. The first temptation encountered on the path of prayer is the observation that everything conspires against the decision to remain in prayer. The purpose of the evil one is to steal our prayer; he uses everything to prevent us from being in prayer. Does one feel compassion for others? The evil one suggests: What are you doing standing here? God knows your needs even if you don't show them to him, go help others! Does one feel tired? The evil one suggests: Rest a bit, you don't want to overdo it! Is one agitated? The evil one whispers: It is not the one who says "Lord, Lord" who

[27] See the beautiful commentary on this prayer by Fr. Petronie Tănase in Ioanichie Bălan, *Volti e parole dei padri del deserto romeno*, ed. Fratelli Contemplativi di Gesù (Bose: Qiqajon, 1991), 90–108. Fr. Daniil also ties it to the mystery of the cross: *Taina Sfintei Cruci*, Caietele 3 (Bucharest: Editura Christiana, 2001), 40–41.

will enter the kingdom of heaven, but the one who fulfills the commandments! He uses everything to prevent us from being in prayer. This spirit of laziness is contrasted with the spirit of purity, that is, the desire to work on one's own sanctification, to cultivate one's inner man and the initial effort is resolved by directing thoughts and desires towards a unique and holy purpose. However, if he does not react to this spiritual indolence, he becomes a victim of despondency, of dispersion into a thousand worries, in a thousand vain thoughts; he becomes agitated, restless. We begin to notice, and the gap between the enthusiasm at the start and the poverty of the results, between what we dreamed of and harsh reality, increase more and more. The remedy then is humility, humiliation, which, as Tudor wisely explains, consists in accepting oneself with peace while standing before the Lord, accepting one's own weakness and fragility. The less man fights against these first two temptations, the more easily he stumbles upon the third temptation, more terrible and more difficult to overcome, the temptation to escape from attention to himself in order to judge what is outside. He hides his own littleness with the haughtiness of criticizing others, falling into a certain taste for dominating others. This taste replaces the desire for repentance. The remedy is patience; the means to exercise it is to make fun of oneself, to ridicule one's own claims even with harsh words in order to return to the first desire to work on one's inner man. If the person instead prefers to take cover in his bigoted nature he, suffice it to say, ends up becoming a chatterbox, a talker. Tudor perhaps knew this stage of temptation well because here he places those who make themselves beautiful with their knowledge, who boast of their studies, and of their spiritual knowledge, without however enjoying life. At this point only God's mercy will overcome their evil. And they will have to start again from their small things to transform them into big things, that is, to move from sadness to humility, to return to desiring the beauty of holy things, until the love of the Lord reveals itself as a thief in their hearts. The prayer continues as if to assure the truth of that love which cannot be guaranteed except by seeing one's own sins and not accusing one's brother—that is, it asks for the humility of charity, so that in this way everyone can bless their Lord. To confirm this profound intuition that the main path is always the humility of a fiery repentance and not simply the fire of our love, which could also be ambiguous, I will offer this saying from one of the desert fathers:

> A brother questioned an elder saying: "If I fast am I saved?" The old man told him: "No." He said to his brother: "If I flee from men, am I saved?" The old man told him: "No." He said to his brother: "If I practice brotherly love, am I saved?" The old man told him: "No. Being saved means this: bringing the accusation against oneself and not afflicting one's brother in anything. In fact, this is how God shows mercy to man."[28]

This means rooting love in humility and humility in love, which is the very meaning of Jesus's prayer combined with incessant interior work, according to that desire for purity which is the first good disposition required by the prayer of St. Ephrem.

In the spirit of the Burning Bush movement, which did not disdain to also refer to mystical authors of other religions, I find, in agreement with the prayer of St. Ephrem, this prayer of Ansari, a Persian Muslim mystic (1006–1088):

> O You who sow the pain of repentance in the hearts of those who have met You! You who make the hearts of those who do penance burn! You who welcome sinners who confess their guilt! No one converts until You convert him; no one finds the path until you take them by the hand. Take us by the hand, for we have no other savior but You! Come to our aid, because we have no other refuge than You! To our questions, only You can give the answer. Only You can remedy our sufferings. To our torments, only You can bring rest.[29]

Behold: You who sow the pain of repentance in the hearts of those who have met You! It is the second beatitude: "blessed are those who mourn, for they will be comforted" (Matt. 5:4). "Mourning, repenting, weeping" is the spring that triggers the movement of the Spirit within us, it is the gateway to the inner man, the beginning of spiritual perception that imposes itself on worldly perception. The prayer of the heart leads to

[28] *The Book of the Elders. Sayings of the Desert Fathers. The Systematic Collection,* trans. J. Wortley (Collegeville, MN: Cistercian Publications/Liturgical Press, 2012), 175.

[29] Ansari, *Cris du cœur. Munajat,* ed. S. de Laugier de Beaurecueil (Paris: Sindbad, 1988), 103–4.

experiencing in all its mysterious depth and radicality that "only Thee," as Jesus says in his priestly prayer: "This is eternal life, that they know thee the only true God, and Jesus Christ whom thou hast sent" (John 17:3).

However, the signal that the heart has reached that depth always has to do with the extremity of repentance, as underscored by a famous Hasidic saying:

> Once when young Zusya was in the house of his teacher, Rabbi Baer, a man came before the Great Maggid and begged him to advise and assist him in an enterprise. Zusya saw that this man was full of sin and untouched by any breath of repentance, he grew angry, and spoke to him harshly, saying: "How can a man like yourself, a man who has committed this crime and that, have the boldness to stand before a holy countenance without shame, and without the longing to atone?" The man left in silence, but Zusya regretted what he had said and did not know what to do. Then his teacher pronounced a blessing over him, that from this moment on, he might see only the good in people, even if a person sinned before his very eyes. But because Zusya's gift of vision could not be taken from him through words spoken by man, it came to pass that from this time on he felt the sins of the people he met, as his own, and blamed himself for them. Whenever the rabbi of Rizhyn told this about Rabbi Zusya, he was likely to add: "And if all of us were like him, evil would long since have been destroyed, and death overcome, and perfection achieved.[30]

FINAL CONSIDERATIONS

Clearly Fr. Daniil's patristic references are almost exclusively eastern. He lists them himself, beyond the scattered quotes he utilizes especially from the apostle John, in a precise series: Macarius the Great, Maximus the Confessor, Simeon the New Theologian, Gregory of Sinai, Gregory Palamas, Nil Sorsky and Paisius Velichkovsky. However, the teaching that he presents is not the exclusive prerogative of the Christian East, especially that on prayer. It is a common tradition of the Church, East and West. Unfortunately, we have become accustomed to underscoring the theological differences between East and West more than underscoring the power of the saints' experience who are the glory of those traditions. When it comes

[30] Martin Buber, *Tales of the Hasidim*, 277.

to explaining differences, at times, misunderstandings emerge, but when it comes to determining the living experience that forms the object of the explanations, then only the splendor of the mystery of man emerges, which finds its raison d'être only in the revelation of Jesus. Holiness can only be essentially ecumenical, radically united in humanity. As evidenced by the accounts of life in the communist prisons at the time of Ceausescu where tragedy had knocked down every fence.[31]

In the history of the Western Church there is a curious case of a Greek saint, canonized only by the Latin Church, St. Nicholas the Pilgrim or Nicholas Kyrieleison, who witnessed to that prayer of the heart which in subsequent centuries would be codified in its complete form: "Lord Jesus Christ, Son of God, have mercy on me" (the Slavs add: "the sinner"). He was born in Stiri, Greece, in 1075. Since a boy, he always repeated *Kyrie eleison*, so much so that he was considered crazy and was chased away by the Greek monks who took care of his education. He repaired to Otranto in 1092, then to Trani where he died in the odor of sanctity in 1094. He was recognized as a saint by Pope Urban II in 1099.[32] He splendidly highlights how the

[31] As Nicolae Steinhardt recalls in his *Diario della felicità* (Bologna: Mulino, 1996).

[32] Cf. the contribution of Father Guglielmo Spirito: *San Nicola Kyrieleison, testimone della preghiera del cuore* at the recent Italian-Greek symposium held at Assisi in August 2018: *La spiritualità come provocazione per il mondo di oggi*, ed. Luca Bianchi and Guglielmo (Padova: Edizioni San Leopoldo, 2022), 97–115. The Catholic Church canonized St. Nicholas the Pilgrim in 1099. In October 2022, Nicholas's sanctity was also recognized by the Greek Orthodox Church, through the initiative of Metropolitan Polycarp of the Holy Orthodox Archdiocese of Italy and Exarch of Southern Europe, and the Ecumenical Patriarchate of Constantinople. It was decided to celebrate in a single celebration the common memory of all the Saints of Magna Graecia (Basilicata, Calabria, Campania, Sicily and Puglia): the Synaxis of the Italo-Greek Saints would be celebrated together with the memory of the Holy God-bearing Fathers of the Seventh Ecumenical Council of Nicaea on the Sunday following October 11 each year. In a kind of great "equipollent canonization" (to use a Latin canonical category), they are fully recognized and celebrated as saints by the Greek Orthodox Church in Italy. St. Nicholas the Pilgrim, Kyrieleison, is commemorated on June 2. Contributing to the hymnography for the feast is the monumental hagiographic work by the protopresbyter Basilio Koutsouras, "The Saints of Magna Graecia," published in 2021 by the Orthodox Media Network, based in Thessaloniki (vivlos.net@gmail.com) and translated from Greek into Italian by Hieromonk Benedetto Colucci. All these Saints listed in the book each have their own apolotìkion (a troparion or short hymn said or sung, which summarizes the feast celebrated that day). Recently, in the city of Trani (August 28–30, 2024), which, in its

essence of prayer of the heart is the acquisition of burning repentance. In invoking *Kyrie eleison*, *Lord have mercy*, one does not simply ask for forgiveness, but: "Lord, pour out your love and tenderness on me," "soothe my sufferings," "wrap me in your splendor," "heal me," "bestow on me your light," "take care of me," "give savor to my life," "show me your forgiveness," "give my heart your peace"... Words of prayer have infinite reverberations and intensities, encompassing the totality of being with all its longings. And all those reverberations draw strength from a single root: repentance. This is because the request for mercy corresponds to Moses's request: "Show me your glory!" (Exod. 33:18), after the anguish for the sin of the golden calf when the destruction of the people would have been expected. God's response of revelation instead sounds forth: "The Lord, the Lord, a merciful and gracious God, slow to anger and rich in love and faithfulness" (Exod. 34:6). That God forgives is the essential dimension of his being for us. It should not be forgotten that the adjective *merciful*, in the Old Testament, never refers to man, but only to God. The Jesus Prayer tends to inspire precisely that revelation of God in the heart of man. It seems that the whole drama of our heart consists in not being convinced that this is the essential point, so much so that we never obtain the revelation of the face of God.

That experience of revelation corresponds to what in Eastern tradition is defined as the movement of the mind descending into the heart. In Western tradition, one of the brightest examples of someone grasping the power of repentance in this movement of the mind's descent, to the point where the heart can perceive the presence of the Lord who inhabits it, is a disciple of St. Francis of Assisi, Angela da Foligno.[33]

---

patron Saint Nicholas the Pilgrim, unites the Orthodox of Greece and the Catholics of Italy, the XVII Inter-Christian Symposium was held, organized by the Department of Theology of the Theological School of Thessaloniki and the Franciscan Institute of Spirituality of the Antonianum in Rome. On that occasion, Metropolitan Polycarp celebrated the Byzantine Divine Liturgy in the crypt of the cathedral (for the first time in 930 years), on the altar that holds the body of Saint Nicholas. He also attended the presentation of the book by Don Natale Albino, originally from Trani and current secretary of the Apostolic Nunciature of Jerusalem (*Ad ogni passo, ad ogni battito. Storia del pellegrino Nicola* [Bologna: EDB, 2024]), also published in Greek translation, created on the initiative of the Orthodox Media Network.

[33] See my contribution "Passaggi e tappe nel cammino mistico di Angela da

Repentance is played out in the acceptance of total sharing in the mystery of the abasement of the "passionate" Son of God and prayer is the way to stay in that abasement, united with one's Lord. The beauty of the soul is captured starting from its total unworthiness, which stands out precisely within a love that reveals itself to it and comes to inhabit it. One experiences it in one's heart and the extraordinary thing is that one connects this perception not simply to the forgiveness of sin but to the eternal dimension of God's love for man. In the soul's awareness the two poles are valid simultaneously, its unworthiness and the gratuitousness of the love that visits it and fills it. Angela refers several times to the fact that the Passion of the Son is willed from eternity, since before sin. Our nothingness is dramatically evident, but within a relationship, so that the awareness of nothingness does not destroy but immeasurably expands the boundaries. The understanding of sin within God's love for man from eternity, revealed in his incarnate and passionate Son, allows for a much more radical experience of God and a freer self-awareness. It seems to me that the very possibility of this experience is due to the extraordinarily singular experience of St. Francis of Assisi, who lived the humanity of the Lord Jesus in his extreme poverty of goods, of affections and of himself, in a word, in his annihilation, as Angela always relates, but not as a diminution or hiding of glory, but as "his" glory, as the typical glory of God:

> "But God wanted even more to be revealed to me in his poverty: I saw him poor in friends and relatives, I saw him poor in himself, so poor that it was not clear how to help him. It is usually said that at that moment the power of God was hidden through humility: although this is said, I also say that he was not."[34]

Biographers report this about St. Francis:

> Indeed, so to offer every fiber of his heart to God in a multiple holocaust, he considered the One who is supremely One under different aspects. Often, without moving his lips, he meditated for a long time within himself and, concentrating

Foligno," in Luigi Borriello, ed., *Sant'Angela da Foligno contemplativa, mystica, apostola* (Miscellanea Francescana, 2014), 137–58.

[34] *Angela of Foligno. Complete Works*, trans. P. Lachance (New York & Mahwah, NJ: Paulist Press, 1993), 179.

> his external powers within, he raised his spirit to heaven. In this way he directed all his mind and affection to that one thing he asked of God: he was not so much a man who prays, but rather himself completely transformed into living prayer.[35]

Another singular fact to underscore is that, at the level of our human conscience, the most truthful effect of sincere and ardent repentance is that of not judging anyone and considering ourselves more vile than everyone. This is the very thing that the prayer of St. Ephrem aims at. The soul chooses to comply with God's movement of abasement in his love for man, living it like him in a radical expropriation of oneself, so as to be able to share God's charity always and no matter how. The well-known characteristic of the love found in man will not be ardor, but rather humility and a sweet, benign humility, because "[t]he more [the soul] perceives and knows that it is nothing, the more it will rise up to know and praise the ineffability of the divine goodness which its humility makes it perceive and understand so fully. And from this, all the other virtues begin to blossom."[36]

In conclusion, we could ask ourselves: How is it that the love of the Lord can only be grasped starting from a profound "repentance"? The Jesus Prayer—"have mercy on me, a sinner"—incessantly and ardently invoked? The reason seems to me to be grasped by the apostle Judas, not Iscariot, who at the Last Supper asks Jesus the question: "Lord, how is it that you will manifest yourself to us, and not to the world?" (John 14:22). He understood that Jesus would manifest himself in a way that did not correspond to their messianic expectations. Only with love can the secret of Jesus be welcomed. That secret is not known to the world; the world does not know its scent.

---

[35] Thomas of Celano, *Second Life of Saint Francis of Assisi*, in *Fonti Francescane*, no. 682.

[36] Angelina of Foligno, *Instructions*, V, *Complete Works*, 252–53. This is not about conquering love but attracting it, just as Isaac the Syrian says: "If you practice a beautiful virtue and don't feel the pleasure of his help, don't be surprised. Until man becomes humble, he does not receive the wages of his work. The reward is not given to work, but to humility. Whoever wrongs the second, loses the first. He who precedes it and has received the reward of goods possesses more than he who has the work of virtue. Virtue is the mother of punishment and humility is born from punishment and grace is given to humility. The reward is not for virtue nor for the effort one endures in practicing it, but for the humility that arises from both. If this is missing, the other two are accomplished in vain" (*Ascetical Homilies*, Homily 57, 282).

In fact, there is opposition between the world and the Spirit because the former would like to bend the latter to its purposes of power and glory, pursued for the purposes of dominion over everything and everyone, while for the Spirit power and glory derive only from merciful love for all, which in Jesus shines forth as the revelation of God in the world. If the Spirit is called the Spirit of truth, this is because his action is entirely aimed at having us taste the love of Jesus and incorporating us into the love that he witnessed to the world on behalf of the Father. It is not for nothing that the observance of the commandments always has to do with love, not only in the sense that they can be observed if one loves Jesus, but also in the sense that the commandments are the concrete possibilities for living the love of Jesus towards everyone and thus for enjoying intimacy with one's God, who is love for all. In fact, as we welcome the Spirit, the world withdraws within us or, better yet, becomes Church, that is, more and still more extensively everything in us supports the work of Jesus, which is to show how great is the Father's love for us, a love bringing together the scattered children at the same table, making us a place for the transparency of God's love for all, in Christ.

Here we find the Jewish intuition of the scent of paradise, of the scent of the Sabbath, of the scent-holiness connection of God shared with man through the commandments. And for this reason, yes, Ephrem can speak of the aromas of paradise that spread over the earth because the aroma of paradise is the enjoyment of God's merciful love that the humanity of Jesus spreads. The condition is always the same: considering oneself a sinner and asking for mercy. The famous Lenten prayer of St. Ephrem, in fact, defines the conditions for charity to always remain splendid and luminous, that is, for man to consider himself a sinner and not accuse anyone. If I am aware of being a sinner (and not just of committing sins), with my anger and demands of every kind, as soon as I refer to the Lord with the cry "have mercy on me," I discover his face of mercy for me and I can be willing to be kind to everyone. Guarding this connection makes everything bright.

Thus, as soon as the heart is freed from its illusions of power or presumptions of power, by accepting to comply with the movement of self-abasement, it finds itself in solidarity with everyone, in Jesus. Prayer then becomes a lived intercession, not for one or the other, but for humanity, for creation. As Angela of Foligno urges:

> My little children, strive to be charitable toward everyone, because I say to you that my soul truly received more from God when I wept and suffered with all my heart over the sins of others than when I wept over my own sins. Truly, there is no greater charity on earth than to suffer for the sins of others. The world could mock what I say, because it seems to be contrary to nature that someone could suffer and weep over the sins of one's neighbor more than for one's own. But the charity which does this is not of this world. My children, strive to have this charity.[37]

It is the holiness of those like Francis of Assisi,—with uninterrupted prayer, capable of "seeing God" in a heart imbued with a clear and luminous atmosphere, totally absorbed in God in a continuous meditation on the name of Jesus, and surrounded by divine light—that is in accord with the most orthodox hesychastic tradition.

Just read passages such as these:

> The friars who lived with him also know very well how every day, or rather every moment, the memory of Christ surfaced on his lips; with how much gentleness and sweetness he spoke to him, with what tender love he conversed with Him. The mouth spoke out of the abundance of the holy affections of the heart (Matt. 12:34), and that source of enlightened love that filled him within also overflowed without. He was really very busy with Jesus. He always carried Jesus in his heart, Jesus on his lips, Jesus in his ears, Jesus in his eyes, Jesus in his hands, Jesus in all his other members. How many times, while sitting at lunch, hearing or pronouncing the name of Jesus, he forgot the temporal food and, as we read of a saint, "looking, he did not see and listening, he did not hear." What is more, many times, finding himself traveling and meditating or singing about Jesus, he forgot that he was traveling and stopped to invite all creatures to praise Jesus. Precisely because he always bore and kept *Christ Jesus and him crucified* in his heart with a wondrous love, therefore, he was gloriously endowed more than any other with the image of Him, which he had the grace of contemplating, during the ecstasy, in the inexpressible and incomprehensible glory sitting at the "right hand of the Father,"

[37] Angela of Foligno, *Complete Works*, 314.

with whom the co-equal and most high Son of the Most High, together with the Holy Spirit lives and reigns, conquers and rules, eternally glorious God, for all ages. Amen![38]

Or, according to the testimony of St. Bonaventure:

When the man of God was left alone and at peace, he would fill the groves with sighs, sprinkle the ground with tears, strike his breast with his fist and having found there a kind of secret hiding place, would converse with his Lord. There he would answer his Judge, there he would entreat his Father, there he would entertain his Friend; and there also on several occasions the friars who were devoutly observing him heard him groan aloud, imploring the divine mercy for sinners and weeping for the Lord's passion as if it were there before his eyes. There he was seen praying at night, with his hands out stretched in the form of a cross, his whole body lifted up from the ground and surrounded by a sort of shining cloud. The extraordinary illumination around his body was a witness to the wonderful light that shone within his soul.[39]

Or, more modestly, according to this prayer of praise, commenting on Psalm 138, found in an old diary of mine without any reference to date or author:

I give thanks to you, O Lord.
You have fulfilled my heart's desires.
My earth has become heaven,
in your dwelling-place I adore you with the angels.
I bless your Name
because your love for me is great,
more than I had imagined.
You have responded to my affliction;
now, my strength and your grace,
my faithfulness your promise.
Men will give you glory
when my life will speak of You,
inside of my words they will listen to yours,
in the desires of my heart they will smell the scent of You.
They will sing your mercy with me
because I am no longer stolen from You by my sins
and you have made me capable of perceiving the need for You

[38] Tommaso da Celano, *First Life of St. Francis of Assisi*, 115, in Fonti Francescane, no. 522.

[39] *The Life of St. Francis (Legenda Maior)*, 4, in *Bonaventure*, trans. E. Cousins (New York, Ramsey & Toronto: Paulist Press, 1978), 275.

in all my frailty and torment.
You have freed me from enmity with myself
and I no longer find enemies about me,
the paths between us are no longer blocked,
the spaces of the heart no longer have boundaries.
Guard your work in the brothers who live with me
so that I may let myself be looked after by them
and together, giving you thanks, we bless you
because you always fulfill those great desires
that you have placed within us.
May your glory be our torment
and our labors accustom us to your mysteries,
now revealed to our very selves,
free to love and forgive, in your peace.

Hymn to the Prayer of the Heart

INTRODUCTION

1. Publication history

The hymn is known in two versions, a short one and a full one. The short version is that of 1948, signed by Sandu Tudor as the monk Agathon at the Antim monastery. That version, like Sandu Tudor's other writings, was both copied by hand and typed to be distributed among friends who participated in the Burning Bush meetings. The composition consists of eight stanzas plus the final troparion. The printed edition, in Romanian, was published in Madrid in 1983. This is the version known in the West and which appears, in French, in the volume edited by Fr. Romul Ionată, now Metropolitan Serafim of the Romanian Orthodox Church of Germany, with a preface by Olivier Clément, who presents the hymn thus: "[The Romanian hesychast tradition] culminates in a paraliturgical text, composed after the Second World War, the *Akathist of the Burning Bush*, which defines the hesychast dimension as a Marian one and ends in an immense and eternal alleluia," as related in the verses of the eighth stanza:

> But my heart, pierced through with a searing lightning flash,
> sadly yet sweetly
> murmurs Thine invocation in full.
> In the rhythm of breath, without effort,
> the pulsing of the prayer
> wells up towards the light in an *Alleluia*![1]

---

[1] Fr. Romul Ionată, *Roumanie, Tradition et culture hésychastes* (Begrolles-en-Mauges: Abbaye de Bellefontaine, 1987), 267–79. The quote from Olivier Clément is on pages 16–17. Curiously, when Clément sums up the presentation of this hymn, after André Scrima's visit to Paris in 1957, in the article "L'église Orthodoxe Roumaine ou le miracle du Buisson ardent," *Réforme*, no. 644, samedi 20 juillet 1957, he cites a passage from the second stanza in a version different from the one published by Fr. Romul Ionată. He confirms how the hymn, celebrating the Mother of God as an incarnate prayer, constitutes a true poetic sum of hesychasm: concentration linked to internal breathing, the mystery of the divine Name, the birth of the inner Christ, constancy in prayer, sobriety and vigilance, and the encounter with Christ in the place of

The French translation was created around 1960 at Bellefontaine Abbey by a Romanian Orthodox monk staying there, with the help of a monk from the same abbey. It was later revised in Sihăstria in Romania by Fr. Petronie Tănase. The published French version is generally attributed to Fr. Placide Deseille (1926–2018), a Trappist monk of the Bellefontaine Abbey, founder in 1966 of the Byzantine rite monastery of Aubazine, then welcomed into the Orthodox Church in 1977 at the Simonopetra monastery of Mount Athos and founder of the Orthodox monastery of Saint-Antoine-le-Grand at Saint-Laurent-en-Royans, the following year, in 1985, then of the Monastery of the Protection of the Mother of God (Solan Monastery). André Scrima, in a letter from Benares in 1957 to Fr. Benedict Ghiuș, while telling him the events of his stay in Switzerland and France, informs him that he had spoken with the Orthodox intellectuals in exile about the Burning Bush movement and Sandu Tudor's akathist hymn. Scrima had even translated it on the spot for his listeners, accepting the proposal to publish it in the French version, entrusting the work to a poet. Listening to it, Vladimir Lossky commented: "I believe this belongs to the spiritual family of the *Spiritual Canticle* of St. John of the Cross." One of the listeners was Professor Olivier Clément, who, without André Scrima's knowledge, published information about the Burning Bush movement in the ecumenical weekly *Réforme*, which also included a stanza from the akathist translated by Scrima.[2]

The Italian edition, with the translation of the hymn from French, edited by Professor Luciana Mirri, appears in the volume *Gloria a Dio per tutto. Inni acatisti*, edited by the Russian Monastery of the Dormition of the Mother of God, with

the heart. The expanded version with additions to the 1987 book by Fr. Romul, now Metropolitan Serafim of Germany, is published in English: *Treasures of Romanian Christianity: Hesychast Tradition and Culture* (Whitby, Ontario: Cross Meridian, 2013). The English version is taken from the expanded Romanian edition, compared to Bellefontaine's original French edition of 1987, which appeared with the title: *Isihasmul, traditie și cultură românească* (Bucharest: Ed. Anastasia, 1994). The English translation appearing on this page is from Fr. Jonată's *Romania: Its Hesychast Tradition and Culture*, trans. R. Ionată (Wildwood, CA: St. Xenia's Skete, 1992).

[2] Cf. André Scrima, *Ortodoxia și incercarea comunismului* (Bucharest: Humanitas, 2008), 394–417. The text of the French translation of the akathist is found in the volume *Recueil d'Acathistes* (Saint-Laurent-en-Royans: Monastère saint-Antoine-le-Grand, metochion de Simonos Petra, 1996).

the title "Inno acatisto alla Madre della preghiera continua" (Akathist Hymn to the Mother of Ceaseless Prayer).[3]

The complete version of the hymn was found among the manuscripts confiscated by the *Securitate* on the night of Fr. Daniil de la Rarău's arrest in 1958. Those manuscripts bear the words: "Found in the search of Sandu Tudor." The manuscript of the *Akathist Hymn to the Burning Bush of the Mother of God*, a thirty-seven-page typescript, with an annotation at the bottom of the page, "composition of the humble monk Agathon of the holy monastery of Antim, 1948. Correction and completion by the hieroschimonk Daniil Tudor, staretz of the Saint John the Theologian skete of the Rarău mountains, 1958," bears an autograph annotation dictated by the *Securitate* agents who carried out the arrest: "Found by me during the search, V. Anania. 14-VI-1958." This is the testimony of Bartolomeu Anania. In 1959, all the manuscripts discovered by the Securitate were entrusted to Fr. Petronie Tănase, for keeping until the release of Fr. Daniil, who instead died in prison in 1962. And when political prisoners were amnestied in 1964, Father Petronie, with the consent of Patriarch Iustinian Marina, went to Slatina bringing with him the manuscripts and volumes from Father Daniil's library, which he then handed over to the Patriarchal Library and which then found a place in the Holy Synod Library. The first complete edition of the hymn, in twelve stanzas, each divided into a kontakion, an ikos and a litany of praise, plus the final thirteenth kontakion, appeared in Bucharest in 1999.[4] It is this complete version that is presented here for the first time in the West.

[3] *Gloria a Dio per tutto. Inni acatisti*, ed. Russian Monastery of the Dormition of the Mother of God (Roma: Appunti di viaggio, 2011), 125–35. In the Italian version, the stanzas, composed in the original of kontakia, ikoi and litany, are called *prelude* and *stanza*.

[4] Ieroschimonahul Daniil Tudor (Sandu Tudor), *Scrieri*, I, ed. A. Dicea (Bucharest: Asociația filantropică medicală crestină/Christiana, 1999), 15–78; with a preface, "Hermeneutic Point of View," and a summarizing epilogue by Fr. Daniil himself. The text is reproduced, in a critical edition, in the volume *Ieroschimonahul Daniil Tudor* (Sandu Tudor), *Acatiste*, (Bucharest: Editura Christiana, 2009). The five akathists composed by Sandu Tudor are presented there, in the complete edition, edited by Alexandru Dimcea and Gabriela Moldoveanu: the akathists of St. Demetrius the New, St. John the Theologian, St. Callinic of Cernica, the Annunciation and the Burning Bush (139–198, the edition that I follow for my translation). We have news of another akathist, that of the Holy Cross, from the papers of Fr. Daniil, but it is only a first draft with many annotations: *Caietele Preacuviosului Părinte Daniil de la*

2. Structure of the Hymn

First of all, let us address the name. It is not simply called akathist, but "akathist hymn." The poet's intention is to consider it a hymn, which defines its specific identity which is not simply a poetic composition on a certain theme. There are many akathists in the Byzantine liturgical tradition, but this akathist was composed as a hymn in which the faithful themselves recognize what is most singular and most secret according to tradition. Its full title reads "Akathist Hymn to the Burning Bush of the Mother of God." In fact, the hymn lays out, in all its theological depth, the whole treasure of tradition in reference to the place and role that the Mother of God has in relation to the spiritual tension of man until his divinization in Christ.

The akathist is set in the mystical dimension of the Liturgy. It has concentrated in its poetic stanzas mankind's heartbreaking nostalgia for God, describing, around the figure and interior experience of the Virgin Mary, in the grace of divine love, the meeting of two hearts: that of God and that of man, as a mysterious preparation for the Kingdom of Heaven.

Each stanza is subdivided into three parts according to the Byzantine structure: a kontakion (in Romanian, *condac*), which introduces the theme in the form of a prayer; an ikos (in Romanian, *icos*), which develops the theme narratively, and a litany, which transforms the theme developed into a song of praise to the Mother of God.

The rhythm of the composition unfolds over twelve passages marking the life of the Mother of God. There are twelve stanzas that make up the hymn, with a final invocation, the thirteenth stanza, composed only of a kontakion, which must be repeated three times, and then a return to the hymn's first stanza to repeat the journey on a deeper level. There is also an emphasis on the dual, ascending and circular, movement that characterizes prayer, and which thus becomes an uninterrupted movement of the heart in its longing for God and in his all-pervading love for us. It is the same movement that

---

Rarău (Sandu Tudor), 3, *Taina Sfintei Cruci*, ed. Alexandru Dimcea (Bucharest: Editura Christiana, 2001), 166–209, from the title "Acatist al Semnelor Sfintei Învieri. Pentru sfânta și minunata Cruce a Sihăstriei Sfintei Milostiviri din Crasna Gorjului," Agathon monah, 12/II/1950.

tradition has discerned in the evangelical beatitudes, read in their sequential and circular movements: having arrived at the last one, one is sent back to the first to resume the same path in an ever-deeper way.

The hymn is like Jacob's ladder which rests on the earth and reaches heaven. The biblical reference is Gen. 28:12: "he had a dream: a ladder rested on the earth, while its top reached heaven; and behold, the angels of God were ascending and descending upon it."[5] On that ladder man ascends to God and God descends to man. It has twenty-four rungs (twelve stanzas subdivided into twelve *kontakia* and twelve *ikoi*) traversed by man in his ascent to God and traversed by God in his pouring of uncreated energies into man to bring him to full union with Himself, according to the three traditional stages of spiritual progress: the purification of the incipient, the enlightenment of the proficient, and the union of the perfect. The three stages of the descent of divine energies on man correspond to these: purity as the effect of the power of transfiguration, light as the assimilation of grace, and the fruit as the grace of union.

The hymn thus appears as a cycle of hymnological icons (this is Fr. Daniil's hermeneutic innovation with respect to the Byzantine tradition) which introduce the meeting of God and man in the mystery of prayer, a mystery which, unlike a theological exposition with concepts, has the advantage of being presented as a theology in action, as a ladder of contemplation. The hymn aspires not simply to be enjoyed for its poetic power (Fr. Daniil has said that poets are, like the ancient prophets,

[5] To this passage must be joined those of Exodus 3:2: "The angel of the Lord appeared to him in a flame of fire from the midst of a bush. He looked and behold: the bush was burning with fire, but that bush was not consumed," Isaiah 11:1–2: "A shoot will grow from the trunk of Jesse, a shoot will sprout from its roots. The spirit of the Lord will rest on him, a spirit of wisdom and understanding, a spirit of counsel and fortitude, a spirit of knowledge and fear of the Lord," and Ezekiel 44:1: "he then led me to the outer door of the sanctuary facing east; it was closed. The Lord said to me: 'This door will remain closed: it will not be opened, no one will pass through, because the Lord, the God of Israel, has passed through it. Therefore it will remain closed.'" These four Old Testament episodes are the very ones depicted at the four corners on the "Burning Bush" icon before which Fr. Daniil would have prayed during the composition of the Burning Bush akathist, and which are included in the hymn. The episode of the seraphim cleansing Isaiah's lips with a burning coal (Isa. 6:6–7) is also depicted on some versions of this icon and is mentioned twice in the course of the hymn.

capable of communicating the inspiration that startled them, just as it is not fine words that characterize a man of culture, but his theophoric consciousness), but to introduce us to the mystery of prayer in the Spirit, what he calls not holy prayer, but sanctified prayer, pneumatic prayer, the prayer of the heart.

The central image is that of the Burning Bush, fundamental in the experience of Moses as told in the book of Exodus, chapter 3, a type of Mary's perpetual virginity, a figure of the knowledge of the heart. It is the image of love enjoyed, of the mystery of prayer in the heart in relation to the encounter with God who lives there, attracting man to himself.

3. A Poetic Theology

The hymn presupposes a lyrical energy that must be awakened and has the aim, in contemplating the Mother of God, of bringing the soul back to its primordial intuitive capacity in its nostalgia for the love of God. A Romanian poet, Liliana Ursu, has aptly observed that Pico della Mirandola (1463–1494) had wanted to compose, but never did so, a book on poetic theology. She thought that Fr. Daniil could be seen as the person who has come the closest to creating this kind of book. And she cites three authors, a theologian, a monk, and a poet. Paul Evdokimov has written:

> Only prophets and poets—the priests of the word—know the frontiers of being in which the mysterious life of the word has its source. "You explain nothing, O poet, but thanks to you all things become explicable," notes Claudel, at the height of the enigmatic shudder that overcame him. Perhaps Peguy has given us the key to the enigma: "I don't invent, I discover." Adam, when he pronounces the name of his wife (Gen 2:23), does not invent, but discovers the meaning and humanizes it, he makes it a word.[6]

Every discovery is rooted in the capacity for wonder, a typical attitude of angels who contemplate God's love for man.

It is extraordinary to listen to a Greek monk, Elder Porphyrios, who defines the path of the Christian as the path of a poet:

[6] P. Evdokimov, *L'uomo icona di Cristo* [Man the Icon of Christ] (Milano: Ancora, 1982), 51. John Paul II, in his *Mulieris dignitatem*, expressed the same vision.

> The soul of the Christian needs to be refined and sensitive, to have sensibility and wings, to be constantly in flight and to live in dreams, to fly through infinity, among the stars, amidst the greatness of God, amid silence. Whoever wants to become a Christian must first become a poet.... You must suffer. You must love and suffer—suffer for the one you love. Love makes effort for the loved one. She runs all through the night; she stays awake; she stains her feet with blood in order to meet her beloved. She makes sacrifices and disregards all impediments, threats and difficulties for the sake of the loved one. Love towards Christ is something even higher, infinitely higher. And when we say "love," we don't mean the virtues that we will acquire, but the heart that is pervaded by love towards Christ and others.[7]

The akathist of the Burning Bush is permeated by this tension of the loving energy of the heart.

And in the experience of a Spanish poet, Ramón del Valle-Inclán (1866–1936), however contradictory his writings, we grasp the intuition that underlies the akathist's entire development:

> Beauty is the intuition of unity and all its paths are mystical paths that lead to God. Only poets cross this world of evocations since, in their eyes, all things have a religious meaning. Where other men find only differences, poets discover luminous bonds of divine harmony. The poet reduces the multitude of immanent allusions to a single divine allusion full of understanding. A bee laden with honey.

Honey here alludes to pure prayer through which the divine fire is rekindled within us; we experience the kingdom of heaven that is within us. This is the basic teaching of Fr. Daniil, corroborated in this by the whole tradition, the hesychast one in particular. The famous saying of Basil the Great applies to everyone: "Man is a creature who is bidden by God to become God by grace."[8]

The words of the poet, who aspires to have his words become the same as those of the reader, are like the echo of his heart lit

---

[7] *Wounded by Love. The Life and Wisdom of Elder Porphyrios*, trans. J. Raffan (Chrysopigi: Holy Convent of the Life-giving Spring, 2005), 107.

[8] Cf. Cleopa Paraschiv [heir to Fr. Daniil de la Rarău and promoter of the interest in him and his work], *Rugul Aprins și staretul Danül (Sandu Tudor)* (Vatra Dornei: Editura Panaghia, 2007), 79–84. The characteristic expression of Basil the Great 'θεός κεκελευσμένος' ("bidden to become god") is reported by Gregory of Nazianzus, *In laudem Basili Magni*, oration 43, 48 (PG 36, 560).

by prayer, by the spiritual joy that arises from an understanding of the mystery of the life of the Mother of God, defined with this extraordinary metaphor: "body woven with prayer, eternal unconsumed Bush" and which is shown at the akathist hymn's very beginning: "Who is this, pure and radiant as the dawn? She is the Queen of prayer, she is prayer incarnate." It is with the reality of the Virgin Mary that the supreme joy for humanity begins, and the litany of praise, which ends each stanza, unceasingly repeats the angel's greeting that is the anticipation of joy for all humanity: "Rejoice, you who conceived the Pledge of Fire," "Rejoice...," and, for all twelve stanzas, always ending with the self-same leitmotif: "Rejoice, O Holy Bride weaver of ceaseless prayer."[9] According to the explanations of Tudor himself, the akathist, a typical Byzantine liturgical piece that had to be sung while standing, was assumed to be never-ending since it always begins anew, like a flame that burns in everlasting praise. Conceived as a spiritual ladder, it gives you the power to climb up *there*, up to that horizon where the contemplated divine Image can descend upon you, without becoming corrupted and without losing its purity, like the cherubic wheel of praise and humility that ascends, always ascends. It remains clear that no one can participate in this ascent or understand how joy can arise from this kind of poetic composition if they have not first been tormented by the hunger and thirst for contemplation.

In the web of cryptic references, placed as a hermeneutic introduction to his composition and to help us to decipher it in the appropriate perspective, Sandu Tudor notes:

> Our most appropriate activity, our most powerful and victorious testimony is singing. Singing from the depths, singing with total sincerity, singing in holiness, singing the truth of life. In other words, praying in the most perfect way cannot

[9] Usually the akathist leitmotif, "Bucură-Te, Mireasă urzitoare de nesfârșită rugăciune" is translated in French as "Réjouis-toi, Épouse, Mère de la prière continuelle!" or, in English (Ionată), "Rejoice, O Bride, Mother of continuous prayer!" Its precise meaning is, however: "Rejoice, O Holy Bride, weaver of ceaseless prayer!" The Romanian term *urzitoare* is not the usual term for weaver (*filator*); it bears a deep folkloric resonance. The three *urzitoare* are said to come to a newborn's cradle to weave the "fabric" of the child's life-long destiny, much like the Greek *Moirai* or Fates. Here, Father Daniil seems to allude to the power of prayer—under the sponsorship of the Holy Virgin—to invest us with a new, decidedly Christ-ward destiny.

be a sign of weakness; it is a sign of immense spiritual power, the power that arises from weakness.

Every pure devotion is based on a similar lyrical yearning for the luminous recognition of the Truth. For millennia the Church has known and mastered the great and sacred art of glorification, the holy art of praise. It is necessary, however, that such praise be so total and full as to completely quench our thirst for holiness and grace, and that it have such vigor and lucidity that it can, unfailingly and powerfully, prove to be our most comprehensive and most exalted act of praise and salvation: Holy Praise.

Pure devotion is hunger and thirst for God, hunger and thirst for his glory, but, since our ordinary, everyday man is petty, limited, quickly impoverished inwardly, the healing springs of Holy Praise must be awakened from the beginning and continually stirred up from the depths.

Pure devotion, the longing and secret yearning for wonder and eternity, which are, in fact, inherent to the profound ontological nature of man, require, according to their ineffability, an incessant prayerful impulse towards the state of a fullness of Holy Praise.

Unceasing prayer is as necessary to us as bread, as air, as water, as freedom.... In our great ignorance we must convince ourselves that "without the truth there is no salvation." Unceasing prayer is our very bread, air, and water, together with freedom in its perfected state, the divine food of the angels and saints, unceasing heavenly praise. How will the ignorant, having come to the very brink of decadence, still be able to understand the objectivity of such a testimony?[10]

I will note here, incidentally, that the language of the akathist is deliberately archaic, refined, with bold metaphors both from a theological and linguistic point of view. It is clear that, in any necessarily approximate translation, the arcane flavor of the original is lost, as is the musicality of the words and the rhyme, which should be instead an integral part of the charm of the composition.[11]

[10] See remarks nos. 5–9 of "Punct ermeneutic la imnul acatist al 'Rugului Aprins.' Argument," in *Akatiste. Acatistul Sf. Dimitrie Cel Nou. Acatistul Sf. Ioan Bogoslovul. Acatistul Sf. Calinic de la Cernica. Acatistul Rugului Aprins. Acatistul Bunei Vestiri.* First complete edition, ed. Alexandru Dimcea and Gabriela Moldoveanu (Bucharest: Editura Christiana, 2009), 142–43.

[11] Those who would like to enjoy the musical sound of the akathist, as well as Sandu Tudor's other poetic pieces listed in the appendix, can access our site www.contemplavi.it and go to the "Sandu Tudor audio" page.

4. The Figure of the Mother of God

The figure of reference for the entire akathist is the "unwedded" Mother of God about whom the song of the poet and the praying person pours forth in a double ascending and descending movement. As on a ladder, one goes up and down, in the mysterious sense of the evangelical expression of John 1:51: "Then he said to him, 'Truly, truly, I say to you, you will see heaven opened and the angels of God ascending and descending upon the Son of man,'" where the strangeness is in the fact that the angels ascend and descend, and not vice versa. Thus, in the akathist, in considering the Mother of God, one climbs all the steps up to the supreme contemplation of the Trinity and, from above, all the charisms descend as uncreated divine energies poured out on men, leading them to be like the Mother of God. The entire pattern of the akathist's composition is based on a powerful intuition, even if not expressed directly, capable of introducing the reader and the person praying to an understanding of the mystery of the union between God and man in prayer. The hymn is nothing but the unfolding of the encounter between the humility of the Virgin and the humility of God. The Virgin Mary is not only the one through whom the Word takes shape, thus entering this world incarnate, but she is also she who represents the direct and positive condition for the incarnation of the Word, in which we can glimpse the entire path of man's divinization. Said with a bold but theologically sound image, God has found in the Virgin the entire mystery of humility, where human dignity finds all its fullness, so much so as to induce him to give himself in the same way, in his most total divine humility. Through the meeting of these two humilities, the Word descended and became flesh. The divine Word took on a body.

Fr. Daniil is following in the wake of the Eastern tradition according to the intuition of Gregory Palamas regarding his Marian theology. In fact, Marian reflection is not a marginal theme in Gregory Palamas. The Virgin is at the center or, rather, at the peak of his theology. Following the way in which the Byzantine theologian reflects on the figure of Mary we can touch on some of the main nodes of Palamite thought: hesychia, pure prayer, contemplation, divinization, light.

The place of the heart is seen by Eastern tradition as the Holy of Holies, the place of the Presence of the Lord, a place to enter, leaving behind all sensory and mental dispersion, to praise the name of the Lord, as the Psalms often repeat. Now Fr. Daniil's position regarding prayer might be expressed in a question like this: are people today still capable of praising God, of seeing the glory of the Lord who came into the world, still capable of being amazed? The discovery of the place of the heart introduces us to this capacity for praise, to the amazement that makes us remain there in silence, a silence of fullness and not of lack. The prayer of the heart becomes like the door to a fourth dimension, the one through which the heart receives the divine fire that burns and does not consume, like the fire of the Burning Bush (cf. Exod. 3:2–3), which Father Daniil calls "the fire of glory," with which the Virgin is totally occupied. For those praying, however, it is not a beatifying fire; it is a fire that burns, and yet leaves traces of joy that makes the heart impervious to evil, even though one sees this evil stirring in the abyss of one's consciousness.

The text by Gregory Palamas which best explains the depths of Father Daniil's poetic and theological intuitions in the composition of his akathist is homily 53, *For the entry into the Holy of Holies and the life of a divine kind lived in it by our most pure Lady, the Mother of God and ever virgin Mary.*[12] It comments on the feast of Mary's entry into the Temple of Jerusalem, based on stories from some apocryphal gospels, such as that of the *Nativity of Mary* (or *Protoevangelium of James*) and the *Gospel of Pseudo-Matthew*, which have long been incorporated into theological doctrine. The homily is a treatise on hesychast doctrine; in it Mary is portrayed as the perfect model of the spiritual life and, in particular, as the prototype of every monk and every hesychast: the description of the path of reclusion and *hesychía* experienced by the Virgin in the Holy of Holies is nothing but the realization of the envisioned hesychast ideal. Mary made the incarnation possible and in this way actively collaborated in the realization of God's plan whose aim is the divinization of man: God came down to earth through Mary, so that we could ascend to heaven through him by regarding

[12] Gregory Palamas, *Mary the Mother of God. Sermons by Gregory Palamas*, ed. C. Veniamin, homily 53 (South Canaan, PA: Mount Tabor Publishing, 2005), 16–50. It is the same text that Basil of Poiana Mărului and Paisius Velichkovsky also followed, whose writings Father Daniil knew perfectly well.

her. This is the path outlined in Father Daniil's akathist, which our poet-orator distributes over the three traditional stages to arrive at divinization: the stage of the beginners, of the progressing, of the perfect, Palamas's homily has divided up the Virgin's experience into an ascetic life, a life of prayer, and a life of union. We find many expressions from this homily in the various sections of the akathist, such as, for example, the victory over the curse that had weighed on man:

> "With profound understanding she listened to the writings of Moses and the revelations of the other prophets when, every Saturday; all the people gathered outside, as the Law ordained.... When the holy Virgin Maid heard and understood this, she was filled with pity for humanity and, with the aim of finding a remedy to counteract this great affliction, she resolved at once to turn with her whole mind to God. She took it upon herself to represent us, to constrain Him Who is above compulsion, and quickly draw Him towards us, that He might remove the curse from among us, halt the advance of the fire burning men's souls, weaken our enemies, answer our prayers, shine upon us with light that never sets and, having healed our sickness, unite His creature with Himself."[13] Or, that of the union with God by her supreme purity: "You alone fulfilled all their visions, surpassing our common human nature by means of your union with God, not just when you gave birth in a marvelous way, but also through the preceding fellowship with Him in everything good, which resulted from your utter purity."[14]

Thus Mary is not only the perfect model for renunciation of the world, but also that of true contemplation because it is not the same thing to say something about God and to meet with God:

> It is absolutely impossible, however, to truly encounter God unless, in addition to being cleansed, we go outside, or rather, beyond ourselves, leaving behind everything perceptible to our senses, together with our ability to perceive, and being lifted up above thoughts, reason, knowledge and even the mind itself... the Virgin found that holy quietness [*hesychia*] was her guide: quietness, in which the mind and the world stand still, forgetfulness of the things below, initiation into heavenly secrets, the laying aside of ideas for something better. This

[13] Ibid., 41.

[14] Ibid., 23.

is truly something we actively do, a means of approaching contemplation or, to state it more aptly, the vision of God, which is the only proof of a soul in good health.... Contemplation... is the fruit of a healthy soul, an outcome and a state which divinize a man... under the guidance of stillness. Continuing in our life's upper room [cf. Acts 1:13–14], as it were, in prayers and supplications night and day; in some way we touch that blessed nature that cannot be touched. Thus the light beyond our perception and understanding is diffused ineffably within those whose hearts have been purified by holy stillness [*hesychia*], and they see God within themselves as in a mirror [cf. 2 Cor. 3:18].[15]

Mary lived this journey in such an extraordinary way as to become "capable" of bearing God himself as a child within herself. Not only she, but she also becomes the mediator for every divine illumination; she who has fully welcomed the light, makes it reverberate on all those who are worthy of it:

Just as it was through her alone that He came to us, and "appeared on earth and lived among men" (Baruch 3:37), whereas previously He was invisible to all, so in the unending age that follows, any progress towards divine illumination, every revelation of the mysteries of the divine order, and every kind of spiritual gift is beyond the capacity of anyone, without her. Being the first to receive "the fulness of him that filleth all" (cf. Eph. 1:23), she brought Him within the grasp of all, sharing with each according to his strength and in proportion to the measure of his purity.[16]

Without the Virgin there is no manifestation of divine light. The echo of the invocations to the Virgin with which the akathist shines refers to those of Palamas's homily:

You bear the title of Mother of God. You have united your mind with God. You have joined God with flesh. You have made God the Son of man, and man the son of God.... You gave human nourishment to Him Who nurtures the angels. Through Him Who provides for the angels you have fed us on the truly heavenly and incorruptible food. You have made men live the same life as angels, or rather, you have made them worthy of greater privileges, in that you conceived, of the Holy Spirit, the theandric Form, and mysteriously gave

[15] Ibid., 43–44.
[16] Ibid., 36.

> Him birth, linking man's nature to the divine nature and rendering it, as it were, equally divine [cf. Heb. 10:12], in inexpressible fashion.... [She] made the whole world heaven.... She did not cause us fleeting pleasure..., but brought us the Treasure of all goodness, the everlasting Fount that springs without ceasing from the Father's bosom, the Word Who is seated above the vaults of heaven. Thence He has brought us living water, and bestowed on us food which makes those who partake of it immortal and sons of God, not adopted merely in name, but in the fellowship of the Holy Spirit—Oh ineffable gift!—brought close to God and one to another through God's Flesh and Blood.[17]

Returning to the discussion, we can thus summarize the thoughts of Palamas and of Father Daniil. Mary united her intellect to God, realizing the ideal of every hesychast, but, in a unique way, she united God to the flesh, making the Invisible visible and the Intangible tangible. The Virgin nourished God with earthly nourishment, so that God could nourish us with heavenly food, a food that makes us immortal because it is the flesh and blood of God himself. The incarnation of the Word in the womb of the Virgin is the presupposition for the divinization of man, which is given to us to the utmost degree precisely in the Eucharist. And it is precisely the Eucharistic mystery that is the singular aspect of the definition of the Virgin as a model for hesychast practice. In fact, what eucharistic communion achieves on the level of mystery, the fruit of God's original plan to unite man to himself, created in the image of the incarnate Word—asceticism and the prayer of the heart manifest this at the level of spiritual perception, in the incessant journey towards full and manifest communion with Him, awaiting the final resurrection, to the praise of the Trinity.[18]

In the few commentary notes that Fr. Daniil had prepared for an understanding of his composition, he has also referred to a famous expression of St. Augustine: *Verbum caro factum est, magna pulchritudo est.* The Word became flesh: what extraordinary beauty![19] The Incarnation is the supreme beauty, as will be foreshadowed by the entire path of the divinization of man

---

[17] Ibid., 49–50.

[18] Cf. L. Bianchi, "Maria modello dell'asceta esicasta secondo G. Palamas" in *Theotokos*, Year XX, 2012, no. 1, 171–86.

[19] *Enar. in psalmos*, 44.3.

which results from allowing the Word to become incarnate in us, just as he became incarnate in the Virgin Mary. Dante, in the last canto of the *Paradiso*, after having raised sublime praise to the Queen of Heaven, expresses himself thus: "Those eyes belovéd and revered by God."[20] It is the Virgin who is sought precisely for her radical humility. The same divine paradox of the Trinity is perfectly reflected in the Virgin Mary, under the sign of a grand cross. In the power of her humility, which is indeed the fruit of her fullness of grace, of that spotless humility, she, the flower of the human race, is raised to the dignity of being Daughter of the Father, Mother of the Word, Bride of the Paraclete, remaining totally and simply a servant of God, the wife of a carpenter from Nazareth.

5. Interpretative Scheme of the Akathist

The twenty-four intervals of a musical scale or rungs of a ladder are divided into three triads, which we can call, in musical language, three octaves, each with four ascending and four descending stages. Each octave constitutes a stage of the spiritual path, according to the common patristic tradition: the stage of the beginners, the stage of the proficient, the stage of the perfect. Everything is contemplated with eyes fixed on the Mother of God considered in her ascent towards the mystery of perfect union with God, in praise of the Trinity and in her becoming a means and guide for our journey of gradually obtaining the divinization for which we were created.

Each octave is made up of four stanzas. The ascending movement refers to the very mystery of the Mother of God, caught up in the participation of her humanity in God's will to save us, which is realized with the incarnation of her Son in her womb.

FIRST OCTAVE: THE PATH OF BEGINNERS

I. Symbol of transfiguration and hypostasis of prayer

The Virgin is the wonder obtained with the prayer of humanity that preceded her and which refined the desire for God in the heart of man to such a point that the very existence of the Virgin can be considered the incarnation of prayer: "Who is this, pure and radiant as the dawn? She is the Queen of

[20] *Paradiso*, 33, 40 (Hollander trans.).

prayer, she is prayer incarnate." This is because the Holy Spirit has overshadowed her and all that she is is full of the Spirit, she is pure space for the action of the Spirit. Thus, in her and through her, in whom the fiery song, the very essence of all divine praise, is ever raised to God, humanity is rapt in the contemplation of God's love and tells of its yearning for redemption, calling her: "you who conceived the Pledge of Fire... bush of supreme ecstasy... body and embodiment of overflowing joy... wonder undoing the world's vanity."

II. Entry into the heart and the lifting of the curse

Following the ancient apocryphal account of the presentation of Mary in the Temple, where she lived from an early age in the Holy of Holies, the Virgin is seen as the first person who entered the Holy of Holies of the heart, the place of the Presence, the place of light, by the absolute purity of her heart. Thus, turning to her, the children of men invoke her as the one who dissolved the curse of nature by breaking the yoke of slavery to sin so that they might return to hymn, together with her, the secrets of the longed-for Bridegroom concerning the salvation of man, following the example of Moses before the bush on fire with grace. He then bursts out in praise of the Virgin, calling her: "measure of the eighth day of the kingdom within us... wisdom drawn from the joy hereafter... amazement kissed by the wonders of the Spirit."

III. The name of glory and the inner Christ

In the wake of Isaiah's ancient prophecy of the Virgin giving birth to a child, the song refers to her as the Parent of him who bears an ineffable Name, the Name which the prophet had celebrated with five titles and which Jesus, the son of Mary, will bear. The name Jesus is made up of five letters in both Greek (Ιησού) and Romanian (*Iisus*), the name which the prayer will then repeat incessantly. In the invocation of the name of Jesus, which the akathist hymn sees as an invitation from the Virgin Mary to pronounce it, there is an exhortation to make the journey into the heart, to find the path of the Name of Light, because the Name of the Lord of glory refers precisely to Mary's son, Jesus, who lives in the heart and who revealed himself humbly by riding on the back of an ass's foal to enter Jerusalem. And then the praises pour forth: "foundation that has allowed us also to contain God...intimacy and reconciliation of our hidden nature...solitude in which Heaven unfurls in the heart...transparency through which an angel is taking shape in us...purity by which the Name of glory was manifested to the world." The spiritual path is envisioned as a path of spiritualization, as the growth of an inner angel, as a cherub in the making.

IV. Holy impassibility and the breath of the Spirit

With the image of the Burning Bush, which burns and is not consumed, the Virgin is seen as the model for the art of spiritualization, to the point where she no longer has anything passionate in herself but is moved only by the passion of God's love. This is called "Luminous impassibility," that is to say, as if an ocean of peace for the fiery love of God, which remains unattainable by any stratagem of the adversary and absolutely free from any acquiescence to anything but the fiery love of God. Thus, the invocation rises to her so to enjoy, along with her, the holy trembling in the Spirit who reveals to us the secret of God's love, completely conquering our heart, caught up in the experience of invoking the Name with the participation of the entirety of the inner universe. This is peace of thoughts, rest from wayward and distracting thoughts. And she is then exalted as "the hesychast leap into blessed flight...eternity enclosed in the space of an instant...ardent wisdom blossoming in the *Philokalia*...masterful discovery of the meaning of worship."

SECOND OCTAVE: THE PATH OF THE PROFICIENT

V. The fire of the Spirit and repetition of the Name

The second phase of spiritual progress begins when the heart is no longer disturbed by extraneous thoughts. The fire of the Spirit now acts and fills one with light. This is the time for patience in prayer. The heart of the Virgin is considered to be in the fullness of light for bearing Christ and is invoked so that we too may be filled with light in constant memory of the fiery love of God, with the soul holding fast to the Name of glory. We pray to be made of fire, taken by the love of his Name and set on fire by the joy sealed by the Holy Spirit. This fire in us is ignited with the humble, incessant invocation of the Name of Jesus, carrying it in the same way in which she carried it. Praise now breaks out for the Mother of God, who is invoked by the person praying as a model: "tender boldness for the invoking of the Holy Name... living rosary of the *Kyrie eleison*... flood of the continuous memory of God... charismatic ceaseless repetition of a wondrous invocation."

VI. Inner sky and sobriety

Contemplating the Virgin we learn to see life as belonging to the Spirit far beyond concepts and space, beyond the flow of any temporal chronicle. It is the experience of a pure mind, of the fiery sky that is within us, where the sources of the heart and the entirety of creation well up, and of seeing the world in its meaning as path and incarnation towards eternity. It comes to us from contemplating the Virgin in her state of absolute sobriety and attention to the Spirit in both will and feelings, the vision of the heart where, at its very core, the transparency of pure spiritual states reigns supreme. It is the transparency of a feeling that combines the sharpness of the mind with the ardor of life's impetuosity, according to the image of heat and cold placed like a cross, capable of generating something that goes far beyond thought and passion. It is the return to spiritual childhood, to holy imperturbable simplicity full of wonder, as expressed so admirably in the akathist: sobriety or vigilance of the spirit is that of a child, a key to the depths of the heart. The praise of the Virgin then bursts forth with bold images: "piercing brightness of the memory of God... lute of the heart played with the bow of the mind... ineffable music of the second birth... betrothed of the Name of Wisdom."

VII. The arcanum of Christian initiation and the mystery of adoption: the dowry

The humble, peaceful and pure soul acts as if it were receiving from the very hands of the Virgin, rich in all holiness, the bridal garment for the splendid wedding of the great Bridegroom, a wedding which can only be celebrated in total purity. Only she can render us participants in it. Additionally, invoked as the most philokalic Bride, all possible spiritual goods are obtained from her, since she summarizes in herself the entire economy of blessings that God has established for her children. Thus the praise that is raised, addressed to her, only underscores the fullness of the blessings that she obtains for us: "utmost skill at fostering us all unto theosis...rarest of gifts painstakingly wrought by purifying grace...wondrous light anointing humble minds... inspiriting Presence giving us entry into Sabbath rest...the word that lasts forever in wondrous silence."

VIII. Inner singing and the heart of grace

The ascent becomes ever steeper, but, before entering the realm of prayer as an encounter with the Bridegroom, when He can be touched or sensed, the prayer-poet becomes lost in total amazement while contemplating the heart of the Mother of God, seen as the one and only heart where, incomparably, the heart of man and the heart of God continually beat as one. Her prayer, in accord with the contemplation of Heaven, shapes her inmost being around the mystery of God's love. Here we have a vision of the heart of the Virgin as the heart of the Church. Thus we ask to have a new heart, like hers, a heart of light, a heart of flesh, an immaculate heart, a heart of the Word. Seeing the scattering that our heart has suffered, its hardening, its straying from the ways of God, we ask to be reawakened to life with new and pure hearts, capable of drawing deeply from the dayspring of the morning without evening. Praise is then raised to the Virgin calling her: "music box through which radiance resounds...feast of the heavens in which the spirit is the true celebrant...Church greatly desiring the Triadic wedding feast."

THIRD OCTAVE: THE GOAL OF THE PERFECT

IX. The encounter with Christ and the art of *hesychia*

Here is the last stage of the journey, the one that leads to the ardently desired union with God. The person praying now professes to be of the same lineage as the Mother of God in order to be admitted to the encounter with the sweet Bridegroom of hearts. Then the apostle Thomas makes his appearance before the Risen One, trembling and, just as the Byzantine liturgy sings, extending his hand into His fiery side without being burned. However, there is no sense of exaltation here, but a feeling of extreme humility, because the light, arising from the depths of God and placed in the heart of man, has, like a timeless sun, entirely illuminated the expanse of being. Thus a spontaneous and flowing light rises to the lips in an unceasing invocation of the prayer of the Name. The Mother of God is invoked as the one who knows perfectly all the ways of redemptive transfiguration, even being called the 'holy human accuracy in all things,' that is, the one who in every circumstance and at any time can show the path of transfiguration, giving us access to the meeting with the sweet Bridegroom. Praise for her person implicitly indicates all possible aspects of the spiritual journey in the church with a view to meeting the Bridegroom: "divine sweetness of the Name like out-poured chrism ... drop [of grace] meted out for a seraphic childhood ... golden harshness of asceticism upon the desert mat ... template of the stool for hesychast prayer ... smile emanating from the engolpion that overcomes the heart's aridity."

X. Pneumatic genesis and the blessing of tears

The Virgin now becomes a person's own spiritual Mother, the one who presides over our luminous birth, the new birth from above. The person praying calls her: "Church giving birth to the inner man." It is to her that the person praying confidently turns, as an anchor for one's own weaknesses, as a hidden guide for the heart. It seemed easy to devote oneself to prayer for establishing one's heart in the place of God, in ceaseless repentance, but the clay idol of one's intellect finds it difficult to consent to this. And then he turns to the Virgin for acquiring the gift of tears, the salt of repentance, and to be purified and freed from the weakness of the spirit. And this is how the Mother of God manifests in her generous blessings on the person praying: "dew of benevolence with which you strengthen believers ... help offered even to the ungodly in their ruin ... mantle spread over every weakness."

XI. Theosis and the theophanic ladder

Beyond his own weakness, through the intercession of the Most Clement, man now feels indwelt by the Lord Jesus so that his seeing, speaking and understanding, his very sight, hearing and will, are no longer simply his own actions, his own senses, but the actions and senses of the very Christ who lives within him. With the incessant repetition of the invocation of the Name he has reached the threshold of the silence of his senses and of the will of his heart to belong entirely to the Lord Jesus. He will be able to begin to see the fruits, he will be able to access the angels' song of praise, wholly gathered with the spirit in the light, in the depths of the heart. The poet does not overtly list the series of fruits but alludes to the famous ladder of Theophanis the Monk:

> The first step is that of purest prayer.
> From this there comes a warmth of heart,
> And then a strange, a holy energy,
> Then tears wrung from the heart, God-given.
> Then peace from thoughts of every kind.
> From this arises purging of the intellect,
> And next the vision of heavenly mysteries,
> Unheard-of light is born from this ineffably,
> And thence, beyond all telling, the heart's illumination.
>
> Last comes—a step that has no limit
> Though compassed in a single line—
> Perfection that is endless.
> The ladder's lowest step
> Prescribes pure prayer alone.
> But prayer has many forms:
> My discourse would be long
> Were I now to speak of them:
> And, friend, know that always
> Experience teaches one, not words.
> A ladder rising wondrously to heaven's vault:
> Ten steps that strangely vivify the soul.
> Ten steps that herald the soul's life.[21]

And the Mother of God herself is exalted as a "ladder that rises from a broken heart... the warmth of grace that pervades the flesh... amazing feat that weaves our sanctification... immensity of perfection for a body freed from corruption."

XII. The model of *hesychia* and incarnate gnosis

We have now reached the top of the ladder. The person praying enters the Sabbath rest, which the poet calls "the great peace of ecstatic rest," where he burns without being consumed, resting in the shelter of the contemplated Face, now transfigured by the unspeakable mystery of an existence of prayer. And the

[21] *The Philokalia*, vol. 3, 67.

existence of grace. This is prayer beyond prayer. Addressing the Mother of God, our spiritual *Amma* full of love for the world, all pure and all compassionate, in whom all the treasures of blessing reside, the person praying invokes her so that she might bestow on us, too, that most pure *gnosis* of which she is full. And such gnosis or divine science is found abundantly in the Fathers who followed her on this path of transfiguration. Praise can now burst forth for the one who is the guardian of the hesychast tradition: "arch-strategist of the unseen warfare... gaze that preserves ascetic labors in sweetness... threshing rod that scatters the evil spirits like chaff."

XIII. The embrace of the Trinity

Mother of God and Mother of man, the Virgin presents to Christ the Bridegroom with her own hands the oblation of glory of the person praying, directing him to the Holy Trinity who embraces everything and in whose embrace everything sings. Since the love of the Holy Trinity presided over the incarnation of the Son in the womb of the Virgin, the hymn refers again to the initial praise of the one who appears as the Queen of prayer, incarnate prayer, within whose womb is unfolded all the secrets of God for man.

It is impossible not to recall here the ending of Dante's *Paradiso*:

> At this point power failed high fantasy but,
> like a wheel in perfect balance turning, I felt
> my will and my desire impelled
> by the Love that moves the sun and the other stars.[22]

What is striking in this ladder of ascent towards union with God is the fact that on the last rungs the traits of the Mother of God's compassion for us sinners, called to such high dignity, are accentuated. The person praying is reminded of his fragility, as if he were being warned that it is not a question of merging into God, but of opening up to the fullest and most total praise of his immense love for us. Man loses himself in praise, not in fusion. Not only that, but the ascent of man coincides with the movement of the entire universe, because everything lives from God and on his boundless love. As St.

[22] *Paradiso*, 33, 142–45 (Musa trans.).

Paul says, showing the goal of the tension that moves the heart of man, since all creation is summed up in him in his longing for God, "Now when all things are made subject to Him, then the Son Himself will also be subject to Him who put all things under Him, that God may be all in all" (1 Cor. 15:28). As in the supreme moment of Dante's experience in paradise, there is no longer a path to follow, any reason in the classical sense to be exercised, there is no longer a word that by approximation tries to get closer to the truth. Here everything is full of light, it is beauty, truth. There is no more effort to do anything, love and knowledge coincide perfectly. And it is apophatic knowledge, not in the sense that it is opposed to cataphatic knowledge, that is, as the negation of what was previously affirmed because the reality of God is immeasurably loftier, but in a sense that is beyond both affirmation and negation. One is absorbed in praise, in pure wonder, in pure amazement. But it is always within the reality of a creature totally overwhelmed by the splendor of a boundless love, the meaning of which is always conveyed by the Mother of God, together with her Son. This is why the goal does not resemble a point of arrival, but a root of meaning which, secret, lies hidden in the creature and in the universe, and which the Mother of God would have us discover. Getting there means coming down here, into the heart, where the Holy Trinity dwells and draws everything to itself, welcoming us into the supreme joy of eternal love. Without losing awareness of one's own creaturely being, the rhythm of prayer does not bring us to a halt at the supreme point but sends us back to the initial movement because, as long as we are on earth, that ascent is in perpetual becoming, until everything in us and of us fully expresses, as with the Mother of God, praise of the Holy Trinity.

Akathist Hymn
TO THE BURNING BUSH OF THE MOTHER OF GOD

I
KONTAKION 1
Akathist prelude
the Virgin—symbol of transfiguration

Who is this, pure and radiant as the dawn?
She is the Queen of prayer, she is prayer incarnate.
Our sovereign Porphyrogenita and Lady of the Morning,
Betrothed of the Consoler who transfigures life!
We run to you, parched and consumed with longing!
Let us also partake of Holy Mount Tabor.
    You yourself be for us
    cool shade and dew,
    You, whom the Spirit overshadowed,
    so that our nature might also find
    a regeneration of grace.
And so we cry out to you with our whole being bowed low:
Rejoice, O Holy Bride, weaver of ceaseless prayer!

IKOS 1

The hypostasis of prayer:
the Holy Virgin

For fifty long centuries,
through Abraham and David,
Your prophesying ancestry has filled Heaven with tears and prostrations
preparing the gift of your immaculate body woven with prayer,
O mighty unconsumed Bush.
The Sacred Fire sings in You as in a flower of glory.
Through you, nature tells of its longing for redemption.
You, Lady, are the Hypostasis
of supernatural praises;
so much so that one is rapt in an ecstasy
of divine love
so that our voices resound like this:

Rejoice, fruit enwrapped unto Sinai's harvest
Rejoice, You who conceived the Pledge of Fire
Rejoice, Entrance for the One Word of Scripture
Rejoice, singing string of the Holy Spirit
Rejoice, heavenly masterpiece of salvation's daybreak
Rejoice, life-giving philosophy of true deification
Rejoice, bush of supreme ecstasy
Rejoice, unity and crown of all symbols
Rejoice, string and sound, bow and lyre
Rejoice, body and embodiment of overflowing joy
Rejoice, wonder undoing the world's vanity
Rejoice, O Holy Bride, weaver of ceaseless prayer!

II
KONTAKION 2
Entry into the heart

All-holy consoler,
Holy Virgin Child!
By the striking propriety of Your tender word
and the humble invocation of the mind's prayer,
You were the first to enter the miraculous sanctuary of man,
our emerald place at the altar of the holy Presence.
With bold wisdom You have broken the circle of slavery,
the circle of death, the circle of oblivion,
overcoming the curse of nature,
the oppressive overlord of our life, with the power of purity,
so to Him who has given us the gift of You
will we chant ardently forever: *Alleluia!*

IKOS 2

The music of Jericho:
the lifting of the curse

Virgin of the age without sunset,
Holy Mother of the Light!
Hear also we sinners, unworthy children of the mire.
Most sweet, good, Most Holy Virgin, womb of the Lord Jesus!
Free us from the curse that imprisons us,
open up the path to the heart,
so that we too, through fiery revelation,
can sing the secrets of the longed-for Bridegroom
just as Moses, putting off his sandals,
with his face aglow from the bush on fire with grace,
cried out to You in the dusk with words like these:

Rejoice, stem of light of the unconsumed Bush
Rejoice, fragrant portal of humanity through which God came to light
Rejoice, circle of fire higher than the heavens
Rejoice, freedom from bondage melting all of our inner frost
Rejoice, flowering staff for the heart's journey
Rejoice, freshet of coolness springing up in the inner desert
Rejoice, ember signet impressed upon the hidden recesses of the soul
Rejoice, snow of the intellect unattainable by any passion
Rejoice, measure of the eighth day of the kingdom within us
Rejoice, wisdom emerging from the joy hereafter
Rejoice, amazement kissed by the wonders of the Spirit.
Rejoice, O Holy Bride, weaver of ceaseless prayer!

III
KONTAKION 3
The name of glory
Prophetic gift

Through the ages, O Virgin, I have heard of You,
by the mouth of Isaiah, prophet of the burning coal.
And in the heaven of Scripture Your word resounds as a supreme gift of grace:
"For, behold, a child will be born to us, a son has been given to us.
Sovereignty is on his shoulders and his Name will be:
Wonderful, Angel of the Great Council, Mighty God,
Prince of universal peace and Father of the age to come."
This is his Name, an ineffable name, the holy name of the Lord that Jesus will bear.
Take heed, O my soul, so that all of us together can cry out: *Alleluia!*

IKOS 3

Invitation to the journey of the heart
The inner Christ

It is from an ever Virgin Mother
that he was conceived, that he became incarnate,
He who kept the corporeal reality of the Burning Bush intact.
The Name of the Lord of glory has become
a pronounceable word,
the Invisible One has mysteriously revealed Himself
in the heart of the fire,
the Face of heavenly Beauty, the uncircumscribable Image
has bounded Himself,
measured Himself with measure,
and it is He, the Ineffable One here among us,
who revealed Himself as a humble victor
riding on the foal of an ass.
Therefore, you too seek the path of the Name of Light,
the sublime Journey,
and from death will you pass to life,
deified in your being,
so that we may all sing together with a clear and resolute voice:

Rejoice, foundation that has allowed us also to contain God
Rejoice, power with which we walk with Christ upon the waters
Rejoice, mercy by which Christ gave Himself to us
Rejoice, path along which the Amen has come to us
Rejoice, silence in which the Word is heard within us
Rejoice, intimacy and reconciliation with our silent nature
Rejoice, humble tenderness that makes us alike to our brother Emmanuel
Rejoice, way by which the Spirit Himself pulses in our veins
Rejoice, solitude in which Heaven unfurls in the heart.
Rejoice, transparency through which an angel is taking shape in us
Rejoice, purity by which the Name of glory was manifested to the world
Rejoice, O Holy Bride, weaver of ceaseless prayer!

IV
KONTAKION 4

The Virgin—Holy Impassibility
Purifying prayer

How are we to find rest from thoughts?
Virgin Mother, All-Holy Virgin!
How can we escape the snares of our passions,
the oppressive temptations that grip us?
Make yourself, for us, the longed-for invocation,
the model for the art of spiritualization.
We will thus overcome our enslaved nature,
to the point of reducing all passions to ashes.
And enraptured in You, "Luminous Impassibility,"
we too can raise up in total and sincere praise
a true and psalmic: *Alleluia!*

IKOS 4

The firebird—
The breath

O Theotokos, You flower enkindled by the unconsuming Flame,
You, image of peace encompassed with coolness at the heart of the fire,
bend down now, Most Good One, over us.
And in Your tender mercy grant us the ability to find in abundance
the rare gift of holy trembling in the Spirit,
the deep breath of a tranquil flight from the bosom of the silver Dove,
which the prophet King also contemplated
soaring above the peaks of Bashan
And bestow on your creature, each one of us,
this fiery secret of goodness,
imparted from your very breath.
Seal our impure lips with a glowing measure of that cleansing fire
so that we can ardently sing to you:

Rejoice, hesychast leap of blessed flight
Rejoice, chaste sigh of quiet emotion
Rejoice, lightning bolt of prayer in the silence of the mind
Rejoice, widely soaring dove of the spirit
Rejoice, horizon arched with cherub wings
Rejoice, eternity enclosed in the space of an instant
Rejoice, mighty oar for the appointed ascent
Rejoice, heavenly sip of subtle knowledge
Rejoice, fount overspread with ripples of Living Water
Rejoice, ardent wisdom blossoming in the *Philokalia*
Rejoice, masterful discovery of the meaning of worship
Rejoice, O Holy Bride, weaver of ceaseless prayer!

V

KONTAKION 5

Fire lit by the Spirit
Unceasing utterance

"I have come to cast fire on the earth,"
Christ declared with fiery words.
O Most Pure One, may the conflagration of His love
ignite us with all the scorching power of its flame
and fill us with incommensurable light as it did You,
O Virgin who bore Him.
May our heart ever remember his love
with our very soul cleaving to the Name of glory
And may every humble intake of our breath
kindle within us the invocation of the Name.
In God we become fire, totally ablaze with the love of his Name.
And, burning with joy in the Lord,
as flames of love we will cry out: *Alleluia!*

IKOS 5

The clay jug's monologistic prayer
The transfiguring power in the reciting
of litanies—repetition of the Name

From You we comprehend, O Virgin,
the mystery of incomprehensible constancy
and the strength of the sweet invocations of a humble and limpid prayer.
Yes, water is fluid by nature; yet stone is very hard.
But the clay jug above the stone,
with its continuous dripping, through that small drop of water,
pierces the most resistant stone.
Persist thus, O Virgin, even over our heart of stone.
And overcome us with Your drop of grace,
so that we might sing to You in glorifying hymns:

Rejoice, tender boldness for the invoking of the Holy Name
Rejoice, clay jug that drips with continuous persistence
Rejoice, steadfast radiance from the Lord's white stone
Rejoice, sweetest honeycomb of Jesus Son of Man
Rejoice, nest of thought wherein my Christ reposes
Rejoice, communion by word from the invoking of God
Rejoice, profusion of fragrance given us by the Son
Rejoice, living rosary of the *Kyrie eleison*
Rejoice, surge that carries even me, a sinner, away
Rejoice, flood of the continuous memory of God
Rejoice, charismatic ceaseless repetition of a wondrous invocation
Rejoice, O Holy Bride, weaver of ceaseless prayer!

VI
KONTAKION 6

Pure mind,
inner sky

All-holy Virgin, ever in your presence,
down through the ages,
the thoughts of those wise in their own minds
are confounded
Because You are the seal of incorruptibility,
a closed door for those who boast of their intelligence,
and a living mirror of wondrous conduct.
You know that life was not given to us
to find a meaning of our own making,
that it proves to be far richer than a life merely lived.
It pertains to the Mind far beyond thought and place,
beyond the chain of fleeting moments.
It is a manifestation of the fiery heavens within us,
above the wellsprings of the heart and creation.
It belongs to the world-creating Word
who would be for us the path and incarnation unto eternity:
Alleluia!

IKOS 6

Sober Watchfulness

O Holy Virgin, our most pure Mother!
You are in truth sobriety of spirit,
the myrrh-bundle of the will
gathered in the forehead,
the inner eye open
to the horizon's entire circuit,
the heart where the transparency
of pure thoughts and feelings
reigns supreme at its center.
You are the most righteous spiritual attention,
through which you join together,
by the power of intellect, beyond words,
in a flash of the mind:
the icy keenness of thought with the burning rush of life,
hot and cold set in a cross,
which yields up the loftiest of meanings.
But this alertness of spirit is that of an infant,
a key which opens, with a swift and unexpected turn,
the depths of the heart,
yet which in no way troubles your serene soul;
to the contrary,
it gives You that great and holy simplicity
which ever fills us with wonder
and before which, as much as we can,
we bow down our heads
gathering all of our breath to sing:

Rejoice, cross of fervor and discernment of the chosen one.
Rejoice, axis of heaven with the morning star of knowledge
Rejoice, banisher of thoughts with their vain swarm
Rejoice, invisible mirror in which is reflected He who is beyond the flesh
Rejoice, most clear crystal of my soul
Rejoice, piercing brightness of the remembrance of God
Rejoice, lute of the heart played with the bow of the mind
Rejoice, sounding forth of five strings in unison
Rejoice, ineffable music of the second birth

Rejoice, supreme height of the fullness of knowledge
Rejoice, betrothed of the Name of Wisdom
Rejoice, O Holy Bride, weaver of ceaseless prayer!

VII
KONTAKION 7

The secret teaching
The arcanum of Christian initiation

To the handicraft of your holiness we come, O Mother,
to be clothed anew by your very hands.
At the splendid wedding of the Great Bridegroom
the garment must be of total purity.
No impurity of look or attire is allowed.
None of those unworthy of the holy mysteries ever dare approach.
Who will let pigs feed on pearls or dogs lick sacred vessels?
Only in spirit can one both ask for and receive a grace,
and only through you, our heavenly Mother.
Come, then, humble, reconciled and pure soul,
and together we will soar into the pure
and complete joy of an *Alleluia*!

IKOS 7

The blessing
Adoption and spiritual endowment

Most holy, most exalted, most beautiful,
most philokalic Bride!
O Queen all en-haloed!
You, our benevolent Mother,
are the bestower of all that is holy:
the living dowry of the good things of grace,
in the sacraments of the Church, in the Divine Liturgy,
signified in the sacred fragrances,
in gestures, in words.
You are the most resplendent Great Tradition
of the whole *economia* of blessings,
like the seven-branched lampstand
alight before the Great Throne of God,
for which all the angels and saints glorify You:

Rejoice, Paschal blessing of new fulfillments
Rejoice, might of the Father set above us in a crown
Rejoice, utmost skill at fostering us all unto theosis
Rejoice, rarest of gifts painstakingly wrought by purifying grace
Rejoice, wondrous light anointing humble minds
Rejoice, realization of untold spiritual powers
Rejoice, rapid spiritual progress granted to firmly established hearts
Rejoice, oneness of mind of all the reconciled Churches
Rejoice, sapphire truth inlaid upon our inner senses
Rejoice, inspiriting Presence giving us entry into Sabbath rest
Rejoice, word that lasts forever in wondrous silence
Rejoice, O Holy Bride, weaver of ceaseless prayer!

VIII
KONTAKION 8

Beating heart
The gift of inner singing

O Queen, All-Holy Lady,
Mother untempted by marriage
You are the only human heart
in which the hymning of the Name of glory
in all the fullness of its living and true reality
never falters.
For this reason, Most Pure One,
a crown of praise surrounds you
because in You alone, as never before,
    the heart of man
    with the heart of God
    have beaten and are beating in unison.
Prayer, like a pendulum between contemplation and Heaven,
    sweeps through your inmost being
intertwined with the lucent *ektenia* of the mystery
    nigh unto the love of God.
O You, Chariot of Light, undefiled,
    unsurpassed and unfading!
Amend us too with the gifts of the heart, O Blessed One!
    And so, as a Church, richly endowed and made worthy,
    we will give ourselves to You with our whole being
    to sing rightly and in holiness: *Alleluia!*

IKOS 8

Heart of grace
Heart of stone

Mother of God, Heart of Light,
Mother of God, Heart of the Earth,
Mother of God, Heart without fault,
Mother of God, Heart of the Word!
We yearn for You, ashamed and humbled
with downcast soul and buckling knees.
because of so great a plague of sin.
Our heart has become
hard and chipped as sharp-edged flint,
bleak beyond telling.
"The Lord has let us tread
the paths we have chosen."
Scattered thoughts stray about in mist.
But, behold, now we prostrate ourselves before You
Mother of Jesus, embrace us as living stones
longing for the day-spring of the morning,
the morning without evening,
and revive us with new and pure hearts
so that we might sing to You:

Rejoice, ark of the covenant of my soul
Rejoice, coffer locked with the Name of God
Rejoice, living ship sailing the billows of the world
Rejoice, coffin preserved from all the vanities of the world
Rejoice, throne upon which life is founded
Rejoice, music box through which radiance resounds
Rejoice, temple in which every celebration of grace transpires
Rejoice, tabernacle of thought for the most spiritual of altars
Rejoice, feast of the heavens, in which the Spirit is the true celebrant
Rejoice, chest of fire set in our very souls
Rejoice, Church greatly desiring the Triadic wedding feast
Rejoice, O Holy Bride, weaver of ceaseless prayer!

IX
KONTAKION 9
The countenance of prayer

Lord Jesus Christ, sweet Bridegroom of our hearts!
I too am of the same lineage as the Most Pure,
a newly grafted shoot.
I approach You by bowing my forehead,
and place my hand like Thomas in your holy side.
Tightly curled within myself, I am seated in silence
like a blind man on a narrow bridge
waiting for "the unsetting Light arising from the depths,
placed in man to entirely illuminate,
like an inner sun, the expanse of being."
Since the darkness of the night of my sins
does not allow me to see you,
with timidity I touch you, with the finger of hope,
with the finger of faith, with the finger of anticipation,
with the finger of desire and, at the same time, of doubt,
and if this were not enough, I would place the other hand
as well;
yet the heart, pierced by a searing flash,
painfully, yet sweetly, to the rhythm of the breath
murmurs the entire invocation and, effortless,
the heartbeat of prayer races towards the light
in an *Alleluia*!

IKOS 9

The Mother of God,
The very art of hesychia

All-holy, ever-helping Virgin,
You are the purest, the most exalted above all angelic creatures,
you also know the supernatural order
suitable for redemptive transfiguration.
You are the mastery, the art, the diligence,
the holy human accuracy in all things,
which together compose
the element that favors our salvation.
And this is why our lips so insistently glorify you:

Rejoice, proper knowledge of holiness to the least detail
Rejoice, sophianic science of working with the inner word
Rejoice, divine sweetness of the Name like out-poured chrism
Rejoice, monastic skill of chanting while bathed in tears
Rejoice, drop meted out for a seraphic childhood
Rejoice, golden harshness of asceticism upon the desert mat
Rejoice, crown of litanies invoked on the prayer-rope
Rejoice, hermit's prayer nook beneath the candle's gentle truth
Rejoice, template of the stool for hesychast prayer
Rejoice, you with upraised hands standing upright in rapture
Rejoice, smile issuing from the engolpion that overcomes the heart's aridity
Rejoice, O Holy Bride, weaver of ceaseless prayer!

X
KONTAKION 10
Pneumatic gnosis

O! flawless Lady full of grace,
Virgin with the wings of the Great Eagle,
Apocalyptic sign of the blameless womb,
Church giving birth to the inner man!
Help me to fashion myself in the ineffable nature
with repeated litanies of whispered invocations.
And grant me luminous birth, my Spiritual Mother,
so that in the experience of the Resurrection
I too can cry out: *Alleluia!*

IKOS 10

The blessing of tears
Incessant repentance

You, generous Mother, Guide to the mysteries,
Lady of hope in evening's azure,
Sovereign with the three stars on her mantle
and Holy Anchor of our weaknesses!
Behold, to You again I have hastened!
I am oppressed by the world, by shattered thoughts.
After receiving holy counsel and a blessing
I entered upon the path of my salvation.
I had made the decision, with strength and determination,
to spend my energies praying ceaselessly.
But my intellect, that clay idol,
does not allow me to overcome myself,
to establish myself in prayer as in the place of God
in that contrition of heart for which I yearn.
Help me, therefore, You my Helper
and obtain for me the gift of tears,
the salt of repentance to be purified and freed
from the weakness of the spirit
and so, once more made worthy, may I sing again to you:

Rejoice, rose bathed in the tears of the heart's conversion
Rejoice, tenderness of repentance with light as its garment
Rejoice, theology of tears, revelation of Wisdom
Rejoice, wise response to the sighs of the world
Rejoice, paradise sprinkled with the rains of saving grace
Rejoice, gaze of a child brimming with tears of wonder
Rejoice, purple vesture for the royal passion of the Amen
Rejoice, gem of grace from the Thorn's tears
Rejoice, dew of benevolence with which you strengthen believers
Rejoice, help offered even to the ungodly in their ruin
Rejoice, mantle spread over every weakness
Rejoice, O Holy Bride, weaver of ceaseless prayer!

XI
KONTAKION 11

Through bright shadow to theosis

I thank you, Most Clement, Ever-Virgin Mother,
for saving me from the second death.
Dangers and temptations serve only to test.
Through the incessant invocations of the most luminous, almighty Name,
my senses and the will of my heart have reached the threshold of silence.
Now free from them,
I wait for the divine hearing, sight and speech to prevail.
Only these will express themselves in me from now on.
And let my Beloved himself, Jesus in his glory, see, speak and understand
with my very own sight, hearing and entire will.
May Christ so live using all my faculties
so that He Himself cries out through me: *Alleluia!*

IKOS 11

The theophanic ladder of fruits

O you heart and mind and thought of mine!
Be wounded with questions before the Face of God.
How are we to discern the truth of heavenly fruits?
And what answer will you hear in these spiritual illuminations:
when the appearing of the unseen Vision drenches you with dew,
within the golden expanse of hallowed images,
in the depths of the spirit,
you will be gathered into tabernacled light,
as was the spirit of the Most Pure Virgin in the Holy of Holies.
And thus you will come to utter a song of praise
as lofty and worthy as the one
that sounds forth by the angel's trumpet.
And, with tender love in your heart,
you will be like the flower of righteous Jesse
trembling this way and that in expectancy of the Three.
We hunger for this
and may the Holy Lady herself deign to bestow on us
the gift of her compassionate intercession
so to raise up a song such as this from us all:

Rejoice, You ladder that rises from a broken heart
Rejoice, ascetic purity of serene prayer
Rejoice, warmth of grace that pervades the flesh
Rejoice, amazing feat that weaves our sanctification
Rejoice, You supernal water gushing from the edge of the abyss
Rejoice, peace that vanquishes the entire welter of thoughts
Rejoice, growing brightness of a mind unclouded
Rejoice, vision in the spirit of overwhelming mysteries
Rejoice, mystical brilliance atop the ineffable ladder
Rejoice, inexpressible illumination of the heart
Rejoice, immensity of perfection for a body freed from corruption
Rejoice, O Holy Bride, weaver of ceaseless prayer!

XII
KONTAKION 12
The Paradoxical Model of Hesychia

You are the sovereign Amma of my soul.
Grant me rest beneath the shelter of Your Countenance,
so that under the golden ember of Your gaze
I too may burn without being consumed,
transfigured by the unspeakable mystery of living prayer.
And, ringed with your refreshing coolness,
O sealed Fount,
may I be renewed ever again
with the streams of Your unfailing grace,
in the great peace of ecstatic rest.
And so, my Holy Amma, encompass me
with the living joy of victory
so that I might sing incandescently
in utmost *hesychia* of knowledge: *Alleluia.*

IKOS 12

Holy Tradition is incarnate Gnosis

Mother of God, Spiritual Mother full of love for the world!
Wellspring of the mystery of the tradition of the Word!
You are divinely gentle and humble,
but, as the Song of Songs says,
also unspeakably righteous and terrible
"like armies arrayed for battle."
You are bright, you are serene, you are sharp
as an unyielding sword.
In the heavenly Jerusalem you have ready helpers,
all those self-deniers, Your devoted children,
all those who belong to the ranks
of ascetics, hermits, and anchorites,
Your entire lineage of wise spiritual elders
to whom are entrusted the treasures of blessing,
everything that expresses clarity, purity and righteousness
that comes from Your purity and boundless compassion,
everything that in one word says
"Pure Gnosis" or the Heritage of the Saints
and which you have manifestly placed within our reach
through the writings, deeds and sayings of the Fathers,
for which we will never know how to
praise you, venerate you, glorify you
except by singing thusly:

Rejoice, guardian Sword of the hesychast tradition
Rejoice, immortal pledge of our adoption as sons
Rejoice, cup in which the blessing of the Lord rests
Rejoice, majestic tree standing vigil over the holy transfiguration of man
Rejoice, wonderful artificer of silent masterpieces
Rejoice, arch-strategist of the unseen warfare
Rejoice, gaze that preserves ascetic labors in sweetness
Rejoice, rule that guides with wise acuity
Rejoice, shield that protects the land of the living
Rejoice, gateway that thwarts every kind of impurity
Rejoice, threshing rod that scatters the evil spirits like chaff
Rejoice, O Holy Bride, weaver of ceaseless prayer!

XIII
KONTAKION 13

Twenty-four harps and incense-bowls

O! Mother of God, ever immaculate and blessed Mother of Man!
Like the twenty-four harps and incense-bowls of the elders
so may our own worship be
in its ceaseless outpouring.
And unto the Most Holy Trinity, O uplifting joy,
from Your hands to Christ the Bridegroom,
may our oblation of true glory
be a most fragrant offering,
so that we might cry out with all the heavens
in the immense embrace of a most sublime: *Alleluia!*

Repeated three times, then Ikos 1 *and* Kontakion 1

Akathist Hymn
TO THE BURNING BUSH OF THE MOTHER OF GOD
Annotated

I
KONTAKION 1
Akathist prelude
the Virgin—symbol[1] of transfiguration

Who is this, pure and radiant as the dawn? SONG OF SONGS 6:10
She is the Queen of prayer, she is prayer incarnate.
Our sovereign Porphyrogenita[2] and Lady of the Morning,
Betrothed of the Consoler who transfigures life!
We run to you, parched and consumed with longing!
Let us also partake of Holy Mount Tabor.
You yourself be for us
cool shade and dew,
You, whom the Spirit overshadowed, LUKE 1:35
so that our nature might also find
a regeneration of grace. JOHN 3:3–8
And so we cry out to you with our whole being bowed low:
Rejoice, O Holy Bride, weaver of ceaseless prayer!

IKOS 1

The hypostasis of prayer:
the Holy Virgin

For fifty long centuries,
through Abraham and David,
Your prophesying ancestry has filled[3] Heaven with tears and prostrations
preparing the gift of your immaculate body woven with prayer,
O mighty unconsumed Bush.[4] EXOD. 3:2
The Sacred Fire sings in You as in a flower of glory.
Through you, nature tells of its longing for redemption. ROM. 8:22–23

You, Lady, are the Hypostasis[5]
of supernatural praises;
so much so that one is rapt in an ecstasy
of divine love
so that our voices resound like this:

Rejoice,[6] fruit enwrapped unto Sinai's harvest
Rejoice, You who conceived the Pledge of Fire
Rejoice, Entrance for the One Word of Scripture
Rejoice, singing string of the Holy Spirit
Rejoice, heavenly masterpiece of salvation's daybreak[7]
Rejoice, life-giving philosophy of true deification
Rejoice, bush of supreme ecstasy
Rejoice, unity and crown of all symbols
Rejoice, string and sound, bow and lyre
Rejoice, body and embodiment of overflowing joy
Rejoice, wonder undoing the world's vanity
Rejoice, O Holy Bride, weaver of ceaseless prayer!

II
KONTAKION 2
Entry into the heart

All-holy consoler,
Holy Virgin Child!
By the striking propriety of Your tender word
and the humble invocation of the mind's prayer,
You were the first to enter the miraculous sanctuary[8] of man, HEB. 9
our emerald place at the altar of the holy Presence.[9]
With bold wisdom You have broken the circle of slavery,
the circle of death, the circle of oblivion,
overcoming the curse of nature,
the oppressive overlord of our life, with the power of purity,
so to Him who has given us the gift of You
will we chant ardently forever: *Alleluia!*

IKOS 2

The music of Jericho:
the lifting of the curse

Virgin of the age without sunset,
Holy Mother of Light!
Hear also we sinners, unworthy children of the mire.
Most sweet, good, Most Holy Virgin, womb of the Lord Jesus!
Free us from the curse that imprisons us,
open up the path to the heart,[10]
so that we too, through fiery revelation,
can sing the secrets of the longed-for Bridegroom
just as Moses, putting off his sandals,
with his face aglow from the bush on fire with grace,* EXOD. 3:2
cried out to You in the dusk with words like these:

Rejoice, stem of light of the unconsumed Bush
Rejoice, fragrant portal[11] of humanity through which God came to light*
Rejoice, circle of fire higher than the heavens
Rejoice, freedom from bondage melting all of our inner frost
Rejoice, flowering staff for the heart's journey NUM. 17:1–10
Rejoice, freshet of coolness springing up in the inner desert NUM. 20:1–11
Rejoice, ember signet impressed upon the hidden recesses of the soul
Rejoice, snow of the intellect unattainable by any passion
Rejoice, measure of the eighth day of the kingdom within us
Rejoice, wisdom emerging from the joy hereafter
Rejoice, amazement kissed by the wonders of the Spirit.
Rejoice, O Holy Bride, weaver of ceaseless prayer!

III
KONTAKION 3
The name of glory
Prophetic gift

Through the ages, O Virgin, I have heard of You,
by the mouth of Isaiah, prophet of the burning coal.* ISA. 6:4–7
And in the heaven of Scripture Your word resounds as a supreme gift of grace:
"For, behold, a child will be born to us, a son has been given to us.
Sovereignty is on his shoulders and his Name will be:
Wonderful, Angel of the Great Council, Mighty God,
Prince of universal peace and Father of the age to come."[12]
ISA. 9:5
This is his Name, an ineffable name,[13] the holy name of the Lord that Jesus will bear.
Take heed, O my soul, so that all of us together can cry out: *Alleluia!*

IKOS 3

Invitation to the journey of the heart
The inner Christ

It is from an ever Virgin Mother
that he was conceived, that he became incarnate,
He who kept the corporeal reality of the Burning Bush intact.
EXOD. 3:2
The Name of the Lord of glory has become
a pronounceable word,
the Invisible One has mysteriously revealed Himself
in the heart of the fire,
the Face of heavenly Beauty, the uncircumscribable Image
has bounded Himself,
measured Himself with measure,[14]
and it is He, the Ineffable One here among us,
who revealed Himself as a humble victor
riding on the foal of an ass. MATT. 21:5–7, JOHN 12:14
Therefore, you too seek the path of the Name of Light,
the sublime Journey,
and from death will you pass to life, JOHN 5:24
deified in your being,
so that we may all sing together with a clear and resolute voice:
Rejoice, foundation that has allowed us also to contain God
Rejoice, power with which we walk with Christ upon the waters
Matt. 14:22–33
Rejoice, mercy by which Christ gave Himself to us
Rejoice, path along which the Amen has come to us APOC. 3:14
Rejoice, silence in which the Word is heard within us
Rejoice, intimacy and reconciliation with our silent nature
Rejoice, humble tenderness that makes us alike to our brother Emmanuel
Rejoice, way by which the Spirit Himself pulses in our veins
Rejoice, solitude in which Heaven unfurls in the heart.
Rejoice, transparency through which an angel[15] is taking shape in us
Rejoice, purity by which the Name of glory was manifested to the world
Rejoice, O Holy Bride, weaver of ceaseless prayer!

IV
KONTAKION 4
The Virgin—Holy Impassibility[16]
Purifying prayer

How are we to find rest from thoughts?
Virgin Mother, All-Holy Virgin!
How can we escape the snares of our passions,
the oppressive temptations that grip us?
Make yourself, for us, the longed-for invocation,
the model for the art of spiritualization.[17]
We will thus overcome our enslaved nature,
to the point of reducing all passions to ashes.
And enraptured in You, "Luminous Impassibility,"
we too can raise up in total and sincere praise
a true and psalmic: *Alleluia!*

IKOS 4

The firebird[18] —
The breath

O Theotokos, You flower enkindled by the unconsuming Flame,*
You, image of peace encompassed with coolness at the heart of the fire,
bend down now, Most Good One, over us.
And in Your tender mercy grant us the ability to find in abundance
the rare gift of holy trembling in the Spirit,
the deep breath of a tranquil flight from the bosom of the silver Dove,
which the prophet King also contemplated
soaring above the peaks of Bashan[19] PSALM 68:14
And bestow on your creature, each one of us,
this fiery secret of goodness,
imparted from your very breath.
Seal our impure lips with a glowing measure of that cleansing fire* ISA. 6:6
so that we can ardently sing to you:

Rejoice, hesychast leap of blessed flight
Rejoice, chaste sigh of quiet emotion
Rejoice, lightning bolt of prayer in the silence of the mind
Rejoice, widely soaring dove of the spirit
Rejoice, horizon arched with cherub wings
Rejoice, eternity enclosed in the space of an instant
Rejoice, mighty oar for the appointed ascent
Rejoice, heavenly sip of subtle knowledge
Rejoice, fount overspread with ripples of Living Water
Rejoice, ardent wisdom blossoming in the *Philokalia*
Rejoice, masterful discovery of the meaning of worship
Rejoice, O Holy Bride, weaver of ceaseless prayer!

V
KONTAKION 5
Fire lit by the Spirit
Unceasing utterance

"I have come to cast fire on the earth," LUKE 12:49
Christ declared with fiery words.
O Most Pure One, may the conflagration of His love
ignite us with all the scorching power of its flame
and fill us with incommensurable light as it did You,
O Virgin who bore Him.
May our heart ever remember his love
with our very soul cleaving to the Name of glory
And may every humble intake of our breath
kindle within us the invocation of the Name.
In God we become fire, totally ablaze with the love of his Name.
And, burning with joy in the Lord,
as flames of love we will cry out: *Alleluia!*

IKOS 5

The clay jug's monologistic prayer[20]
The transfiguring power in the reciting
of litanies—repetition of the Name

From You we comprehend, O Virgin,
the mystery of incomprehensible constancy
and the strength of the sweet invocations of a humble and limpid prayer.
Yes, water is fluid by nature; yet stone is very hard.
But the clay jug above the stone,
with its continuous dripping, through that small drop of water,
pierces the most resistant stone.[21]
Persist thus, O Virgin, even over our heart of stone.
And overcome us with Your drop of grace,
so that we might sing to You in glorifying hymns:

Rejoice, tender boldness for the invoking of the Holy Name
Rejoice, clay jug that drips with continuous persistence
Rejoice, steadfast radiance from the Lord's white stone[22]
Rejoice, sweetest honeycomb of Jesus Son of Man
Rejoice, nest of thought wherein my Christ reposes
Rejoice, communion by word from the invoking of God
Rejoice, profusion of fragrance given us by the Son
Rejoice, living rosary of the *Kyrie eleison*
Rejoice, surge that carries even me, a sinner, away
Rejoice, flood of the continuous memory of God
Rejoice, charismatic ceaseless repetition of a wondrous invocation
Rejoice, O Holy Bride, weaver of ceaseless prayer!

VI
KONTAKION 6

Pure mind,
inner sky

All-holy Virgin, ever in your presence,
down through the ages,
the thoughts of those wise in their own minds
are confounded†
Because You are the seal of incorruptibility,
a closed door for those who boast of their intelligence,
and a living mirror of wondrous conduct.
You know that life was not given to us
to find a meaning of our own making,[23]
that it proves to be far richer than a life merely lived.
It pertains to the Mind far beyond thought and place,
beyond the chain of fleeting moments.
It is a manifestation of the fiery heavens within us,
above the wellsprings of the heart and creation.
It belongs to the world-creating Word
who would be for us the path and incarnation unto eternity:
Alleluia!

IKOS 6

Sober Watchfulness [= *Trezia*][24]

O Holy Virgin, our most pure Mother!
You are in truth sobriety [*trezia*] of spirit,
the myrrh-bundle of the will SONG OF SONGS 1:13
gathered in the forehead,
the inner eye open
to the horizon's entire circuit,
the heart where the transparency
of pure thoughts and feelings
reigns supreme at its center.[25]
You are the most righteous spiritual attention,
through which you join together,
by the power of intellect, beyond words,
in a flash of the mind:
the icy keenness of thought with the burning rush of life,
hot and cold set in a cross,
which yields up the loftiest of meanings.
But this alertness [*trezia*] of spirit is that of an infant,
a key which opens, with a swift and unexpected turn,
the depths of the heart,
yet which in no way troubles your serene soul;
to the contrary,
it gives You that great and holy simplicity
which ever fills us with wonder
and before which, as much as we can,
we bow down our heads
gathering all of our breath to sing:

Rejoice, cross of fervor and discernment of the chosen one.
Rejoice, axis of heaven with the morning star of knowledge
Rejoice, banisher of thoughts with their vain swarm[26]
Rejoice, invisible mirror in which is reflected He who is beyond the flesh
Rejoice, most clear crystal of my soul
Rejoice, piercing brightness of the remembrance of God
Rejoice, lute of the heart played with the bow of the mind
Rejoice, sounding forth of five strings in unison
Rejoice, ineffable music of the second birth

Rejoice, supreme height of the fullness of knowledge
Rejoice, betrothed of the Name of Wisdom
Rejoice, O Holy Bride, weaver of ceaseless prayer!

VII
KONTAKION 7

The secret teaching
The arcanum of Christian initiation

To the handicraft of your holiness we come, O Mother,
to be clothed anew by your very hands.
At the splendid wedding of the Great Bridegroom
the garment must be of total purity.
No impurity of look or attire is allowed.
None of those unworthy of the holy mysteries ever dare approach.
Who will let pigs feed on pearls or dogs lick sacred vessels?
MATT. 7:6
Only in spirit can one both ask for and receive a grace,
and only through you, our heavenly Mother.[27]
Come, then, humble, reconciled and pure soul,
and together we will soar into the pure
and complete joy of an *Alleluia*!

IKOS 7

The blessing
Adoption and spiritual endowment

Most holy, most exalted, most beautiful,
most philokalic Bride!
O Queen all en-haloed!
You, our benevolent Mother,
are the bestower of all that is holy:
the living dowry of the good things of grace,
in the sacraments of the Church, in the Divine Liturgy,
signified in the sacred fragrances,
in gestures, in words.
You are the most resplendent Great Tradition
of the whole *economia* of blessings,
like a seven-branched candlestick
alight before the Great Throne of God,
for which all the angels and saints glorify You:

Rejoice, Paschal blessing of new fulfillments
Rejoice, might of the Father set above us in a crown
Rejoice, utmost skill at fostering us all unto theosis
Rejoice, rarest of gifts painstakingly wrought by purifying grace
Rejoice, wondrous light anointing humble minds
Rejoice, realization of untold spiritual powers
Rejoice, rapid spiritual progress granted to firmly established hearts
Rejoice, oneness of mind of all the reconciled Churches
Rejoice, sapphire truth inlaid upon our inner senses
Rejoice, inspiriting Presence giving us entry into Sabbath rest
Rejoice, word that lasts forever in wondrous silence
Rejoice, O Holy Bride, weaver of ceaseless prayer!

VIII
KONTAKION 8

Beating heart
The gift of inner singing

O Queen, All-Holy Lady,
Mother untempted by marriage[28]
You are the only human heart
in which the hymning of the Name of glory
in all the fullness of its living and true reality
never falters.
For this reason, Most Pure One,
a crown of praise surrounds you
because in You alone, as never before,
    the heart of man
    with the heart of God
    have beaten and are beating in unison.
Prayer, like a pendulum between contemplation and Heaven,
    sweeps through your inmost being
intertwined with the lucent *ektenia* of the mystery
    nigh unto the love of God.
O You, Chariot of Light, undefiled, 2 KINGS 2:11
    unsurpassed and unfading!
Amend us too with the gifts of the heart, O Blessed One!
    And so, as a Church, richly endowed and made worthy,
    we will give ourselves to You with our whole being
    to sing rightly and in holiness: *Alleluia!*

IKOS 8

Heart of grace
Heart of stone

Mother of God, Heart of Light,
Mother of God, Heart of the Earth,
Mother of God, Heart without fault,
Mother of God, Heart of the Word!
We yearn for You, ashamed and humbled
with downcast soul and buckling knees.
because of so great a plague of sin.
Our heart has become
hard and chipped as sharp-edged flint,
bleak beyond telling.
"The Lord has let us tread
the paths we have chosen." SIR. 15:14, PS. 81:12–13
Scattered thoughts stray about in mist. BAR. 1:21–22
But, behold, now we prostrate ourselves before You
Mother of Jesus, embrace us as living stones
longing for the day-spring of the morning,
the morning without evening,
and revive us with new and pure hearts
so that we might sing to You:

Rejoice, ark of the covenant of my soul
Rejoice, coffer locked with the Name of God
Rejoice, living ship sailing the billows of the world
Rejoice, coffin[29] preserved from all the vanities of the world
Rejoice, throne upon which life is founded
Rejoice, music box through which radiance resounds
Rejoice, temple in which every celebration of grace transpires
Rejoice, tabernacle of thought for the most spiritual of altars
Rejoice, feast of the heavens, in which the Spirit is the true celebrant
Rejoice, chest of fire set in our very souls
Rejoice, Church greatly desiring the Triadic wedding feast
Rejoice, O Holy Bride, weaver of ceaseless prayer!

IX
KONTAKION 9
The countenance of prayer

Lord Jesus Christ, sweet Bridegroom of our hearts!
I too am of the same lineage as the Most Pure,
a newly grafted shoot.
I approach You by bowing my forehead,
and place my hand like Thomas in your holy side.
Tightly curled within myself, I am seated in silence
like a blind man on a narrow bridge†
waiting for "the unsetting Light arising from the depths,
placed in man to entirely illuminate,
like an inner sun, the expanse of being." APOC. 22:5
Since the darkness of the night of my sins
does not allow me to see you,
with timidity I touch you, with the finger of hope,
with the finger of faith, with the finger of anticipation,
with the finger of desire and, at the same time, of doubt,
and if this were not enough, I would place the other hand as well; JOHN 20:25–27
yet the heart, pierced by a searing flash,
painfully, yet sweetly, to the rhythm of the breath
murmurs the entire invocation and, effortless,
the heartbeat of prayer races towards the light
in an *Alleluia*!

IKOS 9

The Mother of God,
The very art of hesychia

All-holy, ever-helping Virgin,
You are the purest, the most exalted above all angelic creatures,
you also know the supernatural order
suitable for redemptive transfiguration.
You are the mastery, the art, the diligence,
the holy human accuracy in all things,
which together compose
the element that favors our salvation.
And this is why our lips so insistently glorify you:

Rejoice, proper knowledge of holiness to the least detail
Rejoice, sophianic science of working with the inner word
Rejoice, divine sweetness of the Name like out-poured chrism
SONG OF SONGS 1:3
Rejoice, monastic skill of chanting while bathed in tears
Rejoice, drop meted out for a seraphic childhood [SEE IKOS 5]
Rejoice, golden harshness of asceticism upon the desert mat
Rejoice, crown of litanies invoked on the prayer-rope[30]
Rejoice, hermit's prayer nook beneath the candle's gentle truth
Rejoice, template of the stool for hesychast prayer
Rejoice, you with upraised hands standing upright in rapture
Rejoice, smile issuing from the engolpion[31] that overcomes the heart's aridity
Rejoice, O Holy Bride, weaver of ceaseless prayer!

X
KONTAKION 10
Pneumatic gnosis

O! flawless Lady full of grace,
Virgin with the wings of the Great Eagle,[32] EZEK. 17:1–10, APOC. 12:14
Apocalyptic sign of the blameless womb,
Church giving birth to the inner man!
Help me to fashion myself in the ineffable nature
with repeated[33] litanies of whispered invocations.
And grant me luminous birth, my Spiritual Mother,
so that in the experience of the Resurrection
I too can cry out: *Alleluia!*

IKOS 10

The blessing of tears
Incessant repentance

You, generous Mother, Guide to the mysteries,
Lady of hope in evening's azure,
Sovereign with the three stars on her mantle
and Holy Anchor of our weaknesses!
Behold, to You again I have hastened!
I am oppressed by the world, by shattered thoughts.
After receiving holy counsel and a blessing[34]
I entered upon the path of my salvation.
I had made the decision, with strength and determination,
to spend my energies praying ceaselessly.
But my intellect, that clay idol,
does not allow me to overcome myself,
to establish myself in prayer as in the place of God
in that contrition of heart for which I yearn.
Help me, therefore, You my Helper
and obtain for me the gift of tears,
the salt of repentance to be purified and freed
from the weakness of the spirit
and so, once more made worthy, may I sing again to you:

Rejoice, rose bathed in the tears of the heart's conversion
Rejoice, tenderness of repentance with light as its garment
Rejoice, theology of tears, revelation of Wisdom
Rejoice, wise response to the sighs of the world
Rejoice, paradise sprinkled with the rains of saving grace
Rejoice, gaze of a child brimming with tears of wonder
Rejoice, purple vesture for the royal passion of the Amen[35]
APOC. 3:14
Rejoice, gem of grace from the Thorn's tears[36]
Rejoice, dew of benevolence with which you strengthen believers
Rejoice, help offered even to the ungodly in their ruin
Rejoice, mantle[37] spread over every weakness
Rejoice, O Holy Bride, weaver of ceaseless prayer!

XI
KONTAKION 11
Through bright shadow to theosis[38]

I thank you, Most Clement, Ever-Virgin Mother,
for saving me from the second death. APOC. 2:11, 20:6
Dangers and temptations serve only to test.
Through the incessant invocations of the most luminous, almighty Name,
my senses and the will of my heart have reached the threshold of silence.
Now free from them,
I wait for the divine hearing, sight and speech to prevail.
Only these will express themselves in me from now on.
And let my Beloved himself, Jesus in his glory, see, speak and understand
with my very own sight, hearing and entire will.[39]
May Christ so live using all my faculties
so that He Himself cries out through me: *Alleluia!*

IKOS 11

The theophanic ladder of fruits[40]

O you heart and mind and thought of mine!
Be wounded with questions before the Face of God.
How are we to discern the truth of heavenly fruits?
And what answer will you hear in these spiritual illuminations:
when the appearing of the unseen Vision drenches you with dew,
within the golden expanse of hallowed images,
in the depths of the spirit,
you will be gathered into tabernacled light,
as was the spirit of the Most Pure Virgin in the Holy of Holies.
And thus you will come to utter a song of praise
as lofty and worthy as the one
that sounds forth by the angel's trumpet.
And, with tender love in your heart,
you will be like the flower of righteous Jesse* ISA. 11:1
trembling this way and that in expectancy of the Three. GEN. 18:2
We hunger for this
and may the Holy Lady herself deign to bestow on us
the gift of her compassionate intercession
so to raise up a song such as this from us all:

Rejoice, You ladder that rises from a broken heart
Rejoice, ascetic purity of serene prayer
Rejoice, warmth of grace that pervades the flesh
Rejoice, amazing feat that weaves our sanctification
Rejoice, You supernal water gushing from the edge of the abyss
Rejoice, peace that vanquishes the entire welter of thoughts
Rejoice, growing brightness of a mind unclouded
Rejoice, vision in the spirit of overwhelming mysteries
Rejoice, mystical brilliance atop the ineffable ladder
Rejoice, inexpressible illumination of the heart
Rejoice, immensity of perfection for a body freed from corruption
Rejoice, O Holy Bride, weaver of ceaseless prayer!

XII
KONTAKION 12
The Paradoxical Model of Hesychia

You are the sovereign Amma[41] of my soul.
Grant me rest beneath the shelter of Your Countenance,
so that under the golden ember of Your gaze[42]
I too may burn without being consumed,
transfigured by the unspeakable mystery of living prayer.
And, ringed with your refreshing coolness,
O sealed Fount, SONG OF SONGS 4:12
may I be renewed ever again
with the streams of Your unfailing grace,
in the great peace of ecstatic rest.
And so, my Holy Amma, encompass me
with the living joy of victory [over the passions]
so that I might sing incandescently
in utmost *hesychia* of knowledge: *Alleluia.*

IKOS 12

Holy Tradition is incarnate Gnosis

Mother of God, Spiritual Mother full of love for the world!
Wellspring of the mystery of the tradition of the Word!
You are divinely gentle and humble,
but, as the Song of Songs says,
also unspeakably righteous and terrible
"like armies arrayed for battle." SONG OF SONGS 6:4
You are bright, you are serene, you are sharp
as an unyielding sword.[43]
In the heavenly Jerusalem you have ready helpers,
all those self-deniers, Your devoted children,
all those who belong to the ranks
of ascetics, hermits, and anchorites,
Your entire lineage of wise spiritual elders
to whom are entrusted the treasures of blessing,
everything that expresses clarity, purity and righteousness
that comes from Your purity and boundless compassion,
everything that in one word says
"Pure Gnosis" or the Heritage of the Saints COL. 1:12
and which you have manifestly placed within our reach
through the writings, deeds and sayings of the Fathers,
for which we will never know how to
praise you, venerate you, glorify you
except by singing thusly:

Rejoice, guardian Sword[44] of the hesychast tradition
Rejoice, immortal pledge of our adoption as sons
Rejoice, cup in which the blessing of the Lord rests
Rejoice, majestic tree[45] standing vigil over the holy
transfiguration of man
Rejoice, wonderful artificer of silent masterpieces
Rejoice, arch-strategist of the unseen warfare
Rejoice, gaze that preserves ascetic labors in sweetness
Rejoice, rule that guides with wise acuity
Rejoice, shield that protects the land of the living
Rejoice, gateway that thwarts every kind of impurity
Rejoice, threshing rod that scatters the evil spirits like chaff
Rejoice, O Holy Bride, weaver of ceaseless prayer!

XIII
KONTAKION 13

Twenty-four harps and incense-bowls

O! Mother of God, ever immaculate and blessed Mother of Man!
Like the twenty-four harps and incense-bowls of the elders
APOC. 5:8–14
so may our own worship be
in its ceaseless outpouring [of music and perfumes].
And unto the Most Holy Trinity, O uplifting joy,
from Your hands to Christ the Bridegroom,
may our oblation of true glory
be a most fragrant offering,
so that we might cry out with all the heavens
in the immense embrace of a most sublime: *Alleluia!*

Repeated three times, then Ikos 1 *and* Kontakion 1

* Old Testament episodes depicted at the corners of the Burning Bush Icon.

† *Akathist to the Most Holy Theotokos* (Ikos 2).

NOTES

1. The Romanian term is *zaconul*, coined from the Slavic *zakon*, which means norm, rule, law.

2. The title *porphyrogenitos* (from the Greek πορφυρογέννητος), which means "born in purple," derives from the *porphyra*, the special room decorated in porphyry, a purple-colored stone (of Egyptian extraction), or covered with purple drapes, which was built in the Great Palace of Constantinople before AD 750. It was designed as a place where empresses gave birth to their children, who thus assumed the epithet *porphyrogenites*, "born in purple." It was, in fact, a creative expedient, which introduced a new title in order to legitimize imperial authority. In the canon of St. Andrew of Crete, Ode 8, we read: "As from purple silk, O undefiled Virgin, the spiritual robe of Emmanuel, His flesh, was woven in thy womb" (*Lenten Triodion*, 207).

3. Literally: wearied, exhausted.

4. This is a thought by Elia Miniates (1669–1714), the most famous Greek orator of his time, who lived in Venice, appointed in 1704 by the ecumenical patriarch Gabriel III and by the Synod "doctor and preacher of the Great Church of Christ," later metropolitan in the Peloponnese in 1711. In addition to Greek, he knew Hebrew, Latin, Italian and French. His work consists of only two books: the *Didachai* (Teachings) and *Stone of Scandal*, published posthumously. I report the passage in Sandu Tudor's reasoning about the Virgin Mary, taken from Daniil de la Rarău (Sandu Tudor), *Sfintita Rugăciune*, 171–172: "Have you ever taken the trouble with a slightly more alert intelligence to travel that long path that ended in the dignity of such a weak body? Have you ever understood, as the Fr. Elia Miniatis says, that anguish 'that has wearied the heavens for fifty centuries with fervent prayers' and that unstoppable river of 'uninterrupted tears' of our groaning nature that forced Anna's barren womb to conceive a virgin worthy of the Incarnation of God? We must understand this thing well: this legend is true, it really took place among us with incredibly real power. Have you not ever found yourself even thinking about what an immeasurable effort and what human struggle this entailed? How much self-mastery, how much patience, how much hope against all hope and how much complex preparation in humility and 'head-on' spiritual struggle had to be put together to

generate this flower of the heights of the spirit which is the Virgin, the one who was sheltered in the silence of the Holy of Holies at the Temple of Jerusalem."

In the Greek edition of the *Didachai*, ed. Rigopoulou, Thessaloniki 1969, the translated passage is found on page 382 and constitutes the beginning of the homily for the celebration of the birth of the Mother of God, where the author explains the extraordinary joy that the celebration brings. See also, regarding Elia Miniates, *Testi mariani del secondo millennio. Autori orientali, secoli XI-XX* [Marian texts of the second millennium. Oriental authors, 11th-20th centuries], ed. Georges Gharib and Ermanno M. Toniolo, vol. 1 (Roma: Città Nuova, 2008), 625–35.

5. The clarification of St. Thomas Aquinas is useful regarding this term so dear to Eastern theology: "For the Greeks hypostasis, according to the proper meaning of the word, indicates the individual of any substance, but according to usage it indicates only the individual of a rational nature, waiting for the excellence of this nature. Just as we say in the plural that in God there are three Persons and three Subsistences, so the Greeks say that there are three Hypostases. However, since the name of substance which properly corresponds to hypostasis is ambiguous for us, given that sometimes it means the essence and other times the hypostasis, to avoid the risk of error we preferred to translate hypostasis with the term subsistence, rather than with that of substance" (Thomas Aquinas, *Summa Theologiae* I, q. 29, a. 2, solution of difficulties 1–2).

6. This is the greeting of the angel Gabriel to the Virgin, the beginning of joy for all humanity. This greeting became the beginning of the prayer to the Virgin, the Hail Mary. It has the meaning of "rejoice," "exalt with joy."

7. Eschatological = of the morning or daybreak of the Resurrection.

8. Literally: Holy of Holies, with the allusion to the temple of Jerusalem, where only the High Priest could enter once a year.

9. Literally: altar of wonders. This refers to the altar of the heart, compared to the altar of the Eucharistic table, where the holy mysteries are celebrated. In scripture, the emerald is associated both with our origins in the Garden of Eden (see Ezek. 28:13) and our ultimate state in the presence of God (Apoc. 4:3).

10. Literally: the "way from above." As Fr. Daniil himself

explains, in his *Sfintita Rugaciune*, 112, "There would no longer be any need to repeat that this holy and spiritual Art and Science is the royal way of the saints, 'the elevated way,' that of the definitive victories of the Spirit and is none other than the Way itself, Christ."

11. Literally: *veranda*. In the art style of Prince Brâncoveanu, the church is accessed through a portico. Practically at the beginning you entered the church directly, however at the time of the prince-martyr Constantin Brâncoveanu (1654–1714, canonized by the Romanian Orthodox Church in 1992) a particular style arose which introduced the portico into the construction of the church. The Mother of God is seen as this portico of humanity.

12. Cf. Isa. 9:5. In the text of scripture it is said: "a son is born to us," while the poetic verse says: "a son will be born to us."

13. Literally: name of five letters. In Romanian the name of Jesus, *Iisus*, has five letters. This is also an allusion to 1 Cor. 14:19, where Paul says that he prefers to say five words with his understanding rather than ten thousand with the gift of tongues. Tradition has read the Pauline quote in reference to the Jesus Prayer, which in Greek, in its abbreviated form, is composed of five words: Κύριε Ιησού Χριστέ ελέησόν με (Lord Jesus Christ, have mercy on me).

14. The sublime mystery of the Incarnation of the divine Word is being celebrated here. St. John Damascene states: "...when one who, by transcending his own nature, is bodiless, formless, incommensurable, without magnitude or size, that is, one who is in the form of God, taking the form of a slave, by this reduction to quantity and magnitude puts on the characteristics of a body, then depict him on a board and set up to view the One who has accepted to be seen," Treatise I, 8, *Three Treatises on the Divine Images*, trans. A. Louth (Crestwood, NY: St. Vladimir's Seminary Press, 2003), 24.

15. This is how Father Daniil explains: "[this is about creating] a pneumatic metapsychology of Man grasped in his eternity and totality, the realization of the Angel in the body or of the divine creation that Man is called to be," *Sfintita Rugaciune*, 112. In the documents of the trial against the Burning Bush we find this note on the theology of Father Benedict Ghiuș: "For the great solitaries of the East, an angel is taking shape in every man, a cherub in the making ... in the experience of the Eastern saints the image of an angel in the making incarnated in every man took shape. Be that as it may, the matter has remained and remains a fact for the Eastern tradition"; cf. Ioana Diaconescu, *"Rugul Aprins." Studii și documente despre exterminare și supraviețuire* (Bucharest: Fundația Academia Civică, 2018), 74.

16. The Virgin is venerated as the One who has a heart so transparent and full of God that she is not touched by any passionate movement. John Climacus devotes the penultimate step of his *Scala paradisi* to "divine impassibility, which is heaven on earth." Hesychios the Sinaite says: "Dispassion and humility lead to spiritual knowledge. Without them, no one can see God" (*Philokalia*, I, 174: To Theodulus, 67). As Nicetas Stethatos says, applied to the ascent of the monk longing for God: "[the soul] does not grant sleep or drowsiness to the eyelids of his body, nor rest to his temples, until it finds, by dint of toil and tears, a place of impassibility, like a door that overlooks a palace, and enters the sanctuary of the knowledge of God" (*On the Soul*, 60); "This is how God wanted us: impassible, without worries, without any occupation other than that of the angels" (*Contemplation of Paradise*, 13). When Gregory Palamas, in his homily 53 on the presentation of the Virgin Mary in the temple, takes up this conception of the Fathers on impassibility, he will apply it only in the highest degree to the Virgin. Cf. Pierre Miquel, *Lessico del deserto. La parole della spiritualità* (Bose: Qiqajon, 1998).

17. Here are some reflections by Father Daniil: "Salvation is not achieved through a technique, but is achieved by walking on a specific path and through an incarnation, following Christ in everything, in the gift of self moved by grace, through a holy synergy, through the life of the Church, the entry into the life of the Spirit"; "Original sin is never a power, it is not an act, but a state, a fundamental inertia on which the life of natural man is based, as if by mistake. However, being baptized, our dignity gives us the possibility from time to time of enjoying the powers of Grace which can lead us to the continuous dwelling of the Holy Spirit within us" (*Sfințita Rugaciune*, 110, 128). The Orthodox Mariological tradition sees in the Virgin the completed model of spiritual life.

18. See in the appendix the poem by Father Daniil composed at the end of his life: *I heard the song of the inimitable bird.*

The firebird is the Holy Spirit who draws praise to God from the whole universe and the heart participates in this praise until it reaches intimacy with God himself. It is the dynamic of a love that has completely conquered the heart.

19. The passage from Psalm 68 is commented on based on the Greek and Latin versions by the Fathers: "It is said: 'My dove is one' (Song of Sol. 6.8). And she is silver because she is learned in the divine words, which elsewhere are called 'silver refined in the crucible, purified seven times' (Psalm 11:7)." See Ludwig Monti, *I Salmi: preghiera e vita* (Bose: Qiqajon, 2018), 729, note. John Climacus, *The Ladder of Divine Ascent*, Step 4, 1, relates: "With the help of these two virtues, the holy soul steadily ascends to Heaven as upon golden wings. And perhaps it was about this that he who had received the Holy Spirit sang: 'Who will give me wings like a dove? And I will fly by activity [*praxis*], and be at rest by divine vision and humility [Ps 55 (54):7].'" Rev. ed., trans. Holy Transfiguration Monastery (Boston, MA: Holy Transfiguration Monastery, 2001), 20.

20. Monologistic prayer is concentrated prayer, consisting of a single short formula or even a single word (taken from scripture), which expresses and realizes in extreme synthesis the spiritual experience of the person praying, and becomes an essential tool in the fight against "thoughts." John Climacus is perhaps the first to introduce the term on Step 15 of the *Ladder* where he speaks of "*the Prayer of Jesus said as a monologue*" (54), repeated thereafter by numerous authors, one of whom was Hesychios the Priest, *To Theodoulos* (174): "The single-phrased Jesus Prayer destroys and consumes the deceits of the demons. For when we invoke Jesus, God and Son of God, constantly and tirelessly, He does not allow them to project in the mind's mirror even the first hint of their infiltration—that is to say, their provocation—or any form, nor does He allow them to have any converse with the heart" (*Philokalia* vol. 1, 193).

21. Cf. the "word" of Abba Poemen in *The Sayings of the Desert Fathers*, trans. Benedicta Ward (Kalamazoo, MI: Cistercian Publications, 1975), 192–93.

22. Cf. Rev 2:17: "To the one who conquers I will give the hidden manna and a white stone, on which is written a new name, which no one knows except the one who receives it."

23. Literally: solely so that it can be explained.

24. Sobriety can be defined as the attitude of a mind present to itself, vigilant, careful not to be surprised by the devil who tries to insinuate himself into our heart through thoughts, ready to reject them from their first appearance. It is a defensive tactic that is also called by other names: vigilance, attention, guarding the heart or spirit. Referring to the original meaning of the word (sober = not drunk), the term sobriety in itself, unlike the others, underscores the ability of the mind to see clearly, to distinguish correctly, unlike drunkenness which involves blurred vision. However, it remains focused on the constant and warm memory of God. See Philotheos of Sinai, *Forty Texts on Watchfulness* (*Philokalia*, vol. 3, 16–31). Attention is a habitual tension of the mind aimed at preventing access to one's heart of all kinds of thoughts that are not according to God. The aim is to keep the spirit in a state of perfect peace so that prayer can flow perpetually from the depths of one's heart.

25. Two passages from Gregory of Nyssa's *Homilies on the Song of Songs* will help to shed some light on these verses:

> "...the person who intends to dedicate himself to the worship of God will not be frankincense burned for God unless he has first become myrrh—that is, unless he mortifies his earthly members, having been buried together with the one who submitted to death on our behalf and having received in his own flesh, through mortification of its members, that myrrh which was used to prepare the Lord for burial. When these things have come to pass, every species of the fragrances that belong to virtue—once they have been ground fine in the bowl of life as in some mortar—produces that sweet cloud of dust, and he who inhales it becomes sweet-smelling because he has become full of the fragrant Spirit (Homily 6, Norris, 201–3).
>
> "As to me," [the Bride] says, "the bundle that I hang from my neck upon the breast and by which I give my body a sweet smell is not one of the other perfumed herbs, but the Lord himself, become myrrh, lies in the bundle of my conscience, dwelling in my very heart" (Homily 3, Norris, 105).

26. The image is that of a hive in a whirlwind of activity.

27. Mary lived the spiritual journey in such an extraordinary way that she became "capable" of carrying God himself as a child within her. Not only she, but she also becomes the mediator of all divine illumination; she who has fully welcomed the light, makes it reverberate on all those who are worthy of it, as St. Gregory Palamas says in his *Homily 53*, par. 39 and 62–64 (see supra, pp. 192–95).

28. It is one of the characteristic titles of the Virgin in the Byzantine tradition: Mother who "knewest not wedlock," Virgin Mother.

29. Literally: small coffin or bier, a symbol of the burial of all worldly vanities. It recalls the evangelical term used to designate the tomb of Jesus which is closely related to "memorial," "memory," a place where what is remembered and not the present focus of attention is kept.

30. The prayer rope, usually made of wool, is generally composed of 100, 150 or 300 knots (Greek: κομποσκοίνι—"komboskini"; Russian: чётки—"chotki" or вервица—"vervitsa"; Romanian: *metanii*) to count the number of times the Jesus Prayer is said, interspersed with prostrations to the ground. In Romanian, this poetic verse likens the image of knots to braided hair.

31. The engolpion, also transcribed "enkolpion" or "encolpulion," (Greek: ἐγκόλπιον, "engólpion," or "on the chest") is a ritual object worn on the chest by Orthodox and Catholic bishops of the Byzantine rite. The term *engolpion*, once used to also indicate the pectoral cross, is now used in reference to a medallion with an icon placed at the center, worn around the neck by Orthodox bishops and those of the Eastern Catholic Churches. The icon, of Jesus or the Mother of God, is usually surrounded by precious stones and surmounted by an oriental miter. They often have a small pendant, with a precious stone, hanging from the bottom. The engolpion is worn around the neck on a gold chain. The shape of an engolpion can vary from oval to rhomboid, square, or double-headed eagle shape.

32. In his commentary on the Apocalypse (*Scrieri*, I, 133–83), Fr. Daniil dwells on the meaning of the two wings of the great Eagle, recalling the icon of the Virgin with the wings of a Great Eagle at the Govora monastery. In summary, the Eagle is the symbol of divine help, of the power of grace that comes to our aid, as a dynamic of grace and prophecy. St. Maximus the Confessor states that man has two wings: grace and freedom. Knowledge of the great art of spiritual flight is not necessary, nor is it necessary to know the related science. Man must realize himself as a true "angel in a body," he must learn to fly. To learn the rhythms and important steps of flight under the guidance of the Great Eagle, the true "extraordinary bird" [the Holy Spirit], we need at the beginning of that mysterious knowledge, that 'heavenly science and art' of deep longings, of the Johannine legacy, which we have received from the Neptic Fathers, the masters of sobriety (167).

33. In Romanian, *depănarea* = to unwind or unspool, a weaver reference.

34. In his monastic experience, Fr. Daniil received the blessing for the practice of the Jesus Prayer from Fr. Ioann Kulygin, the Stranger, a Russian priest and monk who came to Romania with the entourage that accompanied Metropolitan Nikolai of Rostov in his exile. They had met at the Cernica monastery, which Sandu Tudor often frequented and had invited him to participate in the meetings at the Antim monastery and it is precisely here that Sandu Tudor, the future Fr. Daniil, received the special blessing for the practice of the prayer.

35. The reference is to Gethsemane where Jesus sweats blood.

36. The image refers to the crown of thorns on Jesus's head which intensified the compassion of his mother, co-redemptrix through the pain that united her to her son on the cross.

37. *Omophórion* (or *maphórion*) in Greek, *pokrov* in Slavic = protective mantle. It was a long piece of fabric that covered the women's heads and bodies like a cloak, down to their knees. In the East it was the dress of deaconesses and consecrated virgins. In the West it became the typical dress of the Mother of God and of holy women. In iconography it expresses the protection of the Mother of God. "O our Lady, cover us now with the omophorion of thy mercy... bulwark, protection [pokrov] and might of the faithful... thou coverest us with the omophorion of thy mercy... all-wondrous protection of the whole world (*Little Vespers* for the feast of the icon, October 1).

38. Commenting on the mysteries of the prayer of the Our Father, Maximus the Confessor states: "If the purpose of the divine counsel is the deification of our nature, and the aim of divine thoughts is to supply the prerequisites of our life, it follows that we should both know and carry into effect the power of the Lord's Prayer, and write about it in the proper way.... The Logos bestows adoption on us when He grants us that birth and deification which, transcending nature, comes by grace from above through the Spirit. The guarding and preservation of this in God depends on the resolve of those thus born: on their sincere acceptance of the grace bestowed on them and, through the practice of the commandments, on their cultivation of the beauty given to them by grace. Moreover, by emptying themselves of the passions they lay hold of the divine to the same degree as that to which, deliberately emptying Himself of His own sublime glory, the Logos of God truly became man" (*Philokalia*, vol. 2, 286–87). See also Maximus the Confessor, *Various Texts on Theology, the Divine Economy, and Virtue and Vice*, First Century, 42: "God made us so that we might become 'partakers of the divine nature' [2 Pet. 1:4] and sharers in His eternity, and so that we might come to be like Him [cf. 1 John 3:2] through deification by grace. It is through deification that all things are reconstituted and achieve their permanence; and it is for its sake that what is not is brought into being and given existence" (*Philokalia*, vol. 2, 173). Also by Maximus the Confessor, *Two Hundred Texts on Theology and Incarnate Dispensation of the Son of God. Written for Thalassios*, II Century, 88:

> "Some seek to discover what the state of perfection of the saints in the kingdom of God is like.... [The soul] is nourished by virtue and contemplation, until it transcends all created things and attains 'the measure of the stature of the fullness of Christ' [Eph. 4:13]. Once it has entered this state it ceases from all increase and growth nourished by indirect means and is nourished directly, in a manner which passes understanding. Having now completed the stage of growth, the soul receives the kind of incorruptible nourishment which sustains the godlike perfection granted to it... and it becomes god by participation in divine grace, ceasing from all activity of intellect and sense, and at the same time suspending all the natural operations of the body. For the body is deified along with the soul through its own corresponding participation in the process of deification" (*Philokalia*, vol. 2, 160). And at no. 93: "Some say that the kingdom of heaven is the way of life which the saints lead in heaven; others that it is a state similar to that of the angels, attained by those who are saved; others that it is the very form of the divine beauty of those who 'wear the image of Him who is from heaven' (1 Cor. 15:49). In my judgment each of these three views is correct" (*Philokalia*, vol. 2, 161).

39. Father Daniil refers to the experience of Simeon the New Theologian described in his hymns:

"We are made members of Christ, and Christ becomes our
members, (1 Cor 6.15)
and Christ becomes my hand and the foot of all-wretched me,
and wretched I become the hand of Christ and the foot of Christ.
I move my hand and my hand is Christ entire.
For, understand me, the divine divinity is indivisible!
I put my foot in motion and behold, it flashes as Himself.
Do not say that I blaspheme, but accept these things
and fall down and worship Christ Who makes you like this!
For if you also wish, you shall become his member,
and thus every member of each one of us
shall become a member of Christ, and Christ our members.
(Hymn 15, 141–151)

Thus are they united to God, those who purify
their souls through repentance in this world,
and they are appointed monks who are apart from others.
Those who take on the mind of Christ,
which is also a mouth [1 Cor. 2.16] and
tongue truly without deceit,
with which they converse with the all-powerful
Father, with which they always cry:
'O Father, O Absolute Monarch, O Creator of all things!'"
(Hymn 27, 57–63)

Divine Eros. Hymns of Saint Symeon the New Theologian, trans. D. K. Griggs (Yonkers, NY: St. Vladimir's Seminary Press, 2010), 77–78, 210–11.

He also refers to Nicodemus of the Holy Mountain who, in his *Unseen Warfare*, taking up the Italian text by Lorenzo Scupoli (1530–1610) writes [chap 3, 278]: "I see clearly, O Lord my God, in the light of thy infinite love, that Thou hast but one desire, which most reveals the radiance of Thy love for me, namely that Thou desirest to give me the whole of Thyself as food (and drink) for no other purpose but to transmute the whole of me into Thyself, not because Thou hast any need of me, but because I have extreme need of Thee; for in this way Thou dwellest in me and I in Thee; and through this union of love I become (as) Thou art. In human words: through the union with my earthly heart with Thy heavenly heart a single divine heart is created in me" (trans. E. Kadloubovsky & G. E. H. Palmer [Crestwood, NY: St. Vladimir's Seminary Press, 1978], 230–31—Nicodemus's additions in parentheses). Ambrose of Milan also expresses a similar thought: "let His image shine forth in our profession of faith, let it shine forth in our love, let it shine forth in our works and deeds so that, if it is possible, all His beauty may be represented in us. Let Him be our head, because 'the head of man is Christ'; let Him be our eye, that through Him we may see the Father; let Him be our voice, that through Him we may speak to the Father; let Him be our right hand, that through Him we may bring our sacrifice to God the Father..." See St. Ambrose, *Isaac or the soul* (8.75), in *Seven Exegetical Works* (trans. M. P. McHugh [Washington, D. C.: Catholic University of America, 1972]), 59.

40. Cf. Theophanis quote, supra, 202.

41. The term *amma* originally meant "mother" or "nurse," but starting from the fourth century its meaning expanded. A papyrus from this era applies the title *amma* to Eve and Mary; later the term acquires the technical meaning of "spiritual mother," corresponding to the masculine *abba* which indicates "the spiritual father." The expression: "Abba, tell me a word" is recurrent in the sayings of the Desert Fathers; the disciple or guest asks an abba/amma who is considered to have reached spiritual maturity (an "elder" or "old woman" not so much by age, but by spiritual maturity) for a word that would help on one's human and spiritual journey.

42. Literally: beneath the golden coal [the flame that gilds a burning coal] of your gaze. It seems that the image refers to the charcoal thurible which is used for incensing during liturgical celebrations. In Ephrem the Syrian, in his *Hymns on the Nativity*, we find the image of the burning [golden] coal: "If she embraced You, / the coal of mercy preserved her bosom," *Hymns on the Nativity,* Hymn 11, 5 (Hymns, trans. K. E. McVey [New York & Mahwah, NJ: Paulist Press, 1989], 132). The image alludes to the mystery of the incandescent divine nature present under the veil of the flesh.

43. Here Mary wields the trophy of her "dry" martyrdom as prophesied by Simeon in Luke (2:35): "And thy own soul a sword shall pierce." But this sword also forms a junction with the next part of Ikos 12, which introduces her "lineage of wise spiritual elders," for Simeon continues: "that, out of many hearts thoughts may be revealed." The revelation of thoughts to one's spiritual elder is integral to hesychast practice.

44. The prayer cord is entrusted to the novice in monastic profession with the words:

"Accept, O brother [name], the sword of the Spirit which is the word of God (Ephesians 6:17). Have the name of the Lord in your soul, in your thoughts and in your heart, always saying: "Lord Jesus Christ, Son of God, have mercy on me a sinner."

45. Perhaps the poet is alluding to the larches of the mountainous region where he lived the last years of his life, in the Rarău skete, tall conifers, with broad fronds, of strong, long-lasting and very precious wood, which grow in the subalpine region.

APPENDIX
Poetic Texts

I HEARD THE SONG OF THE INIMITABLE BIRD[1]

In the morning, at prayer time, with dew
still fresh on the branches,
near me I heard
the song of the inimitable bird.
Look! So wonderfully it rises, so clearly and,
in echoes, multiplies
so much so
it seems as if the whole world,
the great, vast World,
is listening to it,
every creature hears it and responds
hears it and accompanies it
until it rises above everything:
to God.
I observe it, on the bud of a branch, inside
a clear drop of dew,
and I listen to that bird-song of light.
In the long, so lofty silence
of this moment, without wanting to
I imagine heavenly joy;
without wanting to,
I discover it now
in the peace of a state of prayer
in which I find myself and which
completely overwhelms me.
I discover it not as a suspension and sinking
of the senses,
not as the loss of self-oblivion
in ecstasy,
but as a keenness of understanding
lived,

---

[1] The last poem written by Fr. Daniil before being arrested in 1958.

clear and pure,
like an infinite, boundless ascension,
ever closer, ever increasing
towards the mysterious and
holy heart of the Lord.

FOR THE GREAT NIGHT OF THE VIRGIN[2]

Rejoice, sunset of infinite longing.
The heart has glimpsed you and humbly sings
of your face silvery-white as a holy rose[3]
blooming within the halo of a virginal ring.
Dead is the beauty of earthly flowers,
a figure for worldly ornaments that become corrupted.
Only You, Tabernacle, are of incorruption
for having welcomed the Uncontainable within yourself.
To you I sacrifice the light of my eyes
so that I might pass inwardly under the night sky
to gaze in my mind upon your immaculate image
waiting for the longed-for dream to come true.
And, over the evening of my mind, your seal,
clear, unique and overwhelming,
rests high upon my brow, guiding me
to the azure-betrothal of the star-*logostea*.[4]
Ever lead me with your gentle smile,
through the peril and harshness of the times,
to the destiny of my life,
blind yet full of wonder,
to touch the threshold of the biblical Amen.

---

[2] Published in *Gândirea,* X (1930), no. 10. The "Great Night" here is that of the Nativity of Christ.

[3] Dog rose, the most common species, which has white petals with pink lobes, pear-shaped red fruit and arched red spines.

[4] In Romanian folklore a *logostea* star (*logo* = speaking, *stea* = star) was thought to have a bearing on one's personal destiny; also, animals with a star-marking on their foreheads were thought to bring good luck (R. Vulcănescu, *Mitologie Română*, 401). In this poem, however, the potency of the "speaking-star" is amplified to become both the star of the Magi at Christ's birth and "the seal of the gift of the Holy Spirit" signed on the forehead during the Orthodox chrismation service (A. Bălan-Mihailovici, in Paraschiv, 95–96).

THE OCTAVE OF TRUTH

The truth can be plundered or just stolen,
imagined, encountered or conquered,
it can also be predicted or even bestowed,
but it does not save unless incarnate.

EUCHARISTIC THOUGHT

O pierced heart of the World,
sacrament of peace in the chalice,
the sacred feeling broken in bread
as a gift of communion,
brings to our vanity
a taste from beyond nature
that we might burst forth
from this hardened clay.

ICHTHYS

Like the wondrous sweetness of a psalm,
God's love envelops us.
Like the fragrance of a hymn,
the joy of life surrounds us
on all sides.
And our hearts,
athirst with the thrill
that floods their depths,
like fish in deep water,
drink the music of His blessing.

MIDDAY TROPARION

My God,
have mercy upon me!
Give me your name,
make yourself known to my soul!
As if completely conquered by the cry
of the thief on the right,
may my being absorb You
in fiery tears of grace,
and my heart possess You
in the midday offering,
overflowing splendor,
most sweet Ineffable One.

MIRACLES FLOURISH[5]

Miracle upon miracle and you are no longer amazed.
You think they are the ones that were not
and you would like to say promptly, fervently
a stunning word exact in meaning.
But your mouth remains cold as stone,
the prophet is struggling with his spent body;
but a thought breaks through
the ashed-over glow of the hearth
giving wings to the fire.
And you do say a word to yourself,
soundless, unaided by lips.
In an internal echo, like thunder,
the words of Scripture ring out within you,
piercing you through and through.

[5] As soon as he was locked up in prison, on 16 June 1958, Fr. Daniil had opened up to a fellow prisoner, an informer for the *Securitate*, saying that he could accept to die for the truth that he had confessed and this would be his salvation. As if foreseeing the end of his life on this earth, to allow a new heavenly beginning, Sandu Tudor had written this poem.

HRISOV [CHRYSOBULL]: THE CHARTER OF MOMENTS
The seal of life and death

This ballad is rooted in Romanian folk sentiment about the symbiosis between creation and humanity, with death (the princess escorted to the city for the celebration of a royal wedding) seen in its noble and beautiful aspect as it weaves through and seals one's life. The archaic and courtly musicality of the language, which continuously creates rhythmic assonances of words and images, brings back to the ear of the heart the melody of an inner time, a lived time, beyond the banality of events, like gold poured onto the sand of moments. In the background, the life of a medieval Moldavian voivodeship unfolds, well-suited, like the plot of a fairy tale, for hinting at parallels with the anguished life of the author's own time, under the communist empire and its cruelties, with the new rulers simply continuing the fateful course of life and death of former times. Although the ending speaks of death, the ballad describes life as a unique adventure, if the gaze becomes sharp enough to grasp the density of life's moments in their mystery of beauty and glory, in the presence of the Lord of all. —FR. ELIA CITTERIO

PRELUDE

To a royal charter
I put my hand,
not to a chronicle of events.
A zodiac and living clock
for a righteous life,
seemingly paltry,
inwardly beautiful
and in which I firmly believe.
How much obvious insignificance
and how much forgotten dignity,
spent at home and on the street,
wasted, lost in smoke!
Filled with the sadness and beauty
of this golden cinder and nothingness,
I have written in humble magnificence
the royal parchment of this document
right down to the end.

1.

Under the moon, the city of Suceava
with towers soaring into the night,
with its stone coat of arms, its furled banner,
continues to tell the tale
of an ancient Moldavian legend.
A deep silence, emptied of whispers
from the iron door, with the raised drawbridge,
peers down from above, under the moonlight,
onto a road that leads to a ravine,
towards the mountains to the west.
Long have the horses' iron-shod hooves
echoed on the pavement
and in the dust and clay.
And wagon wheels are heard
under the bright moon,
and a cracking of whips.
A deep silence stands sentinel.

2.

From the silent tower, from the sentry post,
his gaze stretches out over the road, lingers.
The soldier on watch has a waking dream
beneath his tall helmet, its peak reaching skyward,
clad in steel chain-mail
upon which an ineffable blue is sparkling now,
his spear upraised, ready, in the dead of night.
With a watchful, absorbed gaze,
he hears the rumbling on the pavement.
And, with his mind's eye, he looks ahead
to the message that advances,
one with the heavy clamor of the wagon.
What a round wheel the moon
and as broad as a village green!

3.

Arriving from the Hungarian lands,
yearning for what will be, longing for what was,
the young princess, with childlike eyes,
is escorted by stalwart knights.
From the Hungarian steppe she comes in haste,
a rosy-cheeked, April bride,
defended by the forty swords of valiant paladins.
Swift, on parade horses, at a trotting gait,
the royal companions of the journey
on rough roads
over wild steep crags,
through fearsome forests,
amazed under the golden moon,
escort, in the heavy carriage,
the princess to beloved Moldavia.

4.

The golden carriage with the royal coat of arms
and a green leather roof,
with its hump of luggage on top,
sways and pitches like an old boat,
under the changing colors of the now yellow moon.
At a walk or a gallop, amongst the forest branches,
pulled by four roan horses in red trappings,
the strange carriage patiently travels,
lurching and creaking
behind the hooves
along an all but impossible trace
through perilous terrain.
For four nights it has advanced
under the verdigris foliage.

5.
The morning star pierces with cold,
while the moon is still high and the dream persists.
But something kisses the edge of the forest with its glances,
and induces you to scrutinize the thought that came from afar.
It outlines the long silhouette of the mountains in the air,
it regains its strength and desire surges,
and, with a warlike gesture,
it bursts into shouts
—a glory of light.
Behold, through the courtyard gate,
the enchanted carriage has entered
and the banner dips.
Dressed in green silk
the princess flutters into her home,
like a tiny butterfly.
With a silvery sound
the pendulum beats its timid octave.

6.
In the armory, his chain-mail laid aside,
the soldier, last night's sentry,
tightens a string of his ancestral cobuz [lute]
to sing, from the quiet of his heart,
without hesitating, beyond enchantment,
out of the depths of a rough and vigorous soul,
at the fateful bidding of servant or lord,
with an oval quill pick
with a tender ison,[6]
with a gentle hand,
resoundingly aloud,
the praise of painful truth.
And about the virginal soul,
the one bestowed by love,
he will sing with accents sweet
and hushed
on the thinnest of golden strings.

[6] A drone-note used to accompany a melody.

7.
Let us rise silently on the whisper of that string
from the deep wellsprings of the mind in prayer,
to enjoy rest in soaring peace
beyond all charm, in finest clarity.
And, without delay, let us craft miracles
from tender thoughts and the royal splendor of the sun,
and, with art, compose them into songs,
harbingers of lasting wisdom and future deeds,
and with a heart
vigilant for the sign of awakening,
clear even from afar,
when, the last hour having come,
we will meet
in tears of pure joy,
for our betrothal without customary ring.

8.
The window is open, the singing is clear.
From the balcony above, a falling gillyflower
slips down slowly into the shadow of the tower.
The echo of the cobuz has died away.

9.
The light floats like gold dust
and on the roofs the heat shimmers.
The colors of the flowers in the gardens delicately sparkle,
while festive life fills the streets.
A drum resounds deafeningly in the square
and people crowd about it.
A royal messenger announces what is to occur:
just as in fairy tales,
there will be a wedding with royal guests.
The prince summons the people
and distributes in abundance.
A soldier scatters coins.
A garland will also be given
to the winners in drinking and rich dishes
according to appetite and taste.

10.

At ten o'clock, right at snack time,
someone knocks on the door of the court potter.
A vagabond, dressed in rags,
barefoot, hair unkempt,
beats loudly, grumbling to himself,
hastily eats a measure of corn and,
with the laugh of someone bringing good news,
blurts out:
here, brother, a royal coin,
because I was invited tomorrow
by the prince
to the wedding at the palace.
The crafts-folk of the town come according to custom.
Give me an enameled jug, brimming with wine,
to offer as a gift
from all those who toil.

11.

On the tower with the bronze clock, from afar
the hammer announces noon.
In the summer heat
three half-naked Polish slaves
lick their sweat with hunger at dusk,
circling, yoked to a millstone
with exhausted faces, bent under the weight of their yokes.
How white, how sweet,
how lightly it descends,
passing between three sieves at the bottom,
the very pure and finely milled flour
for the immense cake of His Majesty,
the glorious lord and husband,
for tomorrow evening's blessed wedding.

12.

Hurly-Burly, the most skillful jester,
never stops prancing about the prince.
Hurly-Burly is a wise fool,
with domed forehead, with a cotton skull-cap,
tender of heart, deformed to sight,
he dares like a fool but tells the truth
and the poor of the town
are most dear to him.
Hurly-Burly wreaks havoc at court
but resolves many a plight.
When the prince became engaged
he laughed and joked
about truth in the service of lies,
and, without making anyone angry,
with his finger, in front of everyone,
he pointed directly at the prince.
The greatest farce is expected at the wedding.

13.

After lunch it rains, the ground gets damp.
From the ravines the hunters drag through the woods
a beautiful deer, fair as a damsel.
The servant, imperturbable, with an imposing axe
cleans the mud from the immaculate body
and a child, on the threshold,
trembles in tears
from fear and amazement at its loving glances.
In his simple goodness
and holiness of life,
with a mind bewildered,
he imagines his own head and heart
serene on a golden tray
adorned with tender foliage,
to become at the wedding
the wild joy of the feast.

14.

In the evening, still in the rain,
at the Chalice Gate, the High Chamberlain
tallies up the convoy transporting wine.
They unload about a hundred barrels into the cellar
full of Cotnar's royal vintage.
They start tapping a barrel
to taste the wine before dinner,
but the cup breaks in the prince's hands.
He is so upset
that out of anger
with jug and mug
he gets terribly drunk.
And he strikes about like never before
with mace and boot.
What else should the wedding be bathed in?

15.

"Just as the bitterness of absinthe spoils
and corrupts the sweetness of clear honey
so too revolting sin embitters life."
With this thought the carpenter, tongs in hand,
aligns a crooked board with the coffin
for this morning's hanged man,
found hanging from a tree in the palace garden.
That man, too much of a dreamer,
must be quickly removed
from the house.
It was nothing major.
The prince had only scolded him a little
with his boot,
and he cowered like a child.
He could have postponed the joke.
How inconvenient on the eve of the wedding.

16.

And so it was that
the gardener found them on the sand:
the footsteps of death
imprinted within the footsteps of a man.
Like a temptation,
he swept them from the path,
but over-mastering fear entered
through the windows to the rooms
from the tree branch.
The image of him, livid and dreadful,
invaded the palace
from one corner to the other
with its unending silence.
And in the anguished peace
the true Bride
to each soul, individually,
with secret words,
is reminding them of other weddings
which must be celebrated,
in true royal fashion.

17.

Only he who has collapsed, racked with blows,
the great jester, tied to the stocks,
amid the screeching of the irons, struggles in vain.
For this reason, death did not reach his ears
and so he knows nothing of the hanged man.
Too sure of himself,
he helplessly gnaws at his fetters.
"I have a star and I know
that I will be freed.
I will transform,
I will become a snake
and with honeyed guise
I will smile, I will be silent
and I will gladly arrange,
like the dregs of revenge
my insane wedding prank."

18.

Balance the point, sharpen it well,
shoot the arrow lightly as far as possible—
deft, straight, it flies through the sky.
Life is fulfilled in the dignity of small things,
one does not know the greatness
of what is worthless
so you have no great work to do.
Nock carefully the royal arrows,
until the eventide [of life]
so to make abundant use
of this terrible quiver
of Moroccan green.
With it I will be able to dedicate,
to the Lord and Bridegroom,
my meticulous work.
I will take every care
because I am risking the reputation
of a great warrior.

19.

"Triumph over yourself as over an adversary
so that you can be fully free
even outwardly.
How could one command and guide others,
who is not even master of himself?"
Thus the prince repented in the evening
awakening from his drunken stupor.
He was lying next to his bed, looking at the ceiling
from where he was lying.
But when he sat up,
from behind the window curtain,
as if from behind a veil of dense fog,
a face, the strange face of the Bride
appeared to him.
Then towards and over the prince,
with his gaze lost in vacancy,
stole a deep green shadow.

20.

"Now is your longest, best moment.
Behold, I have adorned you, I have dressed you, I have clothed you
with a white brocaded garment suitable for a wedding.
I understand that you would also like a ring on your finger.
You are more handsome than ever, so still,
you have forgotten about the body, now useless.
Lo, I sense you are
emptied of yourself,
you are thinking endlessly
of how you have to be on your way.
Just now you were called,
right now."
Thus sighed the old chamberlain,
still attending to the needs of his master.

21.

The unusual death, the least understandable,
the least acceptable, the most astonishing,
that humiliates and frightens,
is the sweet, gentle, familiar death,
like this, without reason, which doesn't hurt,
the satiated death, which lays us low
and gently embraces us, like a maiden's dream,
when life is still precious;
the death of a nobleman
on his wedding day,
the death that comes in sleep
without warning,
when you, as life's own bridegroom,
believe that you already have overcome
all obstacles,
but, with arm extended,
the crown has passed you by,
you were unable to lay hold of it.

22.

The light of a peaceful sunset still shines
and the questions that rise to the surface go beyond life.
The candles are guttering into their heavy candlesticks
while, with their sweet alternation, light and shadow
set a violet smile on the face of the deceased.
With his hair flowing down his chest
and his eyelids closed, he seems awake,
listening kindly
to something clear and pure
from the bright morning
of distant times,
when the sovereign aurochs,[7]
free and unfettered,
were neither ferocious nor cruel.
Here he is now, waiting,
listening, humbled,
to the voices about him
singing his funeral laments.

23.

As befits a princely end
at the ringing of the bells
they will accompany him on the road.
Solemn music will resound
to dispel the sadness
so stormily awakened
on the hills of the town,
on the waters of the valley.
There is in man a need for glorious mercy,
to be accompanied with kindness
on the last journey,
by which sorrow has taught us
victory even in defeat.
In the church he founded they will bury him
with a candle that will never go out.
And, in keeping with tradition,

[7] The aurochs is associated with the founding of Moldavia and appears on its flag.

they will cast
a handful of earth in the grave
so that it can be truly understood
what is no longer there,
as our life passes into the Great Story.

24.
The glittering procession of stars is fading.
Suceava stands inscribed in emerald glory.
Then, at the time of awakening,
the shrill blast of clarion trumpets
startles one with dismay,
and a banner, unfurled and soaring on its staff,
displays the shield with a changed symbol for Suceava.
Without delay, everywhere,
news spreads of an accession to the throne,
as a destiny now accepted
in its majesty or misery,
by the strong and vigorous,
the recognized royal heir
summoned to reign.
And, as dawn breaks,
free Suceava shines in the sun.

The royal charter is short,
all that it is possible to write
in one night and one day.
The jester, the bride and the soldier,
on horseback, by stealth,
have crossed the frontier
on paths known only to them.
And so the whole prank of hatred
has unraveled.
Far, far away, the forest verge
welcomes them into its green shade.
Those unfinished hearts
amble together now
like tangled shadows.

25 February 1958
(St. Tarasio, first week of the Great Fast),
Sihastria at Rarau.

[Fr. Daniil sent the ballad to the poet Vasile Voiculescu, who sent him the following note:]

"You left the century and the world to enter the mystery of
the hermitage, longing to be just a simple hieroschemamonk.
But grace accompanies you: and on the Wallachian plain
the Holy Spirit, the prince of poetry, anoints you."

Vasile Voiculescu
Saturday, March 15, 1958, Bucharest,
after the reading of the Charter.

Church of "All Saints"
Antim Monastery

THE PRAYER OF THE HEART
Canon for multiple voices
PAUL CONSTANTINESCU

Each verse, when it ends, begins again
and continues indefinitely:
this is uninterrupted prayer.

BIBLIOGRAPHY

IN ROMANIAN

Works of Sandu Tudor:

Acatistul Preacuviosului Părintelui nostru Sfintul Dimitrie cel Nou, Boarul, din Basarabov. Bucharest: Fundatia Regală pentru Literatură și Artă, 1942.

Imn-Acatist la Rugul Aprins al Maicii Domnului. Madrid: Colectia Cetătuia, 1983.

Scrieri, 1: Imn Acatist la Rugul Aprins al Născătoarei de Dumnezeu. Cartea Muntelui Sfânt. Marea noapte de aur a Maicii Domnului. Apocalipsa lui Ioan (Numai argument de Predoslovie). Am auzit cântecul Pasării Unice (Gânduri din singuratate). Edited by Alexandru Dimcea. Bucharest: Editura Christiana, 1999.

Taina Rugului Aprins. Scrieri și documente inedite. Bucharest: Anastasia, 1999.

Caiete, 1: Dumnezeu Dragoste. Edited by Alexandru Dimcea. Bucharest: Editura Christiana, 2000; second edition 2003.

Caiete, 2: Sfintita rugăciune. Edited by Alexandru Dimcea. Bucharest: Editura Christiana, 2000.

Caiete, 3: Taina Sfintei Cruci. Edited by Alexandru Dimcea. Bucharest: Editura Christiana, 2001.

Caiete, 4: Ce e omul? Edited by Alexandru Dimcea. Bucharest: Editura Christiana, 2003.

Acatiste. Acatistul Sf. Dimitrie Cel Nou. Acatistul Sf. Ioan Bogoslovul. Acatistul Sf. Calinic de la Cernica. Acatistul Rugului Aprins. Acatistul Bunei Vestiri. First integral edition. Edited by Alexandru Dimcea & Gabriela Moldoveanu. Bucharest: Editura Christiana, 2009.

Texts and Studies

Adunare a cuvintelor celor pentru ascultare. Neamț: Mînăstirea Neamţului, 1817.

Bălan, Ioanichie. *Pateric românesc (secole IV-XX).* Second edition. Galați: Editura arhiepiscopiei Tomisului și Dunării de Jos, 1999.

—. *Pateric românesc.* Bucharest: Institutul biblic, 1980.

Călinescu, George. *Istoria literaturii române de la origini pînă în prezent.* Bucharest: Editura Minerva, 1986.

Cernat, Paul. "Chipuri ale poeziei tinere interbelice." In *Revista 22*, no. 108 (9 Aug. 2011).

Četverikov, Serghie. *Paisie stareţul Mânăstirii Neamţului din*

Moldova. Viața, invățătura și influența lui aspra Bisericii Ortodoxe. Neamț: Mînăstirea Neamţului, 1933.

Ciornea, Carmen. *Chipul Rugului Aprins.* Cluj-Napoca: Eikon, 2015.

—. *Sandu Tudor și asociațiile studentești creștine din România interbelica.* Cluj-Napoca: Eikon, 2017.

—. *Să nu fiți caldicei! Sandu Tudor și intemeierea Rugului Aprins (1945–1952).* Cluj-Napoca: Eikon, 2018.

—. "Condamnarea Monahului Agathon (Sandu Tudor)," In *Revista Logos și agape. Revistă crestină de cultură, tradiții și atitudine civică.* Posted online September 30, 2018. https://logossiagape.ro/dr-carmen-ciornea-condamnarea-monahului-agathon-sandu-tudor/.

Crainic, Nichifor. *Cursurile de mistică. I. Teologie mistică. II. Mistica germană.* Sibiu: Deisis, 2010.

Cuviosul Ioan cel Străin (din arhiva Rugului Aprins). Edited by Gheorghe Vasilescu. Afterword by Sofian Boghiu. Bucharest: Anastasia, 1999.

Cuviosul Paisie de la Neamț (Velicicovski), *Autobiografia și Viețile unui stareț, urmate de Asezăminte și alte texte.* Edited by Ioan I. Ică, Jr. Second edition. Sibiu: Deisis, 2002 (1996).

Diaconescu, Ioana. *"Rugul Aprins." Studii și documente despre exterminare și supraviețuire.* Bucharest: Fundația Academia Civică, 2018.

Filocalia [de la Prodromu]. Vol. 2. Edited by Doina Uricariu. New York: Editura Universalia, 2001.

Hasmațuchi, Gabriel. *Nichifor Crainic and the interwar "New Spirituality."* http://www.apshus.usv.ro/arhiva/2011II.pdf.

Ică, Ioan I., Jr, *Maica Domnului in teologia secoluui XX și în spiritualitatea isihasta a secolului XIV: Grigorie Palama, Nicolae Cabasila, Teofan al Niceei. Studii și texte.* Sibiu: Deisis, 2008.

—, editor. *Predania și un Îndreptar ortodox cu, de și despre Nae Ionescu teolog.* Sibiu: Deisis, 2001.

—, editor. Sfântul Nicodim Aghioritul. *Maica Domnului și Intrările ei în Templu în tâlcuiri mistagogice. Cuvinte și poeme.* Sibiu: Deisis, 2022.

—, editor. *Sfinți stareți Gheorghe și Calinic de la Cernica, Viețile, povațuirile, testamentele.* Second augmented edition. Sibiu: Deisis, 2018.

Ionescu, Nae. *Roza vânturilor 1926-1933.* Bucharest: Editura "Cultura Națională," 1937 (facsimile reprint, Bucharest: Editura "Roza vînturilor," 1990).

Jinga, Constantin. *Ieroschimonahul Daniil Sandu Tudor. Omul și opera.* Bucharest: Editura Christiana, 2005.

Manolescu, Anca. *Modelul Antim, modelul Păltiniș. Cercuri de studiu și prietenie spirituală.* Bucharest: Humanitas, 2015.

Maxim, Virgil. *Imn pentru crucea purtata*, Second edition. Bucharest: Antim, 2002.

Mihăilescu, Emanoil. "Organizatia Rugul Aprins." In *Din documentele rezistenței*, no. 4 (Arhiva Asociației foștilor deținuți politici din România, 1992), 40–55.

Mironescu, Alexandru. *Calea inimii. Eseuri in duhul Rugului Aprins.* Preface by Virgil Cândea. Bucharest: Anastasia, 1998.

Nicolau, Nicolae. "Rugul Aprins al Maicii Domnului." In *Din documentele rezistenței*, no. 4 (Arhiva Asociației foștilor deținuți politici din România, 1992), 22–39.

Oprea, Marius. *Adevărata călătorie a lui Zahei. V. Voiculescu și taina Rugului Aprins.* Bucharest: Humanitas, 2008.

Ornea, Zigu. *Anii treizeci. Extrema dreaptă românească.* Bucharest: Editura Fundației culturale române, 1995.

Pandrea, Petre. *Memoriile mandarinului valah. Jurnal 1954–1956.* Bucharest: Vremea, 2011.

Paraschiv, Cleopa. *Rugul Aprins și starețul Daniil-Sandu Tudor.* Vatra-Dornei: Editura Panaghia, 2007.

Plămădeală, Antonie. Sibiu: *Rugul Aprins*, 2002.

Rădulescu, Mihai. "Consemnari despre Rugul Aprins dintr-o convorbire cu p. Dumitru Stăniloae." In *Din documentele rezistenței*, no. 4 (Arhiva Asociației foștilor deținuți politici din România, 1992), 56–58.

—. *Rugul Aprins. Duhovnicii ortodoxiei, sub lespezi, în gherlele comuniste.* Bucharest: Editura Ramida, 1993.

Rădulescu, Mihai. "Sandu Tudor in deriva spre stânga." In *Floarea de foc* no. 5: http://www.hotnews.ro/stiri-arhiva-1217994-sandu-tudor-deriva-spre-stanga-floarea-foc-5.htm.

Scrima, André. *Teme ecumenice.* Bucharest: Humanitas, 2004.

—. *Ortodoxia și incercarea comunismului.* Bucharest: Humanitas, 2008.

—, *Timpul rugului aprins. Maestrul spiritual în tradiția răsăriteană*, Bucharest: Humanitas, 1996 (revised edition 2000).

Simuț, Ion. "Justițiar cu orice risc." In *România Literară*, no. 3, 2004.

Stahl, Paul Henri. "Intâlnirea duhovnicească de la Cernăuți, august 1943." In *Dilema*, IV (September 20–26, 1996), no 193, 2.

Stanciu, Mihail. *Părintele ieroschimonah Daniil Sandu Tudor – o viață de mărturisire și martiriu pentru Hristos.* Posted online on November 17, 2017 at Internet Archive: https://archive.org/details/parintele-ieroschimonah-daniil-sandu-tudor-o-viata-de-marturisire-si-martiriu-pentru-hristos.

Tolcea, Marcel. "De la Marcel Avramescu, la Părintele Mihail Avramescu. Repere ale unei biografii spirituale." In *Trivium—revistă de gândire simbolică*, no. 4 (13) 2012.

Vasilachi Vasile (1909–2003). *De la Antim la Pocrov.* Cluj Napoca: Eikon, 2015 (previously published in 1984 by Cuvântul Vieți, Detroit, Michigan).

Vasile de la Poiana Mărului. *Introduceri în rugăciunea lui Iisus și isihasm.* Sibiu: Deisis, 2009: *Oglinda adevăratului isihasm*, 207–25.

Vasile, Cristian. *Biserica Ortodoxă Română în primul deceniu comunist.* Curtea Veche 2005, 2013 (ePub). Digital version created by Elefant.ro.

Vasileanu, Marius. In *Ziarul Financiar: Modelul Mănăstirii Antim* (January 30, 2014); *Sandu Tudor și "Ideea unei școli noi teologice"* (February 20, 2014); *Rugul Aprins, un simplu cenaclu?* (February 19, 2015).

Vulcănescu, Mircea. *Nae Ionescu. Asa cum l'am cunoscut.* Bucharest: Eikon, 1992.

Vulcănescu, Romulus. *Mitologie Română.* Bucharest: Editura Academiei Republicii Socialiste România, 1987.

B) IN OTHER LANGUAGES

Texts & Studies

Ambrose, Saint. *Seven Exegetical Works.* Translated by Michael P. McHugh. Washington, D. C.: Catholic University of America, 1972.

André Scrima (1925–2000). *Un moine hésychaste de notre temps*, I (*Contacts*, no. 203, 2003), II (*Contacts*, no. 207, 2004).

Angela of Foligno. *Complete Works.* Translated by Paul Lachance. New York & Mahwah NJ: Paulist Press, 1993.

Ansari, *Cris du cœur. Munajat.* Edited by S. de Laugier de Beaurecueil. Paris: Sindbad, 1988.

Balan, Ioanichie. *Volti e parole dei padri del deserto romeno.* Introduction, translation and notes by Fratelli Contemplativi di Gesù. Bose: Qigajon, 1991.

Bodea, Cornelia. "L'esprit du 'Buisson ardent' du monastère st. Anthime-Bucarest." In *Omagiu Virgil Cândea la 75 de ani.* Edited by Paul H. Stahl. Bucharest: Academiei Române—Roza Vânturilor (2002), vol. I, 87–95.

Bonaventure. *The Life of St. Francis (Legenda Maior).* In *Bonaventure.* Translated by Ewert Cousins. New York & Ramsey & Toronto: Paulist Press, 1978.

The Book of the Elders. The Sayings of the Desert Fathers. The Systematic Collection. Translated by John Wortley. Collegeville, MN: Cistercian Publications, 2012.

Braga, Roman. "*Ogni monaco ha un suo segreto con Dio.*" Roma: Lipa, 1999.

Brunton, Paul. *The Secret Path. A Technique of Spiritual Self-Discovery for the Modern World.* London: Rider & Co., 1934.

Buber, Martin. *Tales of the Hasidim.* Translated by Olga Marx. New York: Schocken Books, 1947 & 1975.

Ciornea, Carmen. "From Alexandru Teodorescu to Sandu Tudor. Biographical Benchmarks." In *Law, Society & Organisation*, vol. IV, 6 (1, 2019), 25–33.

—. "Sandu Tudor and the Christian Student Associations during the Interwar Period." In *Law, Society & Organisation*, vol. IV, 7 (2, 2019), 65–75.

—. "From Sandu Tudor to the monk Agaton. Biographical Benchmarks." In *SEA-Practical Application of Science*, vol. VIII, 22 (1, 2020), 67–73.

Citterio, Elia. *La vita spirituale, i suoi segreti.* Bologna: EDB, 2005.

—. "Paisij Veličkovskij e il contributo delle terre romene alla storia della spiritualità ortodossa." In *Storia religiosa dello spazio romeno.* Edited by Luciano Vaccario, general editor Cesare Alzati. Milano: Centro Ambrosiano (2016), II, 515–36.

—. "La dottrina spirituale dello starets Paisij." *Paisij, lo starec.* Edited by N. Kauchtschischwili, A.-Ai. N. et al. Bose: Qiqajon (1997), 55–82. Romanian translation: *Românii în reînnoirea isihastă.* Edited by Virgil Cândea. Iași: Trinitas (1997), 121–48.

—. "La preghiera e la pratica della preghiera. A proposito di alcuni autori esicasti minori." In *L'Athos e l'esicasmo.* Edited by Antonio Manzella. Firenze: Nerbini (2016), 59–82.

—. "La scuola filocalica di Paisij Velichkovskij e la Filocalia di Nicodimo Aghiorita. Un confronto." In Spidlik, Tomas et al. *Amore del bello. Studi sulla Filocalia.* Bose: Qiqajon (1991), 179–207.

—. "La tradizione teologico-spirituale dell'ortodossia romena." In *Chiese e culture nell'Est europeo. Prospettive di dialogo.* Edited by Adriano Roccucci. Milano: Paoline (2007), 101–38.

—. "L'esperienza monastica di Paisij Veličkovskij. La fecondità della sua eredità: una santità come fermento di umanità." In *Il monachesimo tra eredità e aperture.* Edited by Maciej Bielawski and Daniel Hombergen. Roma: *Studia Anselmiana* (2004), 459–69.

—. "Passaggi e tappe nel cammino mistico di Angela da Foligno." In *Sant'Angela da Foligno contemplativa, mistica, apostola.* Edited by Luigi Borriello. Roma: Miscellanea Francescana (2014), 137–58.

Clément, Olivier. "L'église Orthodoxe Roumaine ou le miracle du Buisson ardent." In *Réforme*, no. 644, Saturday 20 July 1957.

Come vivere e praticare l'esichia. Libro di insegnamento del principe romeno Neagoe Basarab per suo figlio Teodosio. Translation, introductory study and notes edited by Adriana Mitescu. Roma: Bulzoni (biblioteca di cultura, 480), 1993.

Costantini, Emanuela. *Nae Ionescu, Mircea Eliade, Emil Cioran. Antiliberalismo nazionalista alla periferia d'Europa.* Perugia: Morlacchi, 2005.

Dostoevsky, Fyodor, *The Brothers Karamazov.* Translation by Richard Pevear & Volokhonsky, Larissa. New York: Vintage Books, 1990.

Dragan, Radu. *La contribution des auteurs roumains à la littérature ésotérique occidentale (xix-xx siècles).* Conferences of Radu Dragan, *Annuaires de l'École pratique des hautes études*, 2005, vol. 114, 379–85.

—. "Une figure du christianisme oriental du XXe siecle: Jean l'Etranger." In *Politica Hermetica* 20 (no. 20 entitled *L'ésotérisme au féminin*). Lausanne: L'âge d'homme (2006), 124–42.

Enciclopedia dei santi. Le chiese orientali. Roma: Città nuova (Bibliotheca sanctorum orientalium), 1998.

Gagliardi, Isabella. *Novellus pazzus. Storie di santi medievali tra il Mar Caspio e il Mar Mediterraneo (secc. IV-XIV).* Firenze: Società Editrice Fiorentina, 2017.

Gloria a Dio per tutto. Inni acatisti. Edited by the Monastero russo della Dormizione della Madre di Dio. Roma: Appunti di viaggio, 2011.

Gregory of Nyssa. *Homilies on the Song of Songs.* Translated by Richard A. Norris Jr. Atlanta: Society of Biblical Literature, 2012.

Ica, Ioan I., Jr. "La posterità romena dello 'starec' Paisij." In Nina Kauchtschischwili, et al. *Paisij, lo starec. Atti del III Convegno ecumenico internazionale di spiritualità russa "Paisij Velickovskij e il suo movimento spirituale."* Edited by A. Mainardi. Bose: Qiqajon (1997), 245–66.

—. "Il 'Roveto Ardente': una fioritura dell'ideale esicasta all'alba del comunismo in Romania." In *Il monachesimo tra eredità e aperture.* Edited by Maciej Bielawski and Daniel Hombergen. Roma: Studia anselmiana (2004), 471–88.

—. "Lo starec Paisij Veličkovskij e la preghiera del cuore." In *La preghiera di Gesù nella spiritualità russa del XIX.* Acts of the 12th International Ecumenical Conference on Orthodox Spirituality, Russian section. Bose, September 16–18, 2004. Edited by Aldaberto Mainardi. Bose: Qiqajon (2005), 71–104.

Ionascu, Gheorghe. *Il Roveto Ardente.* Viterbo: Tagete, 2008.

Isacco di Ninive. *Un'umile speranza. Antologia.* Edited by Sabino Chialà. Bose: Qiqajon, 1999.

Isaac the Syrian, *Ascetical Homilies.* Translated by the Holy Transfiguration Monastery. Boston: Holy Transfiguration Monastery, 1984.

Jonată, Romul (Bishop Seraphim of Făgăraș). *Romania: Its Hesychast Tradition and Culture.* Translated by Romul Ionată. Wildwood, CA: St. Xenia's Skete, 1992.

—. *Roumanie, Tradition et culture hésychastes.* Begrolles-en-Mauges: Abbaye de Bellefontaine, 1987.

Kotelnikov, Vladimir. *L'eremo di Optina e i Grandi della cultura russa. Milano:* Casa di Matriona, 1996.

Le catacombe della Romania. Testimonianze dalle carceri comuniste, 1945–1964. Milano: Rediviva edizioni, 2014.

The Lenten Triodion. Translated by Mother Mary and Archimandrite Kallistos Ware. South Canaan, PA: St. Tikhon's Seminary Press, 1994.

Liceanu, Gabriel. *Le journal de Paltinis, 1977–1981. Récit d'une formation spirituelle et philosophique.* Parigi: La Découverte, 1999. ePub edition, 2013.

Mariotti, Alessandro. *Mircea Eliade.* Roma: Castelvecchi (digital ed.), 2017.

McGinn, Bernard. *The Flowering of Mysticism. Men and Women in the New Mysticism (1200–1350).* New York: Crossroad, 1998.

Metrophanes. *Blessed Paisius Velichkovski.* Translated by Fr. Seraphim Rose. Platina, CA: Saint Herman of Alaska Brotherhood, 1976.

Montanari, Enrico. *La fatica del cuore. Saggio sull'ascesi esicasta.* Milano: Jaca Book, 2003.

—. *Un'umile regalità. Percorsi dell'esicasmo in Occidente.* Milano–Udine: Mimesis, 2022.

Nivière, Antoine. *Les glorificateurs du Nom. Une querelle théologique parmi les moines russes du Mont Athos (1907–1914).* Nancy: Université de Lorraine, 2015.

Paisij Veličkovskij, *Autobiografia di uno starec.* Edited with introduction, translation and notes by the Comunità dei Fratelli Contemplativi di Gesù. Abbazia di Praglia: Scritti monastici, 1988; republished Bose: Qiqajon, 1998.

Paisij Veličkovskij. *La preghiera del cuore e Lettere scelte sulla vita spirituale.* Edited by Fr. Michele Di Monte. Eremo degli Angeli-Vendrogno: Edizione Monasterium, 2019.

The Philokalia, 5 vols. Compiled by St. Nikodimos of the Holy Mountain and St. Makarios of Corinth. Translated by G.E.H.

Palmer, Philip Sherrard and Kallistos Ware. London: Faber and Faber, 1979–2023.

Pilgrim's Tale. Edited by Aleksej Pentkovsky. New York & Mahwah: Paulist Press, 1999.

Popescu, Violeta. *La Chiesa Ortodossa Romena dopo la Seconda Guerra Mondiale. Figure dell'Ortodossia romena nell'Occidente.* Milano: Rediviva edizioni, 2018.

Raccanello, Dario. *La preghiera di Gesù negli scritti di Basilio di Poiana Marului*, Alessandria: n. p., 1986 (Romanian translation: *Rugăciunea lui Iisus în scrierile starețului Vasile de la Poiana Mărului.* Sibiu: Deisis, 1996).

Rigo, Antonio, editor. *Da Teognosto alla Filocalia (XIII–XVIII secolo). Testi e autori.* Bari: Edizioni di pagina, 2016.

—. *Il monaco, la chiesa e la liturgia. I capitoli sulle gerarchie di Gregorio il Sinaita.* Firenze: Edizioni del Galluzzo, 2005.

—. *Mistici bizantini.* Torino: Einaudi, 2008.

Sayings of the Desert Fathers. Alphabetical Collection. Translated by Benedicta Ward. Kalamazoo, MI: Cistercian Publications, 1975.

Schimonaco Ilarione. *Sulle montagne del Caucaso.* Edited by Adalberto Mainardi. Bose: Qiqajon, 2019.

Scrima, André. *L'accompagnamento spirituale. Il movimento del Roveto Ardente e la rinascita esicasta in Romania.* Italian edition edited by Adalberto Mainardi. Bose: Qiqajon, 2018 (first edition, *Il Padre spirituale*, 1999).

[Scrima, André]. Un moine de l'Eglise Orthodoxe de Roumanie. "L'avènement philocalique dans l'Orthodoxie roumaine." In *Istina* 5 (1958), 295–328, 443–75.

—. *L'évangile de Jean. Un commentaire.* Paris: Cerf, 2017.

Scupoli, Lorenzo. *Unseen Warfare.* Edited by Nicodemus of the Holy Mountain. Revised by Theophan the Recluse. Translated by E. Kadloubovsky & G. E. H. Palmer. Crestwood, NY: St. Vladimir's Seminary Press, 1978.

Sedakova, Olga. "The Light of Life. Some Remarks on the Russian Orthodox Perception." In *La Nuova Europa* 2 (2009), 23–41. English translation online: https://www.olgasedakova.com › eng.

Steinhardt, Nicolae. *Diario della felicità.* Bologna: Mulino, 1996.

Thomas of Celano. *First Life of St. Francis of Assisi.* In *Fonti Francescane*, no. 522.

—. *Second Life of Saint Francis of Assisi.* In *Fonti Francescane*, no. 682.

Vasiliu, Anca. *Le Passeur. Voies de l'expression* (typescript).

www.ingramcontent.com/pod-product-compliance
Lightning Source LLC
LaVergne TN
LVHW090555110826
845146LV00001B/131

* 9 7 9 8 8 9 2 8 0 1 6 9 0 *